NARRATIVES OF DOMESTIC VIOLENCE

Domestic violence is an intractable social problem that must be understood in order to be eradicated. Using theories of indexicality, identity, and narrative, Andrus presents data from interviews she conducted with victims and law enforcement, and analyses the narratives of their interactions and the identities that emerge. She gives insight into law enforcement views on violence, and prevalent misconceptions, in order to create resources to improve communication with victims/survivors. She also analyzes the ways in which identity emerges and is performed via narrative constructions of domestic violence and encounters between police and victims/survivors. By giving voice to the victims of domestic violence, this book provides powerful insights into the ways that ideology and commonplace misconceptions impact the social construction of domestic violence. It will be invaluable to students and researchers in discourse analysis, applied linguistics and forensic linguistics.

JENNIFER ANDRUS is an Associate Professor of Writing and Rhetoric Studies at the University of Utah, where she teaches courses on discourse analysis, legal rhetoric, and gender and rhetoric. Dr Andrus's research for the last decade has been on domestic violence and the Anglo-American law of evidence and law enforcement.

T0384520

NARRATIVES OF DOMESTIC VIOLENCE

VIOLENCE

Policing, Identity, and Indexicality

JENNIFER ANDRUS

University of Utah

Shaftesbury Road, Cambridge CB2 8EA, United Kingdom

One Liberty Plaza, 20th Floor, New York, NY 10006, USA

477 Williamstown Road, Port Melbourne, VIC 3207, Australia

314–321, 3rd Floor, Plot 3, Splendor Forum, Jasola District Centre, New Delhi – 110025, India

103 Penang Road, #05–06/07, Visioncrest Commercial, Singapore 238467

Cambridge University Press is part of Cambridge University Press & Assessment, a department of the University of Cambridge.

We share the University's mission to contribute to society through the pursuit of education, learning and research at the highest international levels of excellence.

www.cambridge.org
Information on this title: www.cambridge.org/9781108813280

DOI: 10.1017/9781108884280

First published 2021
First paperback edition 2024

A catalogue record for this publication is available from the British Library

Library of Congress Cataloging-in-Publication data
NAMES: Andrus, Jennifer, author.
TITLE: Narratives of domestic violence : policing, identity, and indexicality / Jennifer Andrus.
DESCRIPTION: First Edition. | New York : Cambridge University Press, 2020. | Includes bibliographical references and index.
IDENTIFIERS: LCCN 2020025106 (print) | LCCN 2020025107 (ebook) | ISBN 9781108839525 (hardback) | ISBN 9781108813280 (paperback) | ISBN 9781108884280 (ebook)
SUBJECTS: LCSH: Family violence. | Victims of family violence. | Social interaction. | Indexicals (Semantics)
CLASSIFICATION: LCC HV6626 .A63 2020 (print) | LCC HV6626 (ebook) | DDC 362.82/9265--dc23
LC record available at https://lccn.loc.gov/2020025106
LC ebook record available at https://lccn.loc.gov/2020025107

ISBN   978-1-108-83952-5   Hardback
ISBN   978-1-108-81328-0   Paperback

To the domestic violence victims/survivors I know, and to those I do not, all my love

Contents

List of Figures	*page*	ix
List of Tables		x
List of Extracts		xi
Notes on the Text		xiii
Acknowledgments		xv

Introduction: Identities, Indexicality, and Ideology – Victims/Survivors and Police Officer Storying of Domestic Violence		1
I.1	Victims, Survivors, Victims/Survivors	6
I.2	Domestic Violence and Police Work	8
I.3	Interaction and Discourse	14
I.4	Narratives and Identity, Narrative Identity	16
I.5	Indexicality, Social Meaning, and Identity	25
I.6	Policing Domestic Violence	28
I.7	Narrative Identities of Domestic Violence	31
I.8	(Critical) Discourse Analysis	37
I.9	Data Collection	41
I.10	Book Structure	43
I.11	Conclusions	45

1	Domestic Violence, Violence against Women, and Patriarchy	47
	1.1 Domestic Violence: Big Pictures	50
	1.2 Domestic Violence: Legal Histories and Patriarchy	53
	1.3 Patriarchal Control: Intimate/Patriarchal Terrorism	60
	1.4 Male Privilege: Coercive Control	62
	1.5 Seeing Emotional and Physical Violence as Working Together	66
	1.6 Domestic Violence, Law Enforcement, and Verbal/Emotional Violence	70
	1.7 Same-Sex Relationships	72
	1.8 Why Doesn't She Just Leave?	76
	1.9 Conclusions	77

2   Toward the Recreation of a Field of Indexicality:
     Domestic Violence, Social Meaning, and Ideology   79
     2.1 The Indexical Field   84
          2.1.1 Violence Stories   85
          2.1.2 Staying/Leaving Stories   89
          2.1.3 Family Stories   91
          2.1.4 Policing   94
     2.2 Mixed Stories: Connecting the Indexical Fields   98
     2.3 Small Story in an Indexical Field   102
     2.4 Small Story: I'm Not a Victim   105
     2.5 Small Story: I'm Not an Abuser   108
     2.6 Small Story about Policing Victim Behavior   110
     2.7 Conclusions   117

3   Storying the Victim/Survivor: Identity, Domestic Violence,
     and Discourses of Agency   119
     3.1 Iconization, Erasure, and Agented Nonagency   121
     3.2 Staying/Leaving Stories of Violence   124
     3.3 Iconization, Erasure, and Agency   125
     3.4 Leaving and Staying: Policing Victim Identity   129
     3.5 Police Iconization of Agented Nonagency   131
     3.6 Victim/Survivor Accounts of Staying/Leaving   139
     3.7 Accounting for Violence   148
     3.8 Conclusions   154

4   Storying Policing: Identities of Police and Domestic Violence   157
     4.1 Interaction and Identity   162
     4.2 Policing Identity   163
     4.3 Procedural Identity   166
          4.3.1 Positioning in Relationship to Domestic Violence Victims:
                 Frustration and Caring   168
     4.4 Recalcitrant Victims   177
     4.5 Conclusions   186

5   Conclusions : Toward a Reconceptualization of
     Domestic Violence   187
     C.1 Indexicality, Ideology, and Agency   191
     C.2 Identity and Narrative   193
     C.3 Identity, Policing Discourse, and Recalcitrant Victims   196
     C.4 Emotional Violence   198
          C.4.1 Coercion and Control, Agency and Choice   198
          C.4.2 Policing Discourse and Power   200
     C.5 Other and Future Topics   201
     C.6 Sexual Assault   206
     C.7 Conclusions   209

References   213
Index   220

Figures

2.1 Violence indexical field   *page* 89
2.2 Staying/leaving indexical field   92
2.3 Family indexical field   95
2.4 Policing indexical field   97
2.5 Staying/leaving + violence + family + police indexical field   102

Tables

I.1	Victims/survivors	*page* 41
I.2	Police officer and staff breakdown	42
1.1	Physical violence (NIPSVS; Black et al., 2011)	53
1.2	Emotional violence (NIPSVS; Black et al., 2011)	54

Extracts

Extract I.1	Nikki	*page* 7
Extract I.2	Killingsworth	9
Extract I.3	Detective Tyler	10
Extract I.4	Officer Riley	12
Extract I.5	Rainbow	21
Extract I.6	Officer Angel	30
Extract I.7	Detective Love	32
Extract I.8	Bubba	35
Extract 1.1	Killingsworth	47
Extract 1.2	Rachel	61
Extract 1.3	Rachel	62
Extract 1.4	Butterfly	64
Extract 1.5	Melissa	67
Extract 1.6	Killingsworth	68
Extract 1.7	Little Bird	71
Extract 1.8	Sasha	74
Extract 2.1	Becky	98
Extract 2.2	Crystal	99
Extract 2.3	Katherine	101
Extract 2.4	Detective Sidwell	101
Extract 2.5	Melissa	103
Extract 2.6	Kate	105
Extract 2.7	Bob	109
Extract 2.8	Detective Jacobs	110
Extract 2.9	Detective Jacobs	113
Extract 2.10	Jessica	114
Extract 3.1	Detective Sidwell	128
Extract 3.2	Butterfly	130
Extract 3.3	Officer McQuaid	131
Extract 3.4	Officer McQuaid	134

Extract 3.5   Officers Roscoe, Oliver, Angel, Winters   136
Extract 3.6   Radiance   139
Extract 3.7   Radiance   141
Extract 3.8   Butterfly   143
Extract 3.9   Butterfly   146
Extract 3.10   Officer McQuaid   149
Extract 3.11   Officers Angel, Roscoe, Oliver   152
Extract 3.12   Officer McQuaid   153
Extract 4.1   Detective Jacobs   164
Extract 4.2   Detective Jacobs   167
Extract 4.3   Detective Sidwell   169
Extract 4.4   Detective Jacobs   174
Extract 4.5   Detective Sidwell   177
Extract 4.6   Detective Tyler   180
Extract 4.7   Detective Jacobs   183
Extract C.1   Killingsworth   187
Extract C.2   Vera   196
Extract C.3   Killingsworth   199
Extract C.4   Crystal   207
Extract C.5   Little Bird   207
Extract C.6   Beth   209
Extract C.7   Nikki   210
Extract C.8   Katherine   211

Notes on the Text

Note on Transcription and Extract Formatting

Every transcript is a representation of the goals and analyses of the person who made and will use the transcript (Ochs, 1979). The narratives transcribed for this analysis are no different. My focus is on narrative, and all of the extracts are analyzed for their narrative qualities. No phonological, morphological, or syntactic analysis is done here, and therefore, I do not use either Jeffersonian Transcription notation nor the International Phonetic Alphabet. Regular orthography is used throughout, with closed em-dashes to indicate speech that is stopped and restarted mid-utterance and self-revision. Because I am not doing conversation analysis, I have simplified the transcripts by filtering out my back-channeling "mm-hmms." I do this because I am not analyzing the back-and-forth conversation between the interlocutors who are in an interviewed conversation. What I am focusing on in this analysis is the performance of the narrative, recognizing the importance of interaction at the level of theory, but not analyzing my back-channeling outright, in most instances. Removing my back-channeling puts the focus on the interviewee and their narratives without losing analytical quality.

The extracts are all broken into lines. "Lines" in this study are meaningful units, typically made up of a noun phrase (NP), a verb phrase (VP), and details that develop the NP, VP, or both. New topics or even shifts in segment focus result in a line break. This facilitates ease of analysis and ease of reading extracts, allowing me to more effectively point to particular pieces of discourse. There are a small number of places where the line break has to do with the size of the page. These material consequences of publication are unavoidable, but hopefully they do not interrupt reader experience.

Trigger Warning

The book deals with the difficult topic of domestic violence by analyzing the real stories of people who are survivors of domestic violence. These stories include references to physical, emotional, and sexual forms of violence. Some are graphically described while others are glossed, depending on the comfort level of and identity work being done by the storyteller. Some readers might find these depictions of violence upsetting and are therefore forewarned. Thank you for reading the victim/survivor stories. They really want to be heard and taken seriously.

Acknowledgments

To my participants. I could not have done this work without the reflective, introspective, honest, and heartfelt participation of the many domestic violence victims/survivors and the police officers who I interviewed. Their stories guide this analysis and the arguments made in the book. To the victims/survivors, many many thanks for sharing your intense and thoughtful stories of abuse. You were candid, caring, smart, and clever in your tellings and compassionate with regard to the topic and other victims/survivors. You are the strongest people I know. You have trusted me with your stories, and I hope I have done you justice. I take shelter in your strength. To the police officers who answer dangerous domestic calls: all my love and appreciation. You have been in my home, and you have saved my life. I would not be doing this work if it were not for the careful, well-planned and well-executed work of a SWAT team answering my final domestic call. I recognize in these pages that police officers put their lives on the line every day, walking into volatile situations that they don't know about, and doing their best to make sense of them. I respect this work. You are impressive.

I am forever in the debt of Chris Weigel, an extraordinary friend. She read every single word I wrote, often two or three times. She supported my efforts with insightful and prompt feedback that also gave me the energy to keep moving forward. She listened to me talk through arguments and publication strategies, and she helped me plan future projects, all while taking care of her own career and family. Selfless and smart to the end. My mentor and friend, Barbara Johnstone, has also been instrumental in making this book come to fruition. She gave me important and helpful advice early in the project, and as always, she asked me the questions that made the argument take shape and cohere. She has nurtured my career with care, leaving me forever in her debt. And to Alyssa Crow, my research assistant, who knows everything about style and formatting and who took a huge burden from me by stepping in to deal with the final stages of the book project, thank you so much. I don't think I would have crossed the finish line without you. Trista Emmer is the finest editor and index-maker that I know. She is also an extraordinary friend.

Many thanks to my department, Writing and Rhetoric Studies, and to the College of Humanities at the University of Utah. My department and college provided me with research funds and a much needed sabbatical that gave me the opportunity and time to complete this important work. I sincerely thank my colleagues, who took on extra work to give me time off. I recognize their sacrifice and hope to repay it in the coming years. I am also grateful for financial support in the form of a University Research Grant from the University of Utah, which helped with data collection and paid for the formatting and indexing of this book. I owe heartfelt thanks to the police precinct that allowed me to interview their police officers and to the domestic violence shelter that facilitated interviews with victims/ survivors. All of these groups provided institutional support in the shape of money, time, and effort, for which I am deeply grateful.

I am eternally grateful to my partner, Larry, whose strength consistently buoyed me. He met me when I was still half a person and breathed life into me. Larry has cherished me and nursed me through this difficult project. He has comforted me while I cried through data collection and analysis. He has helped me push through the hard times and helped me plan exit strategies when I needed them. He has listened to me talk and plan and given me smart and loving feedback. This work exists because of him. Thank you for believing in me. To my three amazing daughters: I apologize for my addiction to my laptop, and I am genuinely thankful that you let me work all of the time that I worked. Young as you are, you somehow understand the weight of this work, and kindly gave me the space to do it while generously loving me through it all.

Special thanks to the two anonymous reviewers for their careful and thoughtful suggestions and corrections. This book is significantly improved because of their input. And finally, to all who have had to listen to me spout domestic violence facts and figures, cry through long anger-fueled diatribes about how socially entrenched domestic violence is, and vigorously discuss the complexity of the problem that is domestic violence: you have nurtured both this project and me to the end, thank you. It is because of you all that I am here.

Though I have received significant help and support institutionally and personally, any remaining errors in this work are mine alone.

Introduction

Identities, Indexicality, and Ideology – Victims/Survivors and Police Officer Storying of Domestic Violence

When I was still very early in my career and in the early stages of research on domestic violence, a young female friend of mine, who I will call Killingsworth, asked to meet with me in my office, as she had many times before. This time, she was in tears. She announced, "I think my husband is abusing me." We cry-talked through the abuse, control, sexual assaults, and cruelty. The rating system that he used for her on a daily basis. The emotional control. The physical abuses. The hidden bruises. The abuse was severe, and it had been going on for years. We discussed the emotional and the physical violence. She wanted to leave, but she didn't know how. How would she pull apart the life she had built with him? How would she dislocate her life from his? How would she stop loving him? How would she afford to live without him? How would she know when his next attack would be if she weren't by his side? What if he knew she was planning to leave? How would she ever feel safe again? We talked about how to keep her and her cats safe. We looked for solutions. We looked for shelters. We were scared. We made a safety plan. The stakes were so high.

Once all of the pieces were in place, Killingsworth left. She showed resolve and power, and she left. She made her way to a tiny, secluded shelter far from where he was, and there she spent six weeks before moving into more permanent housing. The fear slowly ebbed away over the days, weeks, and months, as she did the legal work of a protective order and divorce and as she healed. In many ways, Killingsworth's strength animates this research.

My encounter with Killingsworth years ago was in many ways the beginning of this project. She showed me fear; she showed me vulnerability; she showed me strength. She showed me how hard it is to leave and how hard it is to stay. She showed me caution and planning. She showed me endurance and resoluteness. Since then, I've met a number of men and women willing to share their stories, vulnerability, and strength with me – people engaged in the labor of working through and surviving domestic violence: the control, the fear, and the scars. This book is the result of individuals sharing their life stories with me.

The narratives analyzed in this book are about domestic violence, the social ill that affects more than one million women and men in the United States every year (National Coalition Against Domestic Violence, NCADV), and law enforcement. The narratives were elicited in fifty interviews with police, police personnel, and victims/survivors. All fifty interviews elicit many interlocking, interrelated stories about domestic violence and police interactions. This research works to better understand that moment when police officers and victims/survivors interact, an interaction that is important to understand because the stakes in domestic violence are so high. It is also important to better understand police interactions with domestic violence victims/survivors because, as I show, they can be filled with communicative dysfluency. The police and the victims/survivors bring with them significantly different discursive, ideological, and rhetorical resources, and they very differently understand the products of the interaction. Further, victims/survivors and police officers mean something different when they each talk about domestic violence. One argument that I make here is that the differences between victim/survivor accounts of domestic violence and police officer accounts are substantial and could potentially lead to less-efficient and effective interactions.

Each interview with victims/survivors typically contains narratives about family, staying and leaving, police, and violence, both emotional and physical, and often showing how emotional and physical violence are combined. My conversation with Melissa was no different. When she sat down to talk with me, she was distraught – nervous about the interview but also emotionally troubled, having just exited a very long, very violent relationship. In my interview with her, she described childhood neglect and abuse. She talked about a desperate desire to be married, settled down, and have kids. She described abusive event after abusive event, including broken arms, ribs, shoulder, and jaw, along with emotional abuse, belittling, gaslighting, and verbal attacks. She described an event with police where they helped her get a protective order, and she described an interaction with police where she was arrested as the "primary aggressor," even though she was in the hospital having a broken arm repaired at the time that she received the citation. Through all of this – through the interaction with the interviewer and through the interviewee's recapitulation of past interactions – identities emerge, partial, fluid, and multiple, as well as ratified and semistable. Some of these identities had been performed multiple times. These were identities of victimhood, of motherhood, of struggle, of love, of partnership, of fear, of fear of being alone. All of these identities were performed, framed, recast, and emergent in the process of telling stories about past events for a present audience. They were contextually and narratively complex.

Melissa showcases many of the themes about family, violence, police, and strength that are central to this book. Thinking with and through the stories of those who participated in this study, I make arguments about identity and indexicality – the working relationship between language and societal discourses. According to Johnstone (2008, p. 133), "people need ways to show which set of social alignments is relevant to the moment, and they need ways to create new sets of alignments." These affiliative discourses construct and function via indexicality. Via the processes of indexicality, such discourses give rise to identity work – emergence and performance. As Melissa, Killingsworth, and the other participants talked about their experiences with me, they were doing identity work and drawing on the indexical formations through which their stories are made meaningful. Another way of saying this is that identity work happens indexically, in and through talk; it is interactional and indexical. "Other participants are always involved in shaping discourse through their reactions to it, through the ways in which it is designed with them in mind, and through the ways in which their roles make authors' roles possible" (Johnstone, 2008, p. 129). Meaning and identity are interactionally shaped through talk. As such, talk about domestic violence is part and parcel with the sociocultural climate in which it lives, circulates, makes meaning, and becomes meaningful (Bucholtz & Hall, 2008). What I show in what follows is that police and victims/survivors narrate domestic violence in dramatically different ways, and thus, different meanings of domestic violence and different identities emerge for each group. As Bucholtz and Hall (2005, p. 586) point out, "identity does not emerge at a single analytical level." Nevertheless, in this book, I choose to work at the interactional level, or the point at which people intermingle and relate to each other discursively, using a fine level of granularity. I am interested in what is accomplished in the telling of a story, and what the recasting of a prior interaction teaches us about interactional, narrative, social identity emergence and performance, and agency.

I argue that narratives erupt in, are performed via, and are made meaningful in an indexical field (Eckert, 2008) or, a constellation of potential meanings for any given discursive variable. Thus, as Eckert (2008, p. 455) argues, "We construct a social landscape through the segmentation of the social terrain, and we construct a linguistic landscape through a segmentation of the linguistic practices in that terrain." That is, we break up and understand the layout of the social world with language, which is interwoven with the social world and ideology. "Different ways of saying things are intended to signal different ways of being, which includes different potential things to say" (Eckert, 2008, p. 456). What is sayable and how it is meaningful establishes a field of possible relationships between social meaning, the social world, and linguistic variables that are linked to them.

Ultimately, in this book, I argue that there is an indexical field (Eckert, 2008) of the social meaning of domestic violence stocked with terms, identities, and concepts that can be animated by a speaker. That is, domestic violence exists and is perpetuated indexically and discursively. It is not somehow prior to discourse. The domestic violence indexical field is supplied with a variety of sometimes contrasting and sometimes overlapping meanings that can be animated by different speakers to make domestic violence meaningful in different ways for different groups of speakers. Indeed, what I show is that domestic violence means differently for victims/survivors than it does for police officers.

Police animate different elements in the indexical field of domestic violence than victims/survivors do, and indeed, the resultant indexical fields sometimes conflict with each other. Domestic violence is differently meaningful for each group. This can lead to communication breakdown, due the fact that each participant in the interaction brings different social meaning/s to bear. The indexical field analyzed here is constructed and operationalized in competing narrative recapitulations of domestic violence and interactions between police and victims/survivors. I argue that the indexical field and the storying therein are resources for identity emergence and performance.

Identity in this research is thought of both as emergent and semistable. By semistable, I mean identity work that has been ratified in prior interactions and is thus available for re/performance. Importantly, re/performance is re/emergence, with each performance rhetorically and discursively situated. That is, even though the identity has been performed before, it will re/emerge anew each time that it is re/performed. In the indexical field, particular available identities are re/animated and re/emerge in the process of telling stories about domestic violence and encounters between police and victims/survivors.

In understanding social identity as emergent in narrative, I consider storytelling as a rhetorical activity, following Stokoe and Edward's admonishment that we should study what "people are doing when they tell stories, and therefore, what stories are designed to do" (Stokoe & Edwards,

2007, p. 70). Focusing on the narrative as a rhetorical and discursive formation that is produced in the performance of the story, I avoid treating narrative and identity as fully formed versions of self that are merely operationalized in interaction. Moreover, rather than using large social, institutional classifications, such as gender, sexuality, or socioeconomic class as identity categories, this study looks for locally performed aspects of micro, on-the-ground identities (Bucholtz & Hall, 2005, 2008) available in individual performances. Or as Johnstone (2008, p. 157) puts it, "It is important to remember that no matter how much we know about the social context of discourse, we cannot predict what a particular person will say in a given instance or how it will be interpreted by another person." That is, it would be a mistake to think that all members of a social group, for example "victim," would have the same identity as others in the group or even with themselves in the past or the future. Identity is local, unpredictable, spontaneous, reactionary, and playful. It is not a static demographic characteristic that supposedly predicts behavior. Indeed, because they are not brought up by my participants, and because of the need to fully protect their identities, I give no demographic or personal details that could be used to identify victims/survivors or place them in a particular location. I do not typically talk about or analyze macro categories. Instead, I argue that when considering the stories told by police officers and victims/survivors about domestic violence, it is important to consider the narrator, the telling, and the rhetoricity of narratives.

The domestic violence situation is as high stakes as it is intellectually and emotionally demanding for police and victims/survivors alike. It is a rampant social problem. According to the NCADV, domestic violence is "the willful intimidation, physical assault, battery, sexual assault, and/or other abusive behavior as part of a systematic pattern of power and control perpetrated by one intimate partner against another." Domestic violence occurs when one person uses tactics of power and control in an intimate relationship in a methodical way to dominate the other person in the relationship. Domestic violence includes physical assaults, sexual assaults, emotional abuse, verbal abuse, financial abuse, and other forms of domination. According to the NCADV "1 in 4 women and 1 in 9 men experience severe intimate partner physical violence, intimate partner contact sexual violence, and/or intimate partner stalking with impacts such as injury, fearfulness, posttraumatic stress disorder, use of victim services, contraction of sexually transmitted diseases, etc." These are startling statistics. "Battering is an issue of crime, health, safety, ethics, politics, systems, choices, economics, and socialization. It is an issue of individual, institutional, and cultural significance" (NCADV, quoted in Berry, 2000, p. 11). That is to say, battering, domestic violence, is an institutional, systematic, ideological problem, not or at least not only an interpersonal one. Domestic violence is patriarchal and discursive – patriarchy circulating in discourse, with material consequences. As I show in what follows, domestic violence happens within a field of discourses and social meanings – indexicalities – that maintain and support violence. One discourse that infiltrates the indexical field of domestic violence is patriarchy, the social discourses that presume male privilege and subjugate women. Because nearly all of my participants are women, and because domestic violence impacts women more than men and in ways that are significantly different than for men, the following analysis is necessarily cloaked in feminist thinking.

I.1 Victims, Survivors, Victims/Survivors

Thinking about domestic violence and labels requires me to consider how I label and discuss people who have lived in and survived abusive relationships. In the tapestry of terms that make up domestic violence, there are a number of ways to refer to the people who find themselves the targets for abuse, primarily victim or survivor. Victim is the legal term. There must be a victim in order for there to be a crime. Statutes are written with the term, as are jury instructions, trial transcripts, and precedents. Victim may make individuals legally recognizable, but perhaps not in ways that people find comfortable. That is, being a legal victim places the focus on the crime committed against one. It focuses on a hurt, a vulnerability, a weakness. Individuals may prefer the term survivor, which places focus on the ways in which a victim of domestic violence has moved past the violent relationship, survived, and thrived in the face of adversity. I use the combined term victims/survivors because it captures many of the elements from both the terms victim and survivor that are important to this study, and because it doesn't fall into the trap of a false binary between the terms.

The selection of label is a fraught field itself, with many different positions that are all quite emotionally charged in circulation around the choice between victim and survivor. For every position and label, there is a counterargument and critique of the label. For example, victim is a legally sanctioned and used term in the context of domestic violence. Some scholars have critiqued the term "victim" for focusing on violence and reifying the identity of the person as abused. "Victim" can become iconized as a stable, static subject position, positioned within a field of violence. At the same time, victim is the legal term used. In order to get justice through the legal system, one needs to be the victim of a crime, and thus victim has legal weight (Mulla, 2011). As I noted elsewhere, the term victim can be used to pathologize the individual, and according to Lamb (1999, pp. 108–109) "being victimized has become equivalent to having a chronic mental illness." Survivor is a similarly fraught term. It focuses on the ability of the person to recover and grow after trauma, but it reduces the purchase of the legal response. The bigger problem here is that the debate creates a victim/survivor binary, in which one is either a victim or a survivor. I use the term victim/survivor because it denies the binary and embraces the complex, partial, and fragmented nature of identity of a domestic violence victim/survivor. I do use the term "victim" when I am analyzing policing discourse, because that is their preferred term. In those analyses, I believe the reader will find the use of the term problematic.

Interestingly, one of the study participants comments on the terms victim and survivor (Extract I.1).

Extract I.1 Nikki

1.	*Nikki:*	Um, and, you know, it - it kinda makes it hard when you're a victim or, uh, and then,
2.		before you become to the point of being a survivor
3.	*Jenny:*	Right, right.
4.	*Nikki:*	um, of domestic violence—
5.		— um, where you're still that victim, you're anal— you're analyzing constantly what you did wrong—
6.		— where were the signs that you missed, that you don't make the same mistake, and
7.		then you end up in another one. You're, like, but those weren't fair—
8.		— so you have to refine them, so—

For Nikki, then, being a victim is a mindset in which the victim blames themselves, scrutinizing and "analyzing" their own behavior in the hopes of finding a problem of self that can fix the violent relationship. Being a survivor, by contrast, would be a subject position in which the victim no longer takes the blame for their own abuse. Of course, feeling like a victim and feeling like a survivor may co-occur. One may hope for and think about one's agency in the context of the abuse, while also recognizing that their treatment was wrong and that they have done nothing to deserve the abuse. In order to avoid the false binary between victim and survivor, then, I use the term victim/survivor, because it embraces the nuance and complications of the identities associated with being a victim/survivor of domestic violence that emerge when victims/survivors talk about themselves. Being a survivor doesn't mean one was never a victim, and being a victim doesn't mean that one is not also a survivor. In this work, I will refuse the false binary.

I.2 Domestic Violence and Police Work

Domestic violence will be my preferred term throughout this book, though I will occasionally use the term intimate partner violence. Domestic violence is more common in police and legal discourse and victim/survivor discourse alike. It is how the legal system more generally refers to this crime. Though I will be referring to multiple forms of violence – physical, emotional, verbal, sexual, and psychological – with the phrase domestic violence, for police, domestic violence almost solely refers to a physical attack of some kind. For victims/survivors, domestic violence is more than physical assault, including physical assault, emotional violence, and sexual violence. Violence for them is diverse and inclusive. In my data, abusers use a variety of physical and emotional techniques to gain and maintain control over victims; physical assault is only one tactic. Stark (2007, 2013) calls nonphysical forms of abuse "coercive control." According to Stark (2013, p. 21), "Coercive control [is] a strategic course of self-interested behavior designed to secure and expand [...] privilege by establishing a regime of domination in personal life." In other words, coercive control is the strategic subjugation of another person, established and performed in a routinized fashion in order to control another person's personal life or worldview (Stark, 2007). Coercive control is enacted through strategies of emotional and verbal abuse, which some participants in this study describe as more odious than physical abuse. At the center of coercive control is isolation, intimidation, and control. Linda, one of the participants in the study, experienced all three. As she puts it: the abuses suffered were "mental, physical, sexual. Isolating [me/Linda] from everything I knew, to everything that I knew as myself before, was isolated from everything and anybody, even phone calls, just everything" (Linda). For this and many of the participants in the study, isolation was the lynchpin of abuse, facilitating physical, mental, and sexual abuses.

Of course, emotional and physical violence are not distinct, separate or separable, and I propose that coercive control often involves both forms of violence. In Extract I.2, Killingsworth narrates how emotional and physical abuses co-instantiate each other.

Extract I.2 Killingsworth

1.	*Killingsworth*:	it was all really combined: physical, sexual, uh, and mental.
2.		But I can remember one time when we were doing one of these activities
3.		where, you know, I, quote, unquote, owed him socialization time.
4.		We were driving up to [place name].
5.		And I was driving, and
6.		he grabbed my forearm and he was squeezing it as hard as he could.
7.		And he was totally silent, and
8.		I was saying, "Let go of me. Stop it. That hurts. Stop touching me. I'm driving."
9.		And he was quiet and all he just kept saying was,
10.		"You have to submit. You have to give in. You have to submit. You have to give in."
11.		And I got bruised from that.

Killingsworth tells a story in Extract I.2 in which her abuser uses physical and verbal/emotional tactics in unison. This story is introduced with a statement about abuse in general, of which this story is just one instance. In this story, Killingsworth's ex-husband hurts her by squeezing her arm with enough force to leave a bruise. While he is hurting her, he demands her submission, both physical and emotional. This is an act of subjugation, of "coercive control" (Stark, 2007). Coercive control creates a systematically regulated program of abuse. Killingsworth lived under such a structured program, a regime in which she is explicitly told that she must submit to her abuser. He wants her to give in emotionally as a condition of stopping the physical abuse. This is a program of control, and in this program, physical and emotional abuses are not entirely distinct from each other, but indeed they inform each other. Both strategies are used to control and coerce obedience to the demands of the abuser.

Many, if not all, of the victims/survivors I spoke with had been abused using tactics of coercive control or emotional violence at some point in their lives. They talked about it as worse than physical assault (Becky). However, the law in the region this study was conducted in does not protect against emotional forms of violence. While police officers acknowledge the trauma and anguish associated with emotional and mental abuse in some ways, it is not against the law; these types of abuse do not fall into what they refer to as a "criminal domestic" – or a domestic call that involved physical violence or threats. So, while police officers will help out in civil matters – arguments and verbal abuse – they cannot arrest in those situations, which in their minds, seems to downgrade the significance of the violence. I discuss this issue in Chapter 3 in some detail. This is just one of the many ways the victims/survivors of domestic violence understand domestic violence differently than police officers – differences that impact the qualitative experience of the event of abuse and the police–victim/survivor interaction and that are explicated in this book.

With abuse taking many forms, abusers using a variety of techniques, and victims responding in a myriad of ways, the contexts in which police and victims/survivors interact are fraught, involving unsure footing and heightened emotions. Police readily acknowledge that domestic calls are among the most unstable and dangerous (Det. Love; Sgt. Roberts). The victims are in a state of crisis, which can be affectively performed in a number of ways, ranging from emotionally upset to calm and meticulous; people respond to trauma in different ways. Once police arrive on the scene, the victims/survivors interact with police officers who, often calm, take statements, interview parties, and generally follow procedure. Detective Tyler gives a detailed description in Extract I.3.

Extract I.3 Detective Tyler

1.	*Det. Tyler*:	Well, the first thing we do is, you know, we try to get any kind of history at the address.
2.		The thing about domestic violence calls and
3.		What law enforcement has been taught—and I've been taught—
4.		is that it is the number—one of the top,
5.		if not the number one call that results in officer assaults, officer injuries
6.		They're very dangerous calls to go on so we're pretty diligent in our safety.
7.		Gotta try and make sure that we're safe and,
8.		obviously, the people that were trying to help are safe.
9.		Um, so, we'll usually knock on the door or,
10.		depending upon if we see them—or anything like that—
11.		try and make contact with the people involved.
12.		We'll explain why we're there.
13.		Sometimes, they already know so there's really no explanation needed.

14.	A lot of times, when you show up at the door, and
15.	one of them didn't call you, they wanna know why.
16.	Usually, what I'll do is, I would walk into a room;
17.	I'll make sure that the room is safe;
18.	I'll separate the parties involved;
19.	I'll have one stay and talk with me
20.	while the other one either talks to my partner,
21.	or my partner on this call will stand there and
22.	wait until I'm ready to talk with the other half.
23.	Usually, depending upon what type of call it is,
24.	you can usually tell where this is gonna head, in a way.
25.	Whether it's a criminal violation, domestic violence, or
26.	if it's just a verbal—non-criminal domestic is what we call it.
27.	Then, if we determine that it's criminal,
28.	then we'll start making arrests if—we'll we have to,
29.	Basically, the state requires it. It's one of the very few laws that we do.
30.	We'll get the parties separated.
31.	We'll give the victim of the assault—or the victim of the criminal violation—
32.	a domestic violence pamphlet that lists everything;
33.	people that they need to call they can contact.
34.	On the back of this pamphlet there's a spot for you to put your name—
35.	as well as the case number—
36.	so that when they do call they have something to refer to.
37.	It gives everything from
38.	—what I've read in the pamphlet—
39.	from emergency shelter to victim's reparations—victim services—
40.	to our victim's advocates to assist them; legal aid.
41.	Everything, so it's very—as far as I know, it's very influential;
42.	it's very informative.
43.	At that point, we make a decision as to whether—
44.	if someone's going to go to jail, or
45.	whether they're going to be cited and released.
46.	It isn't always the first choice for someone to go to jail.
47.	To back up a little bit, the protocol—or, at least, the way that we're trained is,
48.	is to determine the predominant aggressor.
49.	Just because someone is considered the predominant aggressor,
50.	it doesn't necessarily mean that they're not a victim as well, or
51.	like that.

52.	They're the difficult calls to go on.
53.	They are hard to sort out or be, I guess I should say, empathetic on.
54.	Because you're watching someone in a torturous situation that
55.	isn't taking steps to get out of it or can't.
56.	Even when you've offered them everything,
57.	they still don't.
58.	It gets frustrating.

Notice how carefully orchestrated the police officer–victim/survivor interaction is from the police perspective. The police operate with planning, experience, and protocol. As Detective Tyler says, the situation is dangerous for all involved, and the police see their job as getting control over a volatile situation and identifying the primary aggressor in order to determine whether an arrest should be made (lines 25–27). Detective Tyler works in a "mandatory arrest" state, or a state where there must be an arrest made in any situation involving assault, as it is defined by the law – typically not only a physical assault but also a threat with a show of force. According to Detective Tyler, the victim needs help and educational resources, which police provide, but it is also the job of the police to determine who the "primary aggressor" is. If the "victim" is determined to be the primary aggressor in the abusive episode, they also gets arrested. This is what happened to Melissa, discussed above. Many of the victims/survivors I spoke with fell into this double-bind – victim and primary aggressor – and were arrested. Detective Tyler also addresses issues surrounding leaving. According to his understanding, when a victim/survivor has been offered all of the resources available and they still won't leave, it gets frustrating. Detective Tyler is not the only police officer to use the word frustrating. Victims/survivors staying in relationships make police officers feel frustrated, largely because they misunderstand the intricacies and dangers of leaving. Frustration is one of the things that creates dysfluency in interactions between victims/survivors and police officers (see Chapters 3 and 4).

Other descriptions of police protocol are much shorter and position the victim in a different light. Take, for example, Officer Riley's explanation of procedure.

Extract I.4 Officer Riley

| 1. | *Off. Riley:* | A typical? Usually, to me it seems, they call 9-1-1, |
| 2. | | but they don't necessarily… anything criminal to happen or anything to happen to the abuser. |

3.		They mostly just want them to leave for the night, and then they'll come back the next day.
4.		It seems like they want us there just to kick somebody out,
5.		and that's all the action that they want taken, really.
6.		I have yet to come across somebody who's really adamant about getting somebody out for good and
7.		wanting action taken against the abuser.
8.	*Jenny*:	How does that make you feel? What's your response?
9.	*Off. Riley:*	It's frustrating.
10.		I try to understand.
11.		I haven't been in a situation like that myself, so I can't fully put myself in a position like that.
12.		Yeah. It's frustrating to me because
13.		I want them to be able to take care of themselves and be safe,
14.		and obviously they're not if they're calling every other day.

Officer Riley's description in Extract I.4 very quickly moves into a discussion of the victim/survivor and their behavior. As she describes wanting to help and caring, she also shows frustration with victims/survivors who do not leave their abusive situation. "I want them to be able to take care of themselves and be safe, and obviously they're not if they're calling every other day" (lines 13 and 14). Victims are accused of being unable to take care of themselves, as though it is their fault for staying, as though their abuse is a failing of their ability "to take care of themselves" (line 13). There is no blame levied against the abuser. There is no recognition that three quarters of abuse victims are still abused after leaving (Berry, 2000). The officer especially shows frustration in returning to the same house on multiple occasions. As I show in Chapters 2 and 3, these are both typical sentiments for police officers.

The interaction described above – the moment that the police answer a domestic call – is important for victims/survivors, because it is in this moment that they are inaugurated into the criminal justice system. This introduction to police work, law enforcement, and the criminal justice system establishes a tone, expectations, and view of police and law enforcement for the victims/survivors that they carry with them as they move through the system.

In discourse analysis, little has been studied about domestic violence, with notable exceptions (Andrus, 2015; McElhinny, 1995; Trinch, 2003). In previous research, more attention has been paid to contexts such as the protective order interview (Trinch, 2003) or adjudication of crimes involving domestic violence (Andrus, 2015). The present project seeks to add to this growing body of literature, paying special attention to the social meaning of domestic violence and the identities of police and victims/survivors that emerge in narrative interactions about police–victim/survivor exchanges. In what follows, I consider the ways the indexical emergence impacts social identity, identifying the indexical linkages that form the social meaning of domestic violence and the victims/survivors thereof. Identity for each participant emerges and is performed differently. I follow Johnstone (1995, p. 186), finding that "sources of identity expressed in talk and other action are idiosyncratic and particular," to an extent. Though all of the victim/survivor participants have been a victim of domestic violence, the way that identity emerges as well as the other identities that emerge with it are different for each speaker.

1.3 Interaction and Discourse

Interactional analysis situates language, in this case narrative, in contexts – both those of the telling (interview) and those being retold (antecedent interaction with police). According to Hymes (1967, p. 14), "The components of speaking that are taken into account will depend upon a model, implicit if not explicit, of the interaction of language with social setting." That is, the social setting of an interaction is fundamental to the understanding of an event of speech, because, whether functioning implicitly or explicitly, the meaning of the interaction is tied to the context, culture, social setting, and the values, ideologies, and beliefs that the speakers are actively operationalizing. "Ideologies are shared social beliefs and representations that underlie social practices and discourses" (De Fina & King, 2011, pp. 164–165). Ideologies underpin social relationships that also work to form the social relationships. Thus, the discursive practices of police–victim/survivor interaction are constrained by prior knowledges, ideologies, relationships, contexts, and ultimately hopes for future discursive events. From an interactional perspective, then, "the discursive practices" of both police officers and domestic violence victims/survivors must be taken and analyzed "*in their contexts*" (Linell, 1998, p. 7, emphasis in original), in the situations in which they occur.

I am using the concept of interaction in a progressive way that understands discourse as "dynamic and mutual interdependencies between individuals as actors-in-specific-interactions and contexts, the latter seen as invoked by and emergent with (inter)actions" (Linell, 1998, pp. 7–8). Linell aptly connects interaction with discourse here, positioning discourse as both a resource for interaction and emergent from/within interaction. What is sayable emerges in interaction, even as it frames interaction. Discourse provides the resources for interaction at the same time that interaction provides the resources for discourse. According to Bucholtz and Hall (2005, p. 586), "It is in interaction that all these resources gain social meaning." That is, those semantic, semiotic, pragmatic, and rhetorical objects available in the situation emerge as socially meaningful in interaction – not prior to interaction; meaning and identity emerge as interaction unfolds.

Language, meaning, rhetoricity, etc. are not stable objects just awaiting employment by a speaker, but rather they are part and parcel of interaction. "Identities as social processes do not precede the semiotic practices that call them into being in specific interactions" (Bucholtz & Hall, 2005, p. 588). Identity is not a stable form of self-consciousness that exists prior to and outside of interaction, but rather it is performed, constructed, and emergent within interaction. Social meaning and identity are thus emergent, and they are also indexical (Bucholtz & Hall, 2005). To put it more directly, the emergence of identity is an indexical process that can take place in narrative processes. Narratives are stocked with indexical linkages by and through which identities and social meaning of persons and events emerge. According to Johnstone, Andrus, and Danielson (2006, p. 84), "indexical relations link [linguistic] form with 'social meaning' in several ways." There are a variety of indexicals that differ in the way they relate social meaning to linguistic form. As Ochs (1993, p. 297) puts it, "linguistic structures are linked to social identities [indexically] because of systematic cultural expectations linking certain acts and stances encoded by these linguistic structures to certain identities." Indexicality becomes a key location for identifying and analyzing identity work. There are divisions between groups of people, saturated with moral and ideological reasoning that create subject positions and the potential for identity for different speakers. Thus, identity and indexicality are troubled, anxious sites of competing value systems. I propose that a field of indexicality operates ideologically in part through structures of the "semiotic processes" of "iconization" and "erasure" (Irvine & Gal, 2009), in which some positionalities and identities are reified (iconization) and others are overlooked (erasure).

What we find in these data are victims/survivors of domestic violence and police officers storying events of domestic violence. For each group, we see different identities emerge for self and other, and different strategies for assigning identities for the other. The bulk of this book will analyze the different, competing, and occasionally coordinating identities for both police and victims/survivors that emerge in the indexical field of domestic violence. Both groups bring distinct ideological concerns, material concerns, prior experiences, trainings, and procedures with them to their interactions.

1.4 Narratives and Identity, Narrative Identity

Identities are developed in, deployed in, and generally related to narratives. Bamberg (2006, p. 144) defines narrative as "the activity of giving an account." Bamberg importantly frames narrative as an activity – something that is functioning as ongoing and interactive. This process – narrative – is fundamentally a relational description about some prior or anticipated occurrence. Narrative, or storytelling, which I will use as a synonym for narrative, is an activity, rather than a preformed set of ideas, frozen in genre. Creating an account of a past interaction is an endeavor in which meaning emerges in the context and process of telling and in relationship to present interlocutors. Thus, when we analyze narratives, we ask questions about "how we might *define narrative*, on what sorts of *occasions* narratives get told, how analysts *find identity* in instances of storytelling, and what people are *doing* when they tell stories" (Benwell & Stokoe, 2006, p. 130, emphasis in original). That is, narratives are spaces to query identity emergence, places where people do identity work for self and other, and narratives are pragmatic – they do something that includes and goes beyond the simple telling; they build and communicate world views, persuade the listener as to the credibility of the story and the teller, and the like. Just as some phonological variables can come to do identity work in local speech in Pittsburgh, for example (Johnstone, 2013; Johnstone & Kiesling, 2008), some narratives can come to index specific identity formations – in this case "victim." Stories about being a victim, however, emerge alongside other identity formations, survivor, for example, which are unique to each individual storyteller.

Situated pragmatically and indexically, narratives can be seen as "provid[ing] hopes, enhanc[ing] or mitigat[ing] disappointments, challeng[ing] or support[ing] moral order, and test[ing] out theories of the world at both personal and communal levels" (Schiffrin, De Fina, & Nylund, 2010, p. 1). Narratives are places of identity work, places where one can play with ideas about society and community. Testing the "moral order" is a fundamental part of stories that either demonstrate compliance with community/moral standards or that they contest, challenge, and question the communal and moral order. Thus, Ochs and Capps (2001,

p. 4) argue, "All narrative exhibits tension between the desire to construct an overarching storyline that ties events together in a seamless explanatory framework and the desire to capture the complexities of the events experienced, including haphazard details, uncertainties, and conflicting sensibilities among protagonists." There is unease in a narrative – conflicting desires. One desire is to have a polished, glossy, smooth narrative, while a corollary desire is to account for the complexities of interaction and meaning that are recast in and emerge from narrative.

Narratives about domestic violence occur in many settings, from stories swapped among friends to interviews and legal procedures. Indeed, narrative is a fundamental component of domestic violence adjudication. Victims/survivors are asked to tell their stories over and over in different configurations and forms, with different legal goals, and for different legal audiences. According to Trinch (2003, p. 3), "Narrative is especially important in law, because often in cases of gender-related violence, the abusive event occurs privately," leaving little nonlinguistic evidence. The nonlinguistic evidence that exists is on the body of the victim, but there are rarely other witnesses to corroborate accounts of abuse. The narrative of the victim is all there is. Testimony, then, is an essential form of legal narrative that carries the legal weight of evidence. Narrative is also important for the victim/survivor, who uses the process of giving an account to "carve out the meaning of abuse" (Trinch, 2003, p. 3) for himself/herself and for the legal authorities to whom the story is told. Narrative is a central activity for coping with the trauma of domestic violence. It also helps the legal authorities and police hold abusers legally accountable.

This research considers narrative and identity in terms of activity and interaction, as described earlier. It does not look for, identify, or analyze narratives based on their completeness in relationship to a heuristic, nor does it look for a set of "parts" that a narrative must contain. Instead, this analysis is concerned with the fragmented, partial, rhetorical, and pragmatic recapitulation of:

- Past interactions (stories that index a "real" event, something that the author of the story claimed did happen),
- Generalized interactions (stories that index a grouping of stories that the teller finds similar in some way, and thus narrates as a generality), or
- Anticipated interactions (stories that index events and interactions that might happen in the future under certain circumstances or if current circumstances aren't satisfied) (Georgakopoulou, 2006).

I locate and analyze narratives using these broad strokes. This mild definitional structure allows me to capture the messiness of narratives; the ways they move from general to specific and back again; the goals of the teller and the expectations of the audience; and the complexities of the events being narrated. Indeed, narratives do rhetorical work, in that they persuade the listener to take up a particular worldview and to believe the basic framework of the narrative. As such, even though they are elicited in interviews, these narratives are practical, oriented to the tasks of on-the-ground interaction. Such narratives offer and affect explicit and implicit semantic, semiotic, and rhetorical features, giving rise to the identities of the interlocutors and the cast of characters referenced in the narrative using resources available in the discourse.

As I have been suggesting, in a nuanced, interactional view of narrative, the narrative and identity formation go hand in hand. "Narrative is a fundamental construct for understanding the shape of the social world" (Benwell & Stokoe, 2006, p. 136). Narratives help interlocutors to understand the shape of the social world, because narratives offer a space in which social worlds can be developed, troubled, interpreted, and understood. According to Benwell and Stokoe (2006, p. 135), who follow Goodwin (1997), "storytelling accomplishes many different interactional functions: to amuse, inform, accuse, complain, boast, justify, to build social organization and (re)align the social order." A narrative's rhetorical force is varied and complex and always interactional. The tenor of the narrative will respond, at least in part, to the audience of the narrative. Thus, interlocutors work together to build an account. "The content and direction that narrative framings take are contingent upon the narrative input of other interlocutors, who provide, elicit, criticize, refute, and draw inferences from facets of the unfolding account" (Ochs & Capps, 2001, pp. 2–3). The people who listen to a narrative are not passive.

The audience for a story actively participates in and shapes the story being told, either directly through questions and comments, or indirectly with their very presence. The audience brings with them an ideological framework, values, and other framing devices that the storyteller tries to accommodate in their story, all of which impacts what gets told and how it gets told. Indeed, Ochs and Capps (2001, p. 2) explain that "interlocutors build accounts of life events rather than [...] polished narrative performances." The distinction between "accounts of life events" and "polished narrative performances" is an important one. The concentration on "life events" puts the focus on the interaction and world building in narrative, more or less ignoring issues of style or gloss. As an interactive building of a set of life events, "narrative activity becomes a tool for collaboratively reflecting upon specific situations and their place in the general scheme of life" (Ochs & Capps, 2001, p. 2). That is, the interlocutors work together to build a story and a story world that they reflect on together.

The narratives for this study were collected in interviews, either in a conversational setting with multiple people, or an individual academic-style interview. The interlocutor was me, referenced as Jenny in the transcripts. I had a set of questions that I used to guide the conversation, necessarily eliciting certain kinds of information and stories that led to other kinds of information and stories that were more spontaneous. I primarily interjected with indicators that I was listening, "Mm hmm" and the like. I also asked follow up questions to develop points that caught my attention or that the storyteller seemed to weigh heavily. I do want to explain that I am a survivor of domestic violence, which all of the participants knew prior to the interview or learned during the interview. As is always the case, my own subjectivity played a role in the study, impacting the kinds of things I noticed in interviews, the kinds of questions I asked, and the responses to me by those I interviewed. Subjectivity is sometimes associated with bias. Following Roulston and Shelton (2015), I reject that notion, or more softly, strive to alter the relationship. Latour (2000, p. 109) equates objectivity with "something to be looked down and explained, but also something that is to be looked up as the ultimate source of explanation." Objectivity presumes a kind of facticity that is stable for every user of the fact. Subjectivity, by contrast, is something fleeting and personal, stable only for the person whose subjectivity produced the fact. Like Latour, I reject the idea that some facts are stable while others are unstable. Indeed, the relationship between any fact and a user of that fact is subjective. And that's a good thing. It means that people are engaging with and negotiating with others and the ideas that they put into the world. The majority of the participants had knowledge of my status as a survivor, though only a few had detailed knowledge of my experiences. In some situations, this knowledge led to more open discussion with other victims/survivors, as we built a narrative of abuse together. My position as a victim may have been a liability in some ways – it may have altered the kinds of narratives and narrative details given – but it doesn't appear from the interviews that officers or victims/survivors were bothered by my subject status as a victim/survivor. I believe that revealing my victim/survivor status allowed for deeper, sustained conversations with both police and victims/survivors. All of these things shaped and formed the stories that were told to me by police and victims/survivors alike.

Given the all of the variables and complexity that go into identity and narrative, we can say that identity, self, and narrative all go hand in hand because identities are performed and emerge in narrative work. "If selves and identities are constituted in discourse, they are necessarily constructed in stories" (Benwell & Stokoe, 2006, p. 137). Stories are a strata of discourse. Discourse is made up of stories, in significant ways, if not entirely, and in those stories, selves emerge, complex, multifaceted, and partial. Indeed, Ochs and Capps (1996, p. 20) argue that "narrative and self are inseparable." The storyteller and their story emerge together, in the real-time of the interactional telling. Now, in saying this, I do not mean to suggest that narratives give access to deep-seated, static, uniform, and monolithic identity. I take Bamberg and Georgakopoulou's and others' criticisms seriously. Narrative and the identities that emerge in narrative interactions are not the "unmediated and transparent representations of the participants' subjectivities and from there as reflecting back on their identities" (Bamberg & Georgakopoulou, 2008, p. 378). Rather than seeing identity as a reflection of a true self, just waiting to be uncovered, this research sees social identity as contingent, partial, and multiple.

Of course, as Ochs (1993, p. 296) points out, "Social identities have a socio-historical reality independent of language behavior, but, in any given actual situation, at any given actual moment, people in those situations are actively constructing their social identities rather than passively living out some cultural prescription of social identity." Thus, though social categories and identities exist, individuals are not merely dupes who simply occupy preformed identity categories. Nevertheless, some identities are ratified in interaction, which makes them accessible in future interaction, in which they will re/emerge. As Bucholtz and Hall (2005, p. 588) put it, "Resources for identity work in any given interaction may derive from resources developed in earlier interactions (that is, they may draw on 'structure' – such as ideology, linguistic system, or that relation between the two)." Identity categories and performances may become narrative resources for identity formation and performance.

Those prior, ratified identities that emerge and re/emerge are precisely the identity performances that I focus on in this research – prior identity work that becomes a resource for present and future identity work. Though it may seem like this creates durable identities, in fact, in each identity performance, the identity emerges anew, drawing on structures and performances that have worked in the past, but connecting to new interactional spaces, ideologies, and interlocutors. Storytellers learn that certain performances work, and so they may rely on those performances, but they do so by reading the audience, responding to context, and responding to the discourses in play – the indexical field – and thus there is always emergence, even of identities that have been performed in some past situations. I argue, then, that identity is semistable – ratified performances from prior interactions – *and* emergent, responding to the situated requirements of the on-the-ground performance.

Identity is formed and emerges in the relationality between teller, co-teller, and listener, whose responses and input may assist in and shape the telling. In Extract I.5, we see interaction between the interviewer, Jenny, and a participant who has chosen the pseudonym Rainbow – all participants in this study selected their own pseudonyms. In Extract I.5, they are talking about the reasons it is difficult to leave abusive relationships.

Extract I.5 Rainbow

1.	*Jenny:*	Yeah. Wow. What do you think about it the saying? –
2.		some people say, "Why doesn't she just leave? She should just leave."
3.		What do you think about that idea?
4.	*Rainbow:*	I think it's typical for people to say that
5.		- because they don't understand and you won't understand unless you're actually in that situation.
6.		It's so hard.
7.	*Jenny:*	What is it that they don't understand?
8.	*Rainbow:*	To just leave.
9.		They don't understand why you're just going through this.
10.		They feel like you're just going through it like you just want to—
11.		- or you need something out of it. In reality it's really hard.
12.	*Jenny:*	Yeah.
13.	*Rainbow:*	You are with it,
14.		you found this person,
15.		you put it in your head that this is someone that was for you.
16.		You're still trying to figure out what it is about that person that drew you to them.
17.		It's just really hard.
18.	*Jenny:*	That's really interesting. I like the way you put that that. You found this person and

19.		there's this social narrative that says you should make it work. Right?
20.	*Rainbow:*	Exactly. Exactly.
21.	*Jenny:*	All the social pressure to make it work.
22.	*Rainbow:*	Yep.
23.	*Jenny:*	Especially when you have kids together. Right?
24.	*Rainbow:*	Exactly. It's so difficult.
25.	*Jenny:*	That's got to be one of the reasons he wanted to keep you pregnant
26.	*Rainbow:*	Yep, I agree.
27.	*Jenny:*	keep you under lock and key.
28.	*Rainbow:*	All the time. He was just so adamant to go do whatever he wanted to do while I just stayed at home
29.		and took care of kids
30.		and dealt with it, literally just dealt with it.
31.		I didn't leave because, like I said, I wanted to know why
32.		you feel like you see this greater person in them and
33.		you want to reach it before you just back out.

Extract I.5 demonstrates the ways that identity moves and narrative moves relate to and with the interlocutor. These two speakers share something in common: they have both been in abusive relationships. They build this story fragment about what makes leaving difficult together. What is said has as much to do with the audience and the context as the speaker herself. Further, the identity is formed and performed and emerges in the recounting of a prior interaction as much as the interaction of the interview itself. That is, the identity emerges in the on-the-ground interaction, yes, but it also emerges in the ways that the prior interactions are framed and told in the narrative. As Rainbow tells her stories, an identity of hard work and persistence emerges.

In Extract I.5, what the story is about, the prior interaction, means as much to the narrative identity formation as the interaction of the two interlocutors who share knowledge and experiential camaraderie. We begin to see this with Jenny's responses and follow up questions throughout the first portion of the conversation, lines 1–18. The common experiences that these interactants share allow Jenny and Rainbow to swap interactional places in lines 19–33, with Jenny providing key bits of information and Rainbow providing the supportive and agreeing, "Mm hmm"s and "yes"es. Together, in interaction, we see a coordinated identity emerge around the common topic of how hard leaving an abusive relationship really is and indeed the persistence required that both speakers ultimately had and share. They each supply details of what makes leaving "hard," stemming from experience about what it is that makes leaving complicated, and as Rainbow says, "In reality, it's really hard" (line 11). They work together to trouble the common, social idea that leaving is little more than simply recognizing that one's relationship is abusive. For both speakers, it is more than that.

As the discussion above shows, narrative identity emerges in interaction between the teller and the person listening to, adding to, and bringing details to the narrative. In Extract I.5, an identity of abuse victim shared by both is performed. In addition to thinking about narrative as emergent and interactional, it is useful to think about narrative and identity as fragmented and partial. A single teller and telling will not include all of the semantic and rhetorical information of the narrative. That semantic, semiotic, rhetorical, and pragmatic information of the communication will be in part, provided by interlocutors, as we saw in Extract I.5. Further, details and information will be supplied, or not, depending on the needs and expectations of the context of the telling. As Ochs and Capps (1996, p. 22) put it, "Tellings of personal experience are always fragmented intimations of experience." In a narrative, we often get pieces of a story, or a story that is pieced together. Identities that emerge in narrative may also be fragmented and partial, rather than singular, simple, and static. "Narratives have the potential to generate a multiplicity of partial selves. Selves may multiply along such dimensions as past and present" (Ochs & Capps, 1996, p. 22). That is, multiple valences of identities for the teller and/ or protagonist may emerge as they negotiate temporality, rhetoricity, and interactional spaces together.

> Narrative is born out of such tension [the fragmented, partial self] in that narrative activity seeks to bridge a self that felt or acted in the past, a self that feels and acts in the present, an anticipated or hypothetical self that is projected to feel and act in some as yet unrealized moment – any one of which may be alienated from the other. It is this sense that we actualize ourselves through the activity of narrative. We use narrative as a tool for probing and forging connections between our unstable, situated selves. (Ochs & Capps, 1996, p. 29)

According to Ochs and Capps, then, some of the work of narrative is to make identity appear as though it is stable and consistent across time (cf. Benwell & Stokoe, 2006; Johnstone, 2010). Storytellers hope that the listener will overlook competing and partial selves.

In addition to forming selves that reference the past while anticipating the future, tellings also mediate past, present, and future contexts, drawing on and shaping each in and for the individual telling and those present. "Narratives situate narrators, protagonists and listener/readers at the nexus of morally organized, past, present, and possible experiences" (Ochs & Capps, 1996, p. 22). Narrators are doing significant rhetorical work as they weave a tale, drawing on ideology and values for an audience that will also do the same. What a story will mean and which identities will form emerges in the thoughtful, socially meaningful interaction. The meaning of a story and more, including identity and context, "are emergent, a joint venture and the outcome of a negotiation by interlocutors" (De Fina & Georgakopoulou, 2008, p. 381). In this formulation, the weight is taken off of the narrator and distributed across the sociolinguistic context. The semantic and social meaning are formed in and emerge from prior meanings and activities, as well as contexts, assumptions, ideologies, and cultural processes. Social meaning, we might say, emerges in the interaction of the narrative, prior interactions that are gestured to, interlocutors who are present, and those who may hear the narrative second hand. Thus, as Rainbow constructs her narrative in Extract I.5, she was asked to do so against a set of cultural stories about leaving that she indicates she knows exist. Her story addresses the ideology taken for granted in these stories, while it presents a counter-narrative, all for the interviewer's benefit, who Rainbow knows is also a victim/survivor of domestic violence. Ideology, interlocutor, topic, and context all come together to make the segment of speech socially and indexically meaningful.

Identities, partial, fluid, and multiple, emerge in and are performed in narratives. In the telling, narratives provide us a window onto some past moment in time – they provide a window onto a worldview. "Among its many functions, language is the structuring mechanism that we employ to make sense of what has happened to us, to understand what is occurring in our immediate interactions and to predict what might happen to us in our potential encounters" (Trinch, 2003, p. 1). Narratives do more, then, than just tell a story. Narratives about domestic violence, as an event, draw on, recapitulate, and trouble ideological structures that inform cultural and social knowledge about domestic violence and those individuals who are the victims of violence. Both the speaker and the teller are operationalizing such epistemological and ideological structures. As such, "Narrative is an interactional achievement or a co-production" (Trinch, 2003, p. 5). Narrative is a situated activity in which interactional spaces give rise, indexically, to identities and social meaning. In the data described here, we are talking about the social meaning of the event of domestic violence and the victims and survivors thereof. Of note before moving on, nearly all of the victims/survivors that I spoke with, including Rainbow discussed earlier, thanked me for listening to them and making their stories public. Virtually all ached for visibility and voice. If only for them, this project aims at ending the silence around domestic violence, by paying attention to their important stories.

I.5 Indexicality, Social Meaning, and Identity

The view of social meaning presented here is linked closely to the concept of indexicality. The idea of the index comes from Peirce's (1940) three-part conception of the sign: icon, index, and symbol. An icon is visually related to the thing it represents; it "resembles what it means" (Johnstone, 2013, p. 49). An example of an icon is the cross used for worship in some Christian religions. A symbol is an abstract sign that has come to be meaningful and linked to an idea, concept, or object through habitual use. The symbol is conventional. An example of a symbol is the word *file*, which is associated with a file by way of being used to refer to it over time, such that now, it can mean a physical paper file or a digital computer file, and etc. An index is a pointing sort of thing. The meaning of the index comes from proximity with a thing which the index is close to – close enough to point to. The concept indexicality builds off Peirce's (1940) index. According to Johnstone (2013, p. 49) "Indexicality refers to the way signs are related to meaning by virtue of co-occurring with the things they are taken to mean." In the classic example, where there is smoke there is fire (Johnstone, 2013, p. 49), smoke is an index of fire; smoke points to the existence of fire. A linguistic example, borrowed from Silverstein (1995) is the first-person pronoun "I" used by a present speaker to present interlocutors. "I" in this case points back at the speaking self.

The concept of indexicality has recently been extended to think about the ways that social meaning can be indexed by a linguistic or discursive formation, as when a particular accent or way or speaking triggers an ideological presupposition about a group of speakers. "A sign is indexical if it is related to its meaning by virtue of co-occurring with the thing it is take to mean" (Johnstone, 2010, pp. 30–31). Therefore, a linguistic form can come to be connected with a social form through co-occurrence. Here, I want to think about indexicality following Eckert's (2008, p. 454) concept of an indexical field. An indexical field is a "constellation" of "potential meanings" for any given form. That is, social meaning is linked to linguistic form, but there may be multiple social meanings for any given linguistic variable and vice versa. Eckert's argument, then, is about indexical variation and the potential meanings of a variable. She writes, "Meanings of variables are not precise or fixed but rather constitute a field of potential meanings – an indexical field, or constellation of ideologically related meanings, any one of which can be activated in the situated use of the variable" (Eckert, 2008, p. 454). That is, a variable can index any of a number of potential meanings circulating in the indexical field, which is itself saturated with and related to larger ideological structures. "Indexicality relies heavily on ideological structures for associations between language and identity that are rooted in cultural beliefs and values – that is ideologies – about the sorts of speakers who (can or should) produce particular sorts of language" (Bucholtz & Hall, 2005, p. 594). Ideology structures the relationship between social form and linguistic form. "Variation constitutes an indexical system that embeds ideology in language and that is in turn part and parcel of the construction of ideology" (Eckert, 2008, p. 454). Variation creates an indexical system that is at once ideological and value laden, and I will argue, so does narrative.

Like variation for Eckert, I argue that narrative creates an indexical field filled with social meanings that can be activated by the strategic use of a range of variables, in this case word and phrasing choices. For example, there are many potential meanings for "domestic violence" as a social form that is differently constituted depending on other indexical variables. Here, I argue that identity also emerges along with the pathways that are activated in an indexical field. Indexicality and identity go hand in hand. Identity emerges based in part on the variables in the indexical field that are animated in speech.

Indexicality depends on and produces the ideological conditions out of which social meaning and identities emerge. Indexicality thus informs and determines who can speak, what they can say, and what is hearable from them. According to Bucholtz and Hall (2005), the following kinds of issues are important in the study of indexicality, identity, and interaction.

> Identity relations emerge in interaction through several related indexical processes, including: (a) overt mention of identity categories and labels; (b) implicatures and presuppositions regarding one's own or others' identity positions; (c) displayed evaluative and epistemic orientations to ongoing

talk, as well as interactional footings and participant roles; and (d) the use of linguistic structures and systems that are ideologically associated with specific personas and groups. (Bucholtz & Hall, 2005, p. 594)

Analysis of identity through the lens of indexicality runs the gambit from the explicit mention of social categories and groups to more implicit assumptions and discursive and ideological formations about the same. In the present study, we find some explicit mention of categories – for example the police only use the term "victim" to talk about people who have been brutalized by their intimate partners – but we also see more implicit constructions of indexicality and identity formations in how victims/survivors are talked about. We see identities emerge in how stories are told, what elements of narrative arise as important, and how they – victims/survivors and police – story each other.

We find indexical forms in the ways people tell stories about domestic violence, drawing on ideology and cultural notions in order to position their "self" against a social other – the one present in the prior interaction that is being recapitulated and the one who is present for the telling. Indexical identity emerges in this positioning – the relating of the story world to the storytelling context. This is true for the victims/survivors and the police officers and staff alike. "In identity formation, indexicality relies heavily on ideological structures, for associations between language and identity are rooted in cultural beliefs and values – that is ideologies – about the sorts of speakers who (can or should) produce particular sorts of language" (Bucholtz & Hall, 2005, p. 594). These indexical linkages happen differently for different speakers, and importantly, storytellers may make requests of interlocutors to comport with a particular social meaning with which the addressee or object of address may disagree.

Speech, behavior, affect, and identity are constrained and enabled in the ideological and indexical linkages that talk about victims, violence, police work, and social norms in the same breath. Those with more institutional power, in this case police officers, have more access to indexical linkages that have social and institutional weight – they decide who gets arrested. As one police officer put it, "we're the only career that we can literally strip everyone's freedom" (Officer Angel). With this statement, Officer Angel acknowledges that police have a special kind of institutional power, the power to incarcerate.

In order to understand the relationship between stories and indexicality between police officers and victims/survivors, I borrow from Irvine and Gal's (2009) tripartite theory of language ideology to explain the complications of identity emerging and performed through narrative within a field of indexicality. According to their theory, iconization "involves a transformation of the sign relationship between linguistic features or variety and the social images with which they are linked," such that "linguistic features that index social groups or activities appear to be iconic representations of them" (Irvine & Gal, 2009, p. 37). That is, iconization makes an indexical phenomenon like identity formation appear to be fixed and permanent rather than fleeting and emergent. Iconization reduces an individual or activity in limiting ways, constraining how or if a particular identity performance can be recognized within the field of indexicality. Iconization relates directly to the processes of "erasure," or linguistic processes that make it possible to ignore or misrecognize particular identity performances – those that do not comport with iconization. I argue that within the field of indexicality that is domestic violence, we find patterns of iconization and erasure that relate police discourse to victim/survivor talk. For example, in Chapter 3, I show how police create an iconic version of domestic violence victim that occludes some of the performances of identity and agency apparent in the narratives of domestic violence victims/survivors, themselves.

What emerges in the data collected here is a set of indexical, sometimes competing and sometimes coordinating, social identities in and around domestic violence, some of which function via iconization, and others of which function via erasure. We learn what the victim/survivor identity is performed from the perspective of the survivor himself/herself as well as that of the police. Ultimately, we learn what the indexically constructed social meaning of domestic violence is as well as the indexically emerging social identity of domestic violence victim/survivor.

1.6 Policing Domestic Violence

Changes to police policies in the last two decades have led to more arrests of domestic violence perpetrators (Buzawa & Austin, 1993, p. 611). This is true in the Western city in which this study took place. In 2017, a statute was passed in this Western State that requires an arrest if there is an assault. So-called mandatory arrest laws such as these are now common across the United States. A number of the stories told to me happened before this law was passed, and they note that police came and calmed down the situation, but rarely did they arrest the perpetrator. Indeed, Sgt. Roberts corroborates this story, stating that in the past, "We usually routinely sent them to family members. I really rarely remember – unless it was serious injuries – that on your basic domestic anymore that we arrested anybody. We usually separated them and took him to his brother's or his family or his parent's or something." Things have changed since the 1980s when Sgt. Roberts began his career. A study by Buzawa and Austin (1993) showed that the victim's wishes and preferences made some difference in whether an assailant was arrested in a domestic case, but it had to be coordinated with other reasoning used by the police officer. We see a similar pattern with the police studied here. Other research shows that victim cooperation is seen as a pivotal part of making a "good arrest" in a domestic violence case (cf. Berk & Loseke, 1980; Worden & Pollitz, 1984), when taken with other factors such as the severity of the abusive event, the behavior and personality of the victim, and the number of times police answered a call to the residence.

Other research on victim–police interaction focuses on victim reporting behavior in the context of domestic violence. Felson et al. (2002, p. 68) suggest that the decision even to call the police is complicated by the "effects of the victim–offender relationship." They argue that gender and relationship status (married versus unmarried cohabitation) significantly impact the decision to call the police. Hoyle and Sanders (2000) ask what it is victims want when they call the police, in relationship to arrest policies, showing that there is a range of wishes regarding police intervention. Working with post-event interview data, Hoyle and Sanders (2000, p. 21) find that the victim's choices regarding the decision to call the police and their wishes regarding arrest are strategic and rhetorical. They found that while half wanted the offender arrested and charges pressed, the others wanted other things – offender taken away from the house to cool down, police intervention to "teach him a lesson," and the like (Hoyle & Sanders, 2000, p. 22). Coulter et al. are interested in understanding the factors that women take into consideration when they make the decision to call the police. They note that half of the women who report a violent crime do so out of "fear of retaliation" (Coulter et al., 1999, p. 1290). Victim/survivor perception of police attitudes toward victims and domestic violence also plays a role in the decision to call the police. Variable responses to domestic violence and policing aside, according to Coulter et al. (1999), victims who had entered a shelter were overwhelmingly willing to call the police.

My data show a slightly different story. Although more than half of the victim/survivor participants reported negative experiences with police, all, but two, said they would call the police again if they needed them. There was no difference between those participants who were in shelter and those who were not. Some of the participants reported some bullying behavior by police, such as threats of arrest to the victim and threats that they will lose their kids. The police themselves did not express that they would threaten victims/survivors, but many of them did express frustration with victims/ survivors and held the viewpoint that victims are likely to return to abusers.

Another issue that arises in the police discourse is the relationship between public and private. Domestic violence is a crime that happens in the private sphere, which is one of the things that historically protected it and kept it legal, and is one of the things that keeps domestic violence secret (see Chapter 1); it happens behind closed doors. Police feel the public/private binary and respond to it in interesting ways. It came up in the very first interview with Detective Love, who said, "that's something we have to overcome as police officers, too, because we have that on thoughts with us. We do not want somebody coming into our house – [...] and getting into our business, and telling us how we should run our household." Detective Love, a seasoned veteran, recognizes that it's hard to have other people, strangers, in your business, and so he is empathetic. It's also troubling. "We don't want somebody [...] telling us how we should run our households" makes sense in a general sense, but not in the context of domestic violence. Domestic violence is a situation that requires disruption and correction, not a baleful looking away. Police work provides an interruption in crimes, and so it necessarily should interrupt and alter the course of crimes that happen behind closed doors.

The public/private binary doesn't only affect the perpetrators of the crime. It may be difficult and "embarrassing" for victims/survivors to have their private lives placed under public scrutiny. As Officer Angel puts it in Extract I.6.

Extract I.6 Officer Angel

1.	*Officer Angel:*	Other things that I've seen is, and it's not uncommon,
2.		is some of 'em are just embarrassed to continue forward.
3.		They see this major police response to their home;
4.		they're now thinking the neighbors are seeing all these police cars.
5.		If somebody has sustained some type of physical injury,
6.		they may start to think, now I'm gonna be in public like this.
7.		If I show up to work, beaten up, then people are gonna ask questions.
8.		Some of these cases end up on the news, which can cause additional public scrutiny,
9.		and for a victim, that can be even more victimizing in and of itself for that crime

In Extract I.6, Officer Angel is calling attention to the ways that making domestic violence public may be seen by some people as disadvantageous for victims/survivors. They may not want next door neighbors or people at work to know they are in an abusive relationship. Police response to your home, according to Officer Angel, is embarrassing for all involved. Officer Angel goes on to assert that "public scrutiny" may be "even more victimizing" than domestic violence itself (lines 8 and 9). This echoes centuries old reasoning that domestic violence should be legally ignored because the sanctity of the home is more important than this particular brand of violence. Officer Angel appears to support this reasoning, and problematically so. As Dettmer (2004) puts it, "the eradication of domestic violence was not [seen] as important as keeping the home life free from state interference. That is, preventing violence was not as important as maintaining long-held beliefs in the husbands' duty and obligation to maintain control over their wives" (quoted in Woolley, 2007, p. 273). If we follow the reasoning that private matters should remain private, we problematically protect the abuser and the space of abuse.

I.7 Narrative Identities of Domestic Violence

In these data, a number of narrative types emerge, either because they are suggested by the interviewer or because they are brought up by the interviewee. In every interview, police and victim/survivor alike, we find storying of (1) physical violence, (2) emotional violence, (3) staying/leaving in abusive relationships, and (4) policing. In the police narratives, policing discourse takes the form of procedure and explanations of the law and stories about interactions between police officers and victims/survivors. For police officers and victims/survivors alike, there are other stories as well that may relate to or diverge from these four groupings, for example, stories about child abuse from the youth of the participant, cruel parents, abuse of the participant's children, grown children, family responses, and career/work. These stories do not occur with nearly the frequency, and when they are told, it is typically to support one of the four main story types. For example, Butterfly tells a story about the abuse of her son by her partner in order to clarify just how dangerous the abusive partner is. Rainbow narrated her relationship with her abusive mother to explain why she stayed so long with her abusive partner. These stories provide context for the central stories about domestic violence that were shared with me. Indeed, context – from across lived life – is important to many of the victims/survivors. Their narratives draw on experiences, interactions, and relationships from a variety of realms of life and across their lifetimes in order to provide context for stories of violence. In particular, stories about staying in and eventually leaving violent partners required context and background.

Police personnel also have narratives of domestic violence that are sometimes personal – three officers and staff members were victims/survivors of domestic violence. In recounting domestic violence, police officers also oriented toward issues of control, criminality, and frustration. The victims/survivors who were also police officers or staff have responses and stories to domestic violence that are not far off from other victim/survivor stories, orientations, and identities. However, in their discussions of domestic violence from the perspective of a police officer, they are not very far afield from their colleagues who had not experienced domestic violence. Police officer narratives of domestic calls in general focused on the danger of the situation and safety concerns, established protocols, and their desire for victims/survivors to leave and stay out of abusive relationships. Police officers also gave background and context to explain their views on domestic violence.

For police officers and victims/survivors alike, there is a deep and abiding concern with staying in and escaping from abusive relationships. Nearly all police narratives come back to an exposition on why victims should leave as well as critiques of staying. I have labeled these stories "Staying/Leaving stories." I group these two types of stories – staying and leaving – together, because they are related to the participants. Staying is articulated in terms of leaving, and leaving is described as the end of staying. For victims/survivors, these two types of stories are also oriented toward complicating and debunking victim-blaming, cultural discourses about staying in or leaving an abusive relationship. There are social discourses about staying and leaving an abusive relationship that suggest that leaving an abusive relationship is as simple as standing up and walking out the door. Further, it is suggested that abuse victims should do this immediately upon realizing that they are being abused, physically, emotionally, or both. These ideas are referenced by the police officers when they speak about "victimology," and they are indexed by victims/survivors when they talk about how hard it is to leave. In Extract I.7, Detective Love references "victimology" in a description of procedures for answering domestic calls.

Extract I.7 Detective Love

1.   *Det. Love:*   You know, [the call] usually comes in.
2.   Sometimes, it comes and not from the family.

3.		It comes in from the neighbor—
4.	*Jenny:*	The neighbor.
5.	*Det. Love:*	- from the neighbor that—
6.	*Jenny:*	I've called.
7.	*Det. Love:*	Yeah. They hear something going on.
8.		We strongly urge that because of victimology and the mindset of the victim not being—
9.		sometimes, somebody from the outside it needs to have that call come in.
10.		A lot of times, that's how it comes in.
11.		That's how we start our encounters is seeing people who initially don't want to talk to us at all,
12.		even if they are victims.
13.		They don't want to see police there at their home.
14.		It starts off on rough ground.

[…]

15.		- but when we come across victims, they have a certain way of thinking,
16.		whether it be that the denial that they're even a victim,
17.		or the lack of self-confidence to even go through with a case, or just their overall
18.		perception of the situation that they're in.
19.		We talk about toxic and unhealthy relationships.
20.		Again, that the denial is even there that they're even in one because they don't understand.
21.		They may have been raised in a relationship like that,
22.		so what they are experiencing, that violent relationship
23.		that they're in, to them, is completely normal. Yeah.
24.		That's what they know.
25.		That's what they were raised with.
26.		This is the way that things are supposed to be.
27.		It's taking them out of that mindset there and showing them
28.		what could be improved, what could be better,
29.		what could be more healthy for them, and their family, and their children.

This officer's view sees victims/survivors as resistant to police intervention, which he blames on "victimology and the mindset of the victim" (line 8).

This view of the "mindset" of the victim of domestic violence sees victims as having a deficit and being in a state of denial, unwilling, or unable to recognize the abuse that they experience every day (line 8). This resistant victim/survivor does not see that their relationship is "toxic" (line 19), thereby denying themselves something "more healthy" (line 29). Here, we see a piece of the puzzle of the indexical formation of domestic violence "victim." According to police, victims/survivors do not want police intervention, they speak in ways that indicate some level of denial, and thus they are situated in a pathology called "victimology" (line 8). This is opposed to the narratives about staying/leaving told by victims/survivors that are contextually rich and about lived experience.

In victims/survivors' staying/leaving stories, a number of tropes emerge that are different from those available in police stories of staying/leaving. First, the victims/survivors of domestic violence are preoccupied with "not going back." As Butterfly puts it, "I know I'm not gonna go back." Marlo similarly said, "I'm not one of those seven timers," referencing the shared knowledge at the shelter that it can take up to seven times leaving before the victim/survivor stays out of the abusive relationship. Second, the victims/survivors appear to feel socially pushed to articulate why they stayed, for however long they stayed, in an abusive relationship. This social pressure to up and leave is encapsulated in the often judgmentally formulated rhetorical question, "why don't you just leave?" As I discuss in Chapter 3, victims/survivors have good answers that range from not having anywhere else to go (Butterfly), to wanting to maintain paternal relationships for their kids (Denise). What is interesting in these stories is an indexical linkage between an identity of good mother and discourses of staying/leaving. Many participants expressed staying and leaving in stories about their children. Most of the victims/survivors in this study had children that they talked about as they narrated domestic violence.

When police officers story victims, they focus heavily on leaving/staying issues, tending to be obsessed with the victim leaving, riddled with critiques of victims/survivors who stay, and completely ignoring those many women who do leave. Sometimes the focus is on the cooperativeness of the victim. As we will see in Chapter 4, the officers are concerned with compliance and controlling the scene, and the victim is just one more thing to be controlled on scene. As they are narrated, recalcitrant victims are not only "frustrating" but sometimes violent toward officers. Cooperation indicates an acknowledgment of power to arrest, which police equate with their ability to help the victim. Lack of cooperation flouts the expectations of the police officers.

The differences between police officer and victim/survivor stories of leaving/staying are striking. For police, all narratives slip into discussions of leaving and staying that identify valid reasons for leaving and critique victims for not taking exits that present themselves. These narratives also slip into general terms very quickly, wherein they are talking about victims in general, even when they are telling a story about a specific victim (iconization/erasure). Indeed, the police discussed leaving in less contextually rich ways, and they often used the terms "frustrating" and "frustration" in narratives about multiple domestic calls to the same address. The victims/survivors, on the other hand, talked about *why* they stayed or left, and they did not hem "victims" into a small frame.

The victims/survivors are also preoccupied by emotional violence, which correlated in many of their narratives with staying/leaving stories. Importantly, many victims/survivors claimed that emotional violence is worse than the physical violence that they also endured. Becky says it this way, "I actually, I hate to say it, but we were just talking about this outside. I actually think emotional abuse is worse than physical abuse." Becky doesn't just articulate the position that emotional abuse is worse than physical, she presents it as a recent topic of discussion in which multiple victims/survivors were talking and had come to the same conclusion, thereby ratifying the position. Bubba explains the position by telling a small story that contrasts her ex-husband and her ex-boyfriend in terms of emotional versus physical abuse in Extract I.8.

Extract I.8 Bubba

1.	*Bubba:*	The shit that would come out of his mouth.
2.		I'd rather have a black eye, to be honest with you, cause
3.		I healed from my black eye with my ex-husband.
4.		This dude. Man, that's gonna be a lot of therapy to get that outa my head.

Bubba articulately expresses the idea that healing from emotional wounds takes significant time and energy, a position shared by many of her peers. Emotional violence is complicated and vexed for the victims/survivors and police officers alike. Emotional violence is the use of mental and verbal tactics to tear down the person being victimized. Some examples of emotional violence described by the domestic violence victims/survivors include gaslighting (Sasha), put downs (Beth), copious and extreme yelling (Becky, Crystal, Beth), criticism of motherhood abilities (Melissa), and isolation (Melissa, Little Bird, Butterfly). This kind of emotional violence is fundamental to abuse, in as much as it operationalizes control in order to keep the victim down and stop them from leaving. Many of the victims/ survivors explain that they stayed for as long as they did because of the debilitating effects of emotional violence.

Another thing that emerges in the telling of the emotional violence story is its legal unreportability. It is not a crime to yell at your wife for hours a night. It is not a crime to stop your partner from sleeping night after night. Police cannot be called in for help in such cases, which functions to further isolate the victim and do violence. The lack of legal recourse is underscored by the fact that many of the victim/survivor interviews found emotional violence the most egregious form of violence. That is, the victims/survivors interviewed found verbal and emotional abuse heinous, and yet, it is not litigable. Police noted the problem of so-called civil calls or "verbals," but without the recognition that these events trouble victims/survivors as much or more than physical altercations. The distinction between emotional and physical violence is a false dichotomy. A violent action can contain both, and both are violent events. Being strangled or beaten, for example, is often attended by verbal threats and insults, effecting intimidation and control, which I will discuss more in Chapter 4.

Narratives about policing produced by victims/survivors of domestic violence are significantly different than those produced by the police themselves. The differences hinge on a relationship to and account of power and control, as well as histories of interaction with the other. When victims speak about police, a number of things happen. First, the narrative about policing nearly always follows one of a violent episode, establishing the reason for calling the police and providing context for the criminal activity. Second, they evaluate the police officer in some fashion: helpful, compassionate, kind, judgmental, mean, unfair. A few, interestingly enough, do not give a precursor narrative at all; they simply jump to judgment. In the process of narrating a past event, a monolithic identity for police emerges, but interestingly enough, in many ways it coordinates with the identity that police themselves perform, namely, one of procedural expert with authority to enforce law and ultimately arrest.

What we have analyzed in the interviews here is the emergence of identity within interaction in at least two locations. First, we have the emergence of identity for self that occurs in the past interaction that the narrative is recapitulating. In that retelling of a historical interaction, the narrator recounts what happened, but he/she also gives an account of the identity that emerged in that prior interaction – the story world. We see this in both the interactions with victims/survivors and the interactions with police officers. Not only does the narrator give an account of their own earlier identity but they also give an account of their perception of those with whom they are interacting, the other. That is, they give an account of their past self and prior other. Second, we have the emergence of identity of self that happens in the interactional space of the interview – the storytelling world. In Extract I.5, we saw the interaction leading the interviewer to drop her professional self and pick-up and articulate her victim/survivor self. This leads the interviewee, Rainbow, to situate herself in feedback mode, before she moves to reclaim the floor even more boldly. Identities of both content expert and camaraderie emerge for both participants in this conversation, as the interactants orient within an indexical field about domestic violence.

I.8 (Critical) Discourse Analysis

Discourse analysis is an interdisciplinary project in which the details of text and talk are analyzed closely in order to find structures of power (Blommaert, 2005; Fairclough, 1995), identity formation (Benwell & Stokoe, 2006; Bucholtz & Hall, 2005; Johnstone, 2010), language differentiation (Irvine & Gal, 2000), the emergence and performance of gender and sexuality (Bucholtz & Hall, 2005; Cameron, 1998), and so on. It is important to pay attention to the details of text and talk because, language, "though widely misperceived as transparent" actually does work "producing, reproducing, or transforming social structures, relations and identities" (Fairclough, 1995, pp. 208–209). That is, in discursive forms we find social meaning and performance that can only be accessed and analyzed with close attention to the empirical details of discourse. For these reasons, it is essential that I have access to actual, naturally occurring talk produced in and about the police–victim interaction.

A subfield in discourse analysis is forensic discourse analysis, which is the study of legal language. It is common in this analysis to take a component of language and discourse (i.e., intertextuality, indexicality, turn-taking, etc.) and trace an element of legal discourse. In this analysis, language or discourse is not merely a vehicle that carries or transmits information and meaning. Language, according to Matoesian (2001, p. 3), "actually constitutes and transforms evidence, facts, and rules into relevant objects of legal knowledge." That is, law – evidence, testimony, statutes, etc. – are made in and of discourse. Their meaning is in the word.

An important strain of research in forensic discourse analysis for my project here is policing. The research about policing has largely focused on those accused of crimes, their potential innocence, their treatment in the legal process, and so on. Much of the research has been about intertextuality, power dynamics, and turn-taking strategies that function in and impact police–suspect interviews, police–witness interviews, and police–victim interviews. For example, Heydon (2005) analyzes the form and function of linguistic pressure in police interviews. This research works to expose, "assumptions and beliefs underlying the discursive practices of participants in the interview" because such exposure "is an important process in understanding how apparently voluntary confessions can be influenced and guided by the police institution, represented by the interviewing officer" (Heydon, 2005, p. 2) (cf. Haworth, 2009; Newbury & Johnson, 2007; Shuy, 1998; Thornborrow, 2002). An important piece of research on police is Shuy's (1998) study on police–suspect discourse. Analyzing a number of high-profile cases, Shuy describes the discursive differences between interrogation and interview. Shuy also analyzes confessions given in interrogations, and he analyzes the composition of Miranda rights. Rock (2013) takes an intertextual approach to police work. She argues that there are substantial prior texts in police situations – notes, trainings, protocol and procedure, previous experiences, etc. Thus, the resultant narratives produced in interrogation are intertextual. They draw on and anticipate prior texts and future usages (cf. Heydon, 2013). Andrus (2015) also sees police testimony as intertextual, drawing as it always does, on institutional discourse, like statues, that frame and constrain the testimony.

Other research takes up issues of witnessing and victimhood, with regard to police interviews and interactions. In their 2015 article, Dando et al., describe and analyze approaches to interviewing witnesses, especially "vulnerable witnesses." Johnson (2008a) analyzes the ways that stories change during police interviews, attending to the nuances of both suspect and witness interviews. Indeed, Johnson's (2008b) work about police interviews and shifting narratives is important for understanding how police interviews impact the evidence that results from them. MacLeod's (2016) important work on victim–police interactions is concerned with interviews between police and survivors of rape who are reporting the rape, and the ways they mitigate blame in those interviews.

One important discourse analytic study deals with issues of domestic violence and law enforcement. McElhinny (1995) focuses on police–lay person interactions, with some focus on domestic violence. In that study, she rode along with officers over many weeks, even answering calls with them, approaching the door, and interacting with victims and perpetrators. That research shows that female victims of domestic violence interacted with the female researcher and with typically male police officers in ways that were gendered, interacting with the researcher by asking her to recognize the victim's plight, while asking male police officers to agree that the perpetrator's behavior was aberrant (McElhinny, 1995). In more general claims about policing, McElhinny (1995, p. 115) argues that socialization to act like a police officer overrides or supersedes other performances of identity, in part because of other people's presumptions and expectations about police officer ideology and behavior. In fact, McElhinny's (1995, p. 115) research shows, "many police officers believed that the high rate of divorce among police officers is in part a result of their taking their interactional style home." Thus, interaction and interactional style appear to be on the minds of police officers, and they impact their identity emergence and performance. This book builds off of McElhinny's research to think about the ways police officer identity is fairly stable across participants, emerging in similar ways. Because of police culture, discourse, trainings, and interactions, a semistable identity of police officer has emerged and has been ratified. This identity is available to police officers to perform. Of course, the emergence of identity is colored by interaction, personality, and interlocutor, adding depth and nuance to the "police officer" identity.

In addition to a long-standing concern with policing discourses, forensic discourse analysis often takes violence against women as a point of concern, especially focusing on cases involving sexual violence and assault. A prime example of this is Ehrlich's 2003 book, *Representing rape*. In that book, Ehrlich analyzes a rape case, especially focusing on the direct- and cross-examination of both victims and suspects of a rape trial for two rapes that took place on a college campus. She shows how question asking strategies used by the defense attorneys presupposed the sexual promiscuity of the victims, thereby controlling the attempts of the victims to describe the ways they fought during their attacks. The assailants, on the other hand, operationalize a grammar of "nonagency" in their defenses. The result was the discursive revictimization of the young women who had been assaulted and raped (cf. Ehrlich, 2015; Kitzinger & Frith, 1999). Similar work on rape comes from Matoesian (1993), who shows that rape trials tend to blame and revictimize victims of rape. Also focusing on trial discourse and transcripts, he analyzes the ways in which "language use, or discourse, constitutes legal realities in the social construction of rape's legal facticity" (Matoesian, 2001, p. 3). Legal linguistic forms and ideologies are the resources operationalized in the making of legal facticity with regard to allegations of rape. Trinch (2003, 2010) discusses sexual violence in the context of domestic violence. She shows how Latina victims/survivors narrate sexual assault carefully as they navigate the legal social world. Sexual talk is typically avoided by Latina's, according to Trinch (2003). Some of the speakers in Trinch's study use legalese in a euphemistic way to navigate the delicate topic of sexual assault in the legal system. Ultimately, she shows that the legal system and actors in the legal system work to coproduce the narratives. This intertextual work makes the narratives legally recognizable (Trinch, 2003, 2010).

The vast majority of scholarship on violence against women has focused on rape. Only a small group of studies take domestic violence in the United States as their focus (Andrus, 2015; Trinch, 2003). Trinch's (2003) book on the narratives constructed in the context of protective order interviews with domestic violence victims argues that such narratives are co-constructed between the interviewer, the victim, and the institutional surround. Trinch cogently shows the ways in which there is a mismatch between the ways domestic violence victims want to tell their stories and the expectations and requirements of the legal system. In order to create a legally effective narrative, the legal institution, forms, procedures, and expectations necessarily shape the narratives that domestic violence victims bring with them when they ask for help getting a protective order. Of course, there is some push back against the legal institution by victims who are doing identity work in their narratives. At the same time that victims/survivors factually recount what happened and how they feel about what happened, identity emerges. In narrative, then, we find rich data about how situated identities emerge in interaction.

In my previous book (Andrus, 2015) I analyzed the ways that domestic violence victim's words are appropriated, taken out of context, and recontextualized in the legal discourses concerning spoken evidence. Legal language ideology, which is enacted in legal evidentiary discourses, works to frame the speaker as essentially untrustworthy. In that book, the police–victim interaction is fundamental for the use of her words as evidence. However, in the case of excepted hearsay, an utterance only functions as evidence when spoken in court by a police officer, framed with his or her explanations of the incident and the emotional state of the speaker. My previous textual study (Andrus, 2015) has given rise to the present research. In thinking about the effects of police officer restatement of a narrative told in some prior context, I have been led to ask questions about police and victim interaction that are answered in this study on narratives told by police and victims/survivors about their interactions. What the earlier work teaches us are the ways in which criminal justice discourses frame the speech of victims of domestic violence and the ways that police voices give accounts of victim speech in legally sanctioned ways. These findings lead directly to the current study that takes a step closer to the victim–police interaction via police ride-alongs, to identify the epistemological, rhetorical, and discursive resources that are brought by both victims and police in order to (1) make sense of the interaction, (2) move the situation further down the criminal justice pipeline, and (3) do identity work in the moment and later on.

I.9 Data Collection

I primarily collected data in a midsized city in the Western US with a population of just over one million. Because I must maintain the complete anonymity of all participants in the study, domestic violence victims/survivors and police officers alike, I will not disclose the exact location and name of the city, precincts, police force, and shelter in this book. At the request of my university's IRB office, both police and victims/survivors were consented at the beginning of the interview using a Consent Cover Letter. This form of consent does not collect any demographic information. The participants in the study opted in freely and voluntarily, and they were given the option of opting out at any time, freely and without malice. This alternative consenting process allows me to keep my data absolutely private and anonymous (Tables I.1 and I.2).

I interviewed police officers, sergeants, detectives, dispatchers, and domestic violence advocates who worked with the police – twenty-three in total. I worked with a police force, which oversaw a number of unincorporated areas in the larger metropolitan area. I did three police ride-alongs with two officers. I was also able to collect some limited ethnographic data in two police stations. I should note that three of the police personnel disclosed to me that they had also been victims/survivors of domestic violence. Their domestic violence stories were analyzed alongside the other victims/survivors.

Table I.1 *Victims/survivors*

Location	Number	Gender breakdown
Western City, in shelter	15	11 female
National, not in shelter	11	13 female, 1 male
		Totals: 1 male, 24 female

Table I.2 *Police officer and staff breakdown*

	Number	Gender breakdown
Police Officer, Patrol	7	4 male, 3 female
Police Officer, Detective	5	5 male
Police Officer, Sargent	1	1 male
Police Officer, Admin	1	1 male
Dispatcher	6	5 female, 1 male
Victim Advocate	3	3 female
Retired Officer	1	1 male
		Totals: 13 male, 11 female

In the same region, I interviewed fifteen women, living in a large women's shelter. I also interviewed nine victims/survivors over the phone and two in coffee shops in the city. These participants came from across the United States. Victims heard about the research via word of mouth, getting in touch with me via social media. These participants were given the same voluntary opt-in/opt-out. Like the participants interviewed in the shelter, no demographic information was gathered for these participants, with the goal of keeping their identities completely and absolutely secret. If any participant brought up personal information in the interview, it was stricken from the record. All names, including those mentioned in interviews, have been changed to pseudonyms. Based on information from their interviews and the process of meeting with a substantial number of the participants, I will say that the participants were a range of ethnicities, races, socioeconomic backgrounds, educational backgrounds, genders, sexualities, religions, and the like. The victims/survivors were primarily female, except for one male, which is lower than the statistical national averages. I did speak with two other male victims/survivors of domestic violence who declined to give interviews. Only pseudonyms are used in this book. All pseudonyms were selected by the participant.

I.10 Book Structure

I analyze the data described above in four chapters, each taking up a different aspect of domestic violence, discourse, identity, narrative, and indexicality. The goal of all four chapters is to demonstrate the ways in which identity emerges within a field of indexicality that makes the identities and domestic violence in general socially meaningful. Chapter 1, "Domestic Violence, Violence against Women, and Patriarchy," examines heterosexual domestic violence with a female victim from a patriarchal perspective. This chapter argues that two forms of patriarchally styled violence – "patriarchal terrorism" (Johnson, 1995), which is an accounting of physical violence, and "coercive control" (Stark, 2007), which is an accounting of emotional violence – must be brought together in order to understand the depths and terror of domestic violence. This chapter, which is primarily theoretical rather than analytical, argues strongly that police officers need to pay closer attention to "verbal" or "noncriminal domestic" calls, because they involve real forms of violence.

Chapter 2, "Toward the Recreation of a Field of Indexicality: Domestic Violence, Social Meaning, and Ideology," begins the real analytical work, building a theory of indexicality that can be used to analyze and understand the narrative, interactional work done in storytelling about domestic violence. In Chapter 2, I identify the myriad ideas, concepts, values, and ideologies that circulate in narratives about domestic violence and encounters between police officers and victims/survivors of domestic violence. I argue that the field of indexicality functions like a tapestry made out of stories told about domestic violence and police while also informing and shaping said tapestry. For example, nearly every participant in the study, police officer and victim/survivor alike, touches on issues of emotional violence, describing it, dismissing it, or accounting for its effects. Likewise, physical violence is also topicalized in nearly all of the interviews, giving accounts of abuse, while also situating the speaker within the field of indexicality in which the experience is socially meaningful. Family, childhoods, children, and pregnancy figure centrally here as well, with many participants explaining, justifying, and articulating rationale for leaving and staying in abusive relationships in terms of family logics. The analysis in Chapter 2 shows that these family logics often led victims/ survivors to try to stay in the relationship in order to keep a father present for their children, or in order to remain in a position to be a helpmate to an abuser. All of the participants discuss policing in some fashion, negatively, positively, and neutrally. In this variety of stories, a great number of values and topics emerge that identify some of the fundamental ideological structures that underpin domestic violence and keep it a culturally viable structure.

While Chapter 2 considers and maps indexicality, Chapter 3, "Storying the Victim/Survivor: Identity, Domestic Violence and Discourses of Agency," shows how identity and agency emerge in the field of indexicality established and described in Chapter 2. That is, the field of indexicality (Eckert, 2008) is a discursive plane upon which identities emerge. It is also shaped and formed depending on the identities that emerge. It is a recursive relationship between identity and indexicality. What is interesting in these data is the role that agency plays in identity formation. The analysis in Chapter 3 shows that police hold a particular idea about agency in regard to the law – people do things on purpose, and they have the ability to choose to do or not to do things. Further, people can be purposefully effectual. This view of agency, that I call sovereign agency, following Foucault, allows the police to arrest, believing that a person knowingly or purposefully broke the law. Translated in the context of victims, however, this view of agency is entirely problematic. Police believe that victims can just leave an abusive relationship at will – because and if they want/ed to – and that leaving would bring a swift end to the violence. (Neither could be further from the case – see Chapter 1.) In this chapter, I show that victim views on and performances of agency are far more practical and contextual. They are making situated decisions about how to survive every day. I position both models of agency in a theory of discursive agency, to show how the police officers' more institutionally powerful discourse acts on and erases portions of victim identity. Their discourse "iconicizes" (Irvine & Gal, 2009) a particular victim and victim agency, thereby erasing aspects of victim/survivor identity that are performed in their narratives about domestic violence.

Chapter 4 analyzes police officer identities performed and assumed in both the victim/survivor and police officer interviews. For police, there are a number of identities emergent, constrained, and enabled by the network of social meanings and ideologies circulating in the domestic violence field of indexicality. In this chapter, I focus on analyzing police narratives and emergent identities. Most of the narratives told by police are either about procedure, police, and law, or about domestic violence victims. Their identities, then, largely emerge in relationship to an/other, a victim/survivor, who is storied as uncompliant with police wishes and expectations. This chapter argues that identity is formed and emerges via stories told about prior interactions and others. The identity that emerges is not only one of frustration and adherence to protocol but also of caring. In some moments of empathy, police demonstrate concern for victims/survivors and a desire for victims/survivors to get and stay safe.

The conclusion brings together the issues of the book to draw conclusions about identity, indexicality, and narrative; about domestic violence and police work; and about connections between the two. This chapter also takes up and explores the literature on some important topics in domestic violence that did not come up in the book, namely, race, education, and sexuality. Though I touched on them briefly in Chapter 1, in the conclusion I review the extant research on these issues more thoroughly.

I.11 Conclusions

This research is concerned with the ways in which linguistic resources are marshalled within an indexical field in order to do identity work. I am interested in not only how people frame themselves in narratives – how a sense of self emerges through narrative – but I am also interested in how discourses about the other emerge and function within the same field – how a sense of other emerges through narrative. The stories told and analyzed in what follows will give accounts of self and other, and in the process, they define and partially delimit what domestic violence means for this set of speakers. This work is not looking for a "correct" version of events, measuring victim/survivor stories against police officers. I am not looking for the truth or reality. Instead, following Peter Brooks (1996), I am looking to understand to what extent, if anything, the utterance is true. That is, to what other notions, issues, beliefs, lived realities, and values is an utterance true to that beyond the elusiveness of "reality."

One of the objects that some of the statements analyzed here are true to is institutions, in particular the institution of law and police work. Police discourses are powerful, and in some ways, the relationship between police and domestic victim/survivor is asymmetrical, with the police having access to institutional power that the survivor may not. This means that their version of events will become the official version. As Trinch (2003, p. 1) puts it, "While several competing linguistic forms, or representations, may co-exist at any given time, social order in a particular context is produced and reinforced when certain linguistic structures are continually favored over others." Policing discourse is institutionally favored, but not in spaces such as the shelter where victim/survivor discourses are highly valued. The discourses with which the victims/survivors flesh out and complicate the indexical field are beautifully powerful testaments to hope, love, strength, and community.

Domestic Violence, Violence against Women, and Patriarchy

Extract 1.1 Killingsworth

1.	*Killingsworth:*	The other physical things, um,
2.		there were things that I would consider to be just, like,
3.		signals of his dominance and my subordination.
4.		So he might—I might be sitting on the couch watching TV and
5.		he'd be walking by me and
6.		he would just grab me by the throat and just kind of give me a squeeze and a shake.
7.		Uh, just to let me know. And he wouldn't say anything.
8.		So his violence in—
9.		and this is why it was so hard for me to wrap my head around.
10.		It was not explosive.
11.		It was not impulsive.
12.		It was pervasive, and it was calculated to train me into subordination and –
13.		and, like, policing my own behavior constantly.

This small story is (Extract 1.1), at its core, about domination rooted in the patriarchal construct of the heterosexual marriage. Here, Killingsworth (pseudonym selected by the participant) tells a story of abuse, violence, and domination. The violence was both physical and psychological/ emotional. It was cruel, and it was "calculated" and "pervasive," but it was not "explosive." Her husband did not abuse her in the heat of the moment. No, her abuse was designed, calm, and purposeful. It was also constant and ongoing. Her husband put his hands on her maliciously, but not spontaneously. Everything was calculated to gain control. The use of physical and emotional coercion was all in the service of subordinating Killingsworth. Dominating her.

In the story (Extract 1.1), Killingsworth articulately describes emotional abuse, meant to "train [her] into subordination" (line 12). The abuse was ongoing, existing always: a way of being within the walls of the house. As Killingsworth puts it, she was being trained to "police" herself. Trained to prostrate herself to her husband. Killingsworth lived in an environment in which the abusive atmosphere never let up, always aware that some form of violence was just around the corner. This is how abusive households are sometimes structured – consistent and ever-present violence that is both big and small. Violence in Killingsworth's life functioned beyond isolated incidents. Instead, it was a structured regime of control, colored by the patriarchal discourses that infiltrate and run through male-on-female domestic violence. Killingsworth describes a pervasive violence, a violence that permeates every part of her daily life. Indeed, it is a violence that structures her daily life. In her narratives, Killingsworth describes what Stark (2007) calls "coercive control."

> Coercive control entails a malevolent course of conduct that subordinates women to an alien will by violating their physical integrity (domestic violence), denying them respect and autonomy (intimidation), depriving them of social connectedness (isolation), and appropriating or denying them access to the resources required for personhood and citizenship (control). (Stark, 2007, p. 15)

Though I disagree with the division of domestic violence as a separate phenomenon, this description of what Stark calls coercive control accounts for many of Killingsworth's experiences. She was isolated, controlled, intimidated, and abused. Her abusive partner used many different tactics consistently in order to create a structure of violence, in which she was forced to live. Killingsworth's longer story, which will be shared across the pages of this book, teaches us that "violence in abusive relationships is ongoing not episodic, […] the effects are cumulative rather than incident-specific, and […] the harms it causes are more readily explained by these factors than by its severity" (Stark, 2007, p. 12). That is, domestic violence is harmful and awful because some aspect of abuse is always present. The victim/survivor has no space of respite or rest. The harms of domestic violence are seen in the structured regimen of control and intimidation, punctuated with physical violence. These structures make up the everyday of domestic violence. Further, such violence is developed within patriarchal, masculine discourse. Stark (2007, p. 5) argues, "Men deploy coercive control to secure privileges that involve the use of time, control over material resources, access to sex, and personal service." That is, men use coercive control in sync with male privilege to demand time, sex, money, and work.

Though they are commonly divided, Killingsworth's story shows us that different forms of violence – physical and emotional/psychological/verbal – occur in the same events. They are part and parcel of the same thing. Why is it, then, that physical violence tends to get more page-time in the research, in news and other media, laws and legal discourses, and law enforcement policies and procedures? At the center of this book, and indeed this chapter, is a plea to see emotional/psychological/verbal violence as a substantive part of domestic violence rather than ancillary to it. While emotional/psychological/verbal forms of violence are often discussed in the domestic violence literature, these forms of violence are nearly always analytically separated from physical violence. Take, for example, that famous, influential, and important visual developed by Pence and Paymar (1993), often referred to as the "Power and Control Wheel." It very aptly lays out the different forms of emotional/psychological/verbal violence that are used against victims/survivors of domestic violence. In their theory/visual, power and control are broken into eight subtopics of abuse: coercion and threats; intimidation; emotional abuse; isolation; minimizing, denying, and blaming; using children; male privilege; and economic abuse. This list is important as it fairly comprehensively lays out the ways a person can be emotionally/psychologically/verbally abused. The problem with this model for this project is that it separates physical violence out, as though physical violence and emotional violence were discreet, occurring individually.

The division of physical forms of violence from emotional/psychological/verbal violence is a problem because it does not account for the ways that emotional/psychological/verbal violence underpins and is entwined with physical violence. Moreover, for the victims/survivors, the connections, overlaps, and interrelated patriarchal support between physical and emotional/psychological/verbal forms of violence are fundamental to domestic violence. However, law enforcement divides the two legally. Physical violence is criminal, while emotional/psychological/verbal is not (State Statute). Police officers call physical violence "criminal domestics" while referring to emotional/psychological/verbal violence as "noncriminal domestics" or "verbals" (Love, Roberts, Angel, Tyler, Oliver). The literature on domestic violence also separates physical from emotional, focusing on either physical violence (Johnson, 1995; Pence & Paymar, 1993; Stark, 2007; Woolley, 2007) or emotional/psychological violence (Pence & Paymar, 1993; Stark, 2007), but very rarely both together. This is problematic because Killingsworth and others in my data teach us that violence is very often both together.

I am using Johnson (1995) as a corollary to Stark's (2007) theory of coercive control. While Stark (2007) discusses emotional forms of violence,

Johnson (1995) attempts to explain patriarchally styled, physically enacted domestic violence with the concept "patriarchal terrorism." Thus, both are concerned with patriarchally flavored violence, with each focusing on a different manner of violence. For Johnson (1995), "patriarchal terrorism" involves violence in which women are controlled and overpowered violently by their male partners. He contrasts patriarchal terrorism with "common couple violence," or arguments and/or fights in which both parties share culpability. Johnson argues strongly that patriarchal terrorism is different. It involves dominance, and thus, there is no shared culpability. Patriarchal terrorism is about one party in an intimate relationship controlling and subjugating the other. Johnson and Ferraro (2000) argue that patriarchal terrorism is more common and more problematic than common couple violence. It is rare that when a relationship turns physically violent, both parties are equally to blame. Indeed, even in common couple violence, men are far more likely to begin fights, and women are more likely to be more severely hurt (Johnson & Ferraro, 2000).

Taking the stance that physical and emotional violence are part of the same phenomenon, namely, domestic violence, in this chapter, I combine the concepts of patriarchal terrorism and coercive control (Stark, 2007). I create a model for understanding physical and emotional/verbal violence as equal processes that work together in a relationship to create a system of power, control, and intimidation that impacts the victim/survivor's worldview. Police officers especially should understand physical and emotional/psychological/verbal violence as a pair. What I show here, and in the book more broadly, is that law enforcement needs better tools for understanding emotional and verbal forms of violence and would be suited to seeing coercive control as part of patriarchal terrorism rather than separate from it. More broadly, I argue that domestic violence involving female victims/survivors is saturated with patriarchal ideas and values that impact the form and function of domestic violence in heterosexual relationships. Ultimately, I assert that we will understand patriarchal domestic violence with more nuance, sustainability, and pragmatic applicability if we marry theories of patriarchal terrorism with those of coercive control.

1.1 Domestic Violence: Big Pictures

Domestic violence is one of the most intractable problems facing societies worldwide. Before moving to a discussion of patriarchally styled violence, I want to frame the discussion in current and relevant statistics regarding intimate partner/domestic violence. According to the National Intimate

Partner and Sexual Violence Survey (NIPSVS), domestic, intimate partner violence in the United States "includes physical violence, sexual violence, threats of physical or sexual violence, stalking and psychological aggression (including coercive tactics) by a current or a former intimate partner" (Black et al., 2011, p. 37). In the United States, there are more than three million violent attacks reported each year, along with any number of emotionally violent, unreportable encounters (Berry, 2000, p. 7). The National Coalition Against Domestic Violence (NCADV) estimates that approximately 90 percent of abusive events go unreported (Berry, 2000, p. 7). A police officer in this study, Officer Love concurs, stating, "we have a problem with reporting. We don't want to get other family members in trouble or the victim is in denial that this is even happening." He thus gives his opinion on why reporting is so low – people do not want to hurt family members or see them in trouble.

The NIPSVS collected data about domestic violence, which includes physical, emotional, and sexual harms in its measurements. According to the NIPSVS results (Black et al., 2011, pp. 38–39), roughly a third of women in the United States (35.6 percent) have experienced domestic violence in some fashion (physical violence, psychological aggression, stalking, and sexual assault) in their lifetimes, and one in ten women in the United States have experienced sexual violence. It is important to note that the NIPSVS does not distinguish between same-sex and different-sex couples in any of its statistics, so these figures include both homosexual and heterosexual relationships. The figures for men in the United States are somewhat less, with 28.5 percent of men reporting experiences of domestic violence in their lifetimes. Thus, domestic violence impacts women more than men, and it impacts women of color the most. Women of color are particularly at risk for being victims of domestic violence: 35.2 percent of Latinas, 40.9 percent of Black women, 45.9 percent of Native American women, and 50.4 percent of mixed-race women will experience physical violence in their lifetimes. Compare those numbers to 31.7 percent for White women. All of these numbers are too high, but we must ask: Why are women of color so at risk for domestic violence? We need to look at sociocultural factors for this risk and solutions, such as access to education and other resources, education, and residence location. It is a complex picture.

Age also makes a significant difference. Those most at risk for domestic violence are young women between eleven and thirty-four years of age, with the largest risk being between ages eighteen and twenty-four: 47.1 percent (ages 11–17, 22.4 percent; ages 18–24, 47.1 percent; and ages 25–34, 21.1 percent). Thus, adolescents make up a large portion of at-risk females.

Poverty is a key indicator of domestic violence, as well (Coker, 2001; Raphael & Tolman, 1997; Tolman & Rapheal, 2000; Williams & Mickelson, 2004). "Poor women are more vulnerable to repeat violence, yet relatively few dollars are allocated for measures that would render them less vulnerable such as transportation, or education and job training" (Coker, 2001, p. 804). That is, we know that community and material resources make a difference, but money is rarely allocated into those directions. Indeed, money is more likely to be pushed in the direction of law enforcement, even though we know that "changes in women's access to material resources [and community services] can increase their safety" (Coker, 2004, p. 1334). More money is put into law enforcement, which has a fraught relationship with domestic violence victims/survivors. Poor women, especially poor women of color, are "sandwiched by their heightened vulnerability to battering, on the one hand, and their heightened vulnerability to intrusive state control, on the other" (Coker, 2001, p. 1011). That is, domestic violence victims/survivors are vulnerable on multiple fronts: vulnerable to their abusive partner's violence and vulnerable to government and institutional intervention and control that may or may not be in-line with the wishes or best interests of the victims/survivors.

In addition to demographic data and general trends, the NIPSVS collected data on the types of emotional and physical violence experienced by men and women in the United States. This picture into abuse is incredibly important because (1) it provides a sense of the structure of abuse and its variable severity; (2) it demonstrates the severity and high occurrence rates of emotional/verbal forms of violence; and (3) it shows the ways that emotional and physical forms of violence play together. A selection of the statistics for physical and emotional violence for men and women in their lifetimes is represented in Tables 1.1 and 1.2. Table 1.1 catalogues physical harms done to both men and women such as events of hair pulling (W: 10.4%/M: 2.9%), slapping (W: 20.4%/M: 18.3%), beating (W: 11.2%/M: 2.6%), choking (W: 9.7%/M: 1.1%), and more. Table 1.2 catalogues emotional/psychological harms done to both men and women, including threats (W: 45.5%/M: 20.1%), name-calling (W: 64.3%/M: 51.6%), communication and whereabouts monitoring (W: 61.7%/M: 63.1%), forcing the victim/survivor to stay home (W: 36%/M: 19.4%), refusing to let him/her have access to money (W: 22.2%/M: 12.9%), and the like. These two charts demonstrate at least three things: First, the types of violence, both emotional and physical, are experienced by men and women differently. Men are more likely to experience some forms of violence, while women are likely to experience other forms of violence. For example, in the case

Table 1.1 *Physical violence (NIPSVS; Black et al., 2011)*

Type of violence	Women (%)	Men (%)
Slapped, pushed, or shoved	30.3	25.7
Slapped	20.4	18.3
Pushed	27.5	19.4
Severe physical violence	24.3	13.8
Hair pulling	10.4	2.9
Hit with fist or hard object	14.2	9.4
Kicked	7.1	4.3
Slammed into something	17.2	2.7
Choked or suffocated	9.7	1.1
Beaten	11.2	2.6
Burned	1.1	6
Knife or gun	4.6	2.8

of "whereabouts monitoring," men see higher rates of control. Second, the emotional/verbal figures are higher than the physical violence numbers, indicating that more men and women are emotionally/psychologically/verbally abused than they are physically abused. Finally, third, when we see breakouts of types of domestic assaults, both physical and emotional, the numbers are higher for women, nearly across the board. More women are verbally assaulted, physically assaulted, and emotionally assaulted than are men. They are choked, beaten, and socially isolated more than their male counterparts. Thus, the weight and damage of both physical and emotional elements of domestic violence appear to impact women more than men. The story of patriarchy and domestic violence begins in sociolegal discourses.

1.2 Domestic Violence: Legal Histories and Patriarchy

In Section 1.1, I gave a snapshot of the current state of affairs regarding domestic violence. In this section, I will overview the historical development

Table 1.2 *Emotional violence (NIPSVS; Black et al., 2011)*

Type of violence	Women (%)	Men (%)
Expressive aggression		
Acted dangerously angry	57.9	40.4
Called a loser, a failure, and/or worthless	48.9	42.4
Called names like fat, ugly, crazy	64.3	51.6
Insulted, humiliated, and made fun of	58	39.4
Told no one else would want them	39.1	23
Coercive control		
Isolation tactics	43.7	28.3
Abusive partner made decisions that were not theirs to make	41.2	35.5
Kept track of; demanded to know whereabouts constantly	61.7	63.1
Threats of physical harm	45.5	20.1
Abuser threatened to self-harm/suicide	37.1	24.8
Threatened to take the children	21.5	13
Kept victim from leaving the house	36	19.4
Kept victim from having their own money	22.2	12.9
Said things like, "if I can't have you, no one can."	27.4	15.4

of domestic violence so that we can understand how and why patriarchy has come to play such a big role in domestic violence. The history of domestic violence is in many ways told in the law, where it is saturated with patriarchal ideals and values. Law determines what can and cannot be done in a society, which actions and behaviors are permissible, and which will be sanctioned. There is in this history "a congruence between law and what might be called a 'masculine culture'" (Smart, 1989, p. 2). That is, the institutions of male privilege find safe haven in the law, and vice versa. Anglo-American law, working in sync with patriarchal religious discourses, has long commented on, supported, and upheld domestic violence. As Schneider (2000, p. 13) puts it, "Anglo-American common law originally provided that a husband, as a master of his household, could subject his wife to corporal punishment or 'chastisement' if he did not inflict permanent damage upon her." That is, punishment was alright, as long as that punishment did not go too far, an undetermined measurement that was easily ignored and vague enough to be unenforceable. Married women were viewed as their husband's property at worst and one-in-the-same with the husband at best. As Bathurst and Buller (1768, p. 286) put it, "the [husband's and wife's] [i]nterests are absolutely the same." One cannot do violence to one's own interests, and one cannot abuse one's own property. Such ideology reduces women to property, while simultaneously making domestic violence melt invisibly into the tapestry of the domestic sphere.

In the nineteenth century, things began changing, if only slightly. Legal statements were published that sanctioned and limited extreme forms of violence and cruelty. While mild violence was acceptable, extreme violence was to be avoided when punishing one's wife. For example, Judge Scott ruled in favor of the wife in *Holden* v. *Holden* [1810], stating, "For the reason which would justify the imputation of blame to the wife will not justify the ferocity of the husband" (English Reports: Ecclesiastical, Admiralty, and Probate and Divorce, volume 161: 616). That is, the presumed crimes of the wife do not justify the husband's ill temper and heavy hand. Still there are numerous cases in the 1800s and even early 1900s that uphold the rights of the husband to beat his wife. The infamous *State of North Carolina* v. *Black* [1864], hearkening back to seventeenth/eighteenth century reasoning, successfully asserted:

> A husband is responsible for the acts of his wife, and he is required to govern his household, and for that purpose the law permits him to use towards his wife such a degree of force as is necessary to control an unruly temper and make her behave herself.

This US case thus argues that it is the job of the husband to make his wife "behave herself," giving him permission to use whatever form of violence was effective.

Perhaps even more important in nineteenth century lawmaking around domestic violence is the use of reasoning that protected the sanctity home, the domestic sphere, from outside scrutiny. That is, there should be a partition between the public and the private sphere that stops the public from viewing and judging that which happens within the walls of the home. For example, *Bradley* v. *State of Mississippi* [1824] affirmed the innocence of Mr. Bradley for beating his wife severely, stating:

> Family broils and dissentions cannot be investigated before the tribunals of the country, without casting a shade over the character of those who are unfortunately engaged in the controversy. To screen from public reproach those who may be thus unhappily situated, let the husband be permitted to exercise the right of moderate chastisement, in cases of great emergency, and use salutary restraints in every case of misbehaviour, without being subjected to vexatious prosecutions, resulting in the mutual discredit and shame of all parties concerned.

The reasoning goes something like this: In order to be sequestered from public scrutiny, it is appropriate to beat one's wife, and to do so without legal sanction or the prying eyes of the public, which would result in *mutual* shame for the husband who is abusive, and the wife who deserves punishment for some reason. Put another way, it is alright to beat your wife, and such a beating should in no way be under the purview of the public or the law, because the sanctity of the home is more important than that of the female body. Similarly, *Black* [1864] opines, "the law will not invade the domestic forum or go behind the curtain." According to *Black* [1864], then, the inviolability of the domestic sphere is more important than the safety or health of married women, nay all women. Jump forward a hundred years, and it makes sense that the battered women's movement is taking political aim at the public/private divide and that they are making strong arguments that domestic violence is a public, not a private problem.

This short history shows us the reality and truth of Schneider's (2000, p. 5) words when she says, "Heterosexual intimate violence is part of a larger system of coercive control and subordination; this system is based on structural gender inequality and it has political roots." In other words, the violent actions of an abusive partner against an individual woman stand on and are underpinned by sociolegal discourses that have and do support domestic violence and ignore women's bodies. Within this ideological structure and within the pragmatic structure of the home, domestic violence has caused some women to second guess their every move, silencing them in their homes. As Dobash and Dobash (1992, p. 137) put it, "For a woman simply to live her daily life she is always in a position in which almost anything she does may be deemed a violation of her wifely duties or a challenge to her husband's authority and thus defined as the cause of the silence she continues to experience." Anything the abused woman does may be deemed a punishable offense, rendering her most benign act a reason for chastisement.

Responding to issues of domestic violence such as voice and the embodied experiences of abused women, the US feminist movement took notice of domestic violence in the 1960s and 1970s. US feminists began a movement, working to end violence against women, including creating a grassroots shelter network. According to Schneider (2000, p. 182), "many feminists saw battering as the product of patriarchy, as male control over women." Also identifying the state with patriarchy, feminists tended to distrust state interventions in domestic violence and to reject state and federal money (Schneider, 2000, p. 182). Indeed, many feminists "saw the state as maintaining, enforcing, and legitimizing male violence against women" (Schneider, 2000, p. 182). As a patriarchal institution itself, the state was distrusted. Some feminists worried that legal and law enforcement responses to domestic violence would continue to support the rights of the husband and ignore the needs of the victims/survivors. Their worries were proved right in some situations. "Studies [in the 1970s and 80s] revealed that the police were reluctant to respond to battered women's calls and that battered women's experiences were sometimes trivialized as 'non-crimes' by prosecutors and judges" (Murphy, 1993, p. 1263). Domestic violence was thus viewed by police as something that isn't really a crime, that should not be taken seriously. As a noncrime, "criminal justice personnel, including police, [sometimes] view battering in gender-neutral terms as a problem of pathological family interaction" (Ferraro, 1995, p. 265). Police considered domestic violence to be a manifestation of a bad family more than they viewed it as a crime. Much of the police discourse analyzed in this book holds this position, blaming an unhealthy relationship rather than the abuser (see Chapters 4 and 5).

As the history of law and domestic violence discussed earlier shows, law has traditionally supported and enforced violence against women. Further police have historically been poorly trained to handle domestic calls. "Police often exercise their power in ways that reinforce the disadvantages already experienced by women" (Coker, 2001, p. 801). Police discourse is a part of patriarchy, exercising power and authority in ways that may recognize and authorize male power and authority in the home. Police may misunderstand domestic violence, relegating it to the level of an argument (Chapter 3), and they may even arrest the victim/survivor, misrecognizing her defensiveness as the instigator of the fight.

Fears about state interventions into domestic violence, notwithstanding, ultimately, many feminist groups relinquished and began accepting federal funds, which was, of course, a mixed blessing. "Although it helped to legitimize the movement, it also served to undermine shelters' philosophy and organizational structure, requiring the employment of credentialed staff and transforming grassroots shelters into social service agencies serving clients instead of empowering women" (Schneider, 2000, p. 183). And so began the modern shelter system: a network of federally funded facilities that provide crucial social services to people who have been abused by their intimate partners.

As the shelter system developed and moved along, so did the criminalization of domestic violence. The state attacked the problem of domestic violence from two fronts, one social and the other legal. Here, I will talk about two key components in the criminalization of domestic violence: the Violence Against Women Act (VAWA) and mandatory arrest policies. The criminalization of domestic violence has been questioned, critiqued, and criticized in a number of ways. This is largely "because the state has been deficient in protecting women from abuse in the past" (Schneider, 2000, p. 184), leading concerned parties to worry about the efforts and motives of the state in the present and future. Even though changes and trainings concerning domestic violence were underway in police departments and courts of law, during the 1980s and 1990s, there was still much work to be done. Police officers had longstanding procedures and policies in place that would require retraining efforts. "Despite extensive efforts to train police, police continue to resist arresting battering men, and they frequently arrest both battering men and the women they batter" (Schneider, 2000, p. 181). In addition to the necessary changes in on-the-ground police work, more discursive changes were needed as well. "[Law] enforcement is plagued by longstanding tensions: the historic public/private dichotomy, which labels intimate violence as a 'private' matter that should not be litigated [...]; and resistance to the connection between violence and gender" (Schneider, 2000, p. 182). That is, police culture and discourse are slow to change and may continue to follow traditional paths, like those that divide public and private, rather than forging new ones.

A centerpiece in the criminalization of domestic violence is the Violence Against Women Act (VAWA). VAWA, signed into law in 1994, saw the federal criminalization of domestic violence. This was a big coup for feminists and lawmakers concerned with violence against women and the rights of women. VAWA was "a comprehensive legislative effort to address the problem of violence against women through a variety of different mechanisms, including funding for women's shelters, a national domestic abuse hotline, rape education and prevention programs, and training for federal and state judges" (Schneider, 2000, p. 188). Violence Against Women Act dollars are stretched far and wide, with many shelters getting most of their funding from the federal government. The act has practically and pragmatically been a funding boon for shelters and other organizations across the country. At its "core," however, "the Act is embodied in the notion that it is a civil right to be free from violence, and that all persons within the United States have a right to be free from crimes of violence motivated by gender" (Schneider, 2000, p. 189). This is a hugely important point. Freedom from violence, including violence in the home perpetrated by an intimate partner, should be a right provided to every citizen in the United States.

When VAWA was signed into law, many states and regions had already put laws to criminalize domestic violence into place, and over the following years, many more followed. A foundational piece to regional and local legislation regarding domestic violence has been and continues to be so-called mandatory arrest laws. Mandatory arrest laws require police to arrest somebody when there has been an assault. In Western State, police are to arrest the person deemed the "primary aggressor." Sometimes the primary aggressor is determined to be the person who is the victim. As Coker (2001, p. 801) puts it, "State power simultaneously empowers and disempowers women." State power does neither entirely harm women, but neither is it an analgesic for injuries endured by women. Mandatory arrest laws are neither all good nor all bad. On the one hand, mandatory arrest laws treat domestic violence like a real crime, equal to stranger violence. However, on the other hand, mandatory arrest takes decision-making out of women's hands, granting it instead to the state. The introduction of such laws has also led to greater rates of arrests of the domestic violence victims/survivors themselves (Coker, 2004). On domestic calls, police misattribute fault to female victims, misunderstanding defensive wounds and overlooking bruises and black-eyes, which do not immediately show. In my interviews, I heard a number of such stories. Mandatory arrest policies, thus, potentially hurt women more than they help them (Coker, 2004).

Mandatory arrest laws are an instrument of law, authorizing legal, not feminist, action. As Coker (2001, p. 807) puts it, "mandatory policies limit the control of the individual woman," a process I assert, that references and even mirrors the control at work in domestic violence itself. That is, the state takes control over the female victim of domestic violence much the same as the abusive intimate partner, and with similar injurious consequences. "Mandatory policies have [also] been criticized for being paternalistic and limiting women's autonomy" (Coker, 2004, p. 1332). Such policies limit, even exclude, women's decision-making about her intimate relationship.

In addition to being patronizing, such polices "increase the risk of further entanglement in these systems" for female victims of domestic violence (Coker, 2004, p. 1332). Issues with parole, immigration status, and the like come to light in mandatory arrest situations, leading more women to be arrested (Coker, 2004). In addition to the increased likelihood of incarceration, "for women whose partners are unemployed, arrest may actually *increase* their chances of being reabused (Sherman, 1992)" (Coker, 2004, p. 1334). Abusive partners may come home from jail with retaliation on the mind and abuse the victim/survivor again. In short, mandatory arrest laws ignore the social issues of race, poverty, and social vulnerability that run through domestic violence.

Though the laws have changed, the story of domestic violence persists, with millions of women abused in the United States every year. What continues to be divided, overlooked, and even hidden in this story is the interrelationship between physical and emotional violence. That is, feminists and lawmakers alike see domestic violence as a patriarchal problem, but they have tended to focus on physical violence, overlooking the devastating effects of emotional abuse. In what follows, I will develop the concepts of "patriarchal terrorism" (Johnson, 1995) and "coercive control" (Stark, 2007) as co-processes that work together within patriarchal forms of domestic violence to limit access to resources and limit public responses to domestic violence. Just as "patriarchal terrorism" as a concept sidelines emotional violence, coercive control tends to mention but undertheorizes physical violence. The division of physical and emotional violence also occurs in the law in the region that the present study took place, as well as numerous jurisdictions and precincts across the United States. Domestic violence victims/survivors do not see their experiences of both types of violence divided up in this way. Thus, it is problematic for victims/survivors to have their experiences chunked up the way they are in both the domestic violence literature and the law. In the remainder of this chapter, I will explicate patriarchal terrorism and coercive control, before describing the hurt that the division between emotional and physical violence causes and proposing a new paradigm.

1.3 Patriarchal Control: Intimate/Patriarchal Terrorism

Developing out of this history in which domestic violence was understood as wife-beating, domestic violence can be seen as patriarchal violence, in which the victims/survivors are by and large female. "Patriarchal terrorism" (Johnson, 1995) or what Johnson and Ferraro (2000) call "intimate terrorism" "is a product of patriarchal traditions of men's right to control 'their' women, a form of terroristic control of wives by their husbands that involves the systemic use of not only violence, but economic subordination, threats, isolation, and other control tactics" (Johnson, 1995, p. 284). Of course, I extend this theory to all female intimate partners, but the point remains the same: Some men attempt to control their female partners from a position of male entitlement. Put simply, they see it as their right, and this right is facilitated by masculine sociocultural discourses.

At its root, patriarchal terrorism is about control and ownership, enacted with a heavy hand. "The causal dynamic of patriarchal terrorism is rooted in patriarchal traditions, adopted with a vengeance by men who feel that they must control 'their' women by any means necessary" (Johnson, 1995, p. 286). Thus, control is paramount, and abusive behavior is developed and deployed with the goal of maintaining control over one's female partner. Importantly, control is performed through physical and emotional violence. In families experiencing patriarchal terrorism, "beatings occur on average more than once a week, and escalate in seriousness over time. The violence is almost exclusively initiated by the husband" (Johnson, 1995, p. 287). The patterning of control that underpins this style of domestic violence is not only physically violent. Johnson and Ferraro (2000) gesture to other forms of manipulation and control that may be psychological, emotional, and/or verbal, but discussion of these forms of violence is not sustained, nor are these forms of violence explicated or analyzed.

Focusing in on physical violence allows Johnson (1995) to spotlight patriarchal terrorism, a type of domestic violence deeply steeped in patriarchy and emotional control. Extract 1.3 is a story told by Rachel that identifies a moment of patriarchal terrorism, offset and supported as it always is by coercive control (Extract 1.2).

Extract 1.2 Rachel

1.	*Rachel*:	He started, um, just, like, controlling little things. Controlling.
2.		Wanting to know where I was going,
3.		who I was with. Um.
4.		Telling me I couldn't be friends with certain people or do certain things.
5.		And it happened so slowly that I don't even think I knew what was happening.
6.		He framed it in such a way that it was like, his version of--
7.		that meant that he loved me, that he cared.

Extract 1.3 Rachel

1.	*Rachel*:	He, um, pinned me in a closet.
2.		I told him that I wasn't afraid to die, and
3.		he said, "well then, I'm gonna go after your family."
4.		And, I don't even remember how I got out of there.

In Rachel's case, coercive control underpins and enables physical violence. Not only does coercive control precede patriarchal terrorism, it infiltrates the physical violence that was the result of Rachel's abusive relationship. When her abusive boyfriend overpowered her and pinned her in a closet, she was terrified. The physical and the emotional violence co-occur, aggravating and intensifying each other. Rachel is physically weaker than her abusive partner, a fact that he uses against her, time and time again. The control and power moves are part of a structure of abuse that is motivated by male privilege – he felt the girlfriend whom he had been controlling for many years was his possession. Rachel describes a system of control, starting when they were teenagers and lasting into college. Abuse was not episodic; it was constant, involving physical and emotional tactics. Elsewhere in the interview, Rachel recalls hanging sheets and blankets over doors when people came to visit, in order to hide the holes and other manifestations of violence. Violence structured her everyday life.

1.4 Male Privilege: Coercive Control

Like Johnson (1995), Stark (2007) sees domestic violence as a patriarchal issue of male dominance of women. In the introduction to his 2007 book, *Coercive Control*, he explains that he is reframing the conversation about domestic violence "as a course of calculated, malevolent conduct deployed almost exclusively by men to dominate individual women by interweaving repeated physical abuse with three equally important tactics: intimidation, isolation, and control" (Stark, 2007, p. 5). For Stark, then, the big issues in domestic violence that he frames as coercive control are psychological/ emotional issues that result in the political deprivation of rights: isolation, intimidation, and control. Stark divides physical violence out of coercive control, suggesting in at least one place that physical assault is domestic violence while other forms of control are coercive control. Thus, Stark (2007, p. 5) recognizes "assault is an essential part of this strategy and is often injurious and sometimes fatal," but that is not his focal point. Instead, he focuses on the emotional processes of intimidation and isolation and the political processes of rights deprivation. He also frames the issue in a feminist way, focusing on heterosexual violence with female victims/ survivors. He sees coercive control as a problem of sociocultural, masculine ideology, with male perpetrators and female victims.

In addition to being an issue of male privilege, coercive control is also founded on male/female stereotypes. Coercive control operationalizes and heightens stereotypes about male/female labor and behavior. "The main means used to establish control is the microregulation of everyday behavior associated with stereotypic female roles, such as how women dress, cook, clean, socialize, care for their children, or perform sexually" (Stark, 2007, p. 5). Stereotypes about how women should behave and what kinds of activities they should perform fuel and interconnect with the belief that men should have control over women. Thus, Starks argues, "the abuse of women in personal life is inextricably bound up with their standing in the larger society and therefore [domestic violence] can be significantly reduced only if sexual discrimination is addressed simultaneously" (Stark, 2007, p. 14). In other words, violence against women will not stop or change until we recognize and alter the treatment of women in larger sociocultural discourses. Little Bird agrees, saying, "It's more complicated than just the police not responding right to it [domestic violence]. It's society not responding to women calling the police. That's really what I feel like." What Little Bird is getting at are the social factors that stop women from calling the police and stop police from responding to domestic violence with clarity of purpose. It is a social problem, not an individual problem.

Grounded, as it is, in a belief that women deserve the same rights and privileges as men, the focus of Starks' argument is political, aimed at reinstating the fundamental rights of women. "The primary harm abusive men inflict is political not physical, and reflects the deprivation of rights and resources that are critical to personhood and citizenship" (Stark, 2007, p. 5). Coercive control is thus concerned with the deprivation of rights that occurs through intimidation, isolation from social supports and resources, control of mind and body, limitation of communication and mobility, and the like. That is, coercive control is concerned with the ability of a woman to live her life, to function as an autonomous member of society. Coercive control thus impacts how an individual lives. It is more than a single incident or an event. Coercive control is a regime of control that constrains every aspect of a victim/survivor's life and identity. Such a regime subordinates its object. According to Stark, as many as 80 percent of abuse victims/survivors seeking help have been victims of coercive control, including tactics such as "denial of money, the monitoring of time, and restricted mobility and communication" (Stark, 2007, p. 13). Thus, coercive control "is a liberty crime rather than a crime of assault" (Stark, 2007, p. 13). Victims of coercive control have their resources limited, their autonomy and privacy undermined and limited, and access to social relationships and supports curtailed (Stark, 2007).

Take for example Butterfly's (pseudonym selected by the participant) story in Extract 1.4 about living in her father-in-law's basement. Butterfly and her experiences fall between the cracks in a traditional model of domestic violence. She was expected to do household chores, but she was not given space to do them. Instead, she was more or less confined to a small bedroom in the basement. She was only able to leave the small room when her husband saw fit, or when he had been adequately convinced that they needed to go to the grocery store.

Extract 1.4 Butterfly

1.	Butterfly:	He had us in his dad's basement and he wouldn't get us out.
2.		I couldn't do the dishes upstairs.
3.		I did them in my room out of tubs.
4.		I had a hard time going and showering because they were mean to me.
5.		I had to do my laundry at laundromats, and
6.		I had to pay for it and
7.		[ex-husband] would throw a fit to even take us.
8.		There was an LG washer and dryer right in the bathroom that we used.

[...]

9.	Butterfly:	When we would go to the store, he would have really bad road rage.
10.		It was terrible and he would scare me really bad.
11.		In Wal-Mart and stuff, he would embarrass me and
12.		just not cooperate and make the situation feel like it was such a hard thing to do and
13.		make me feel guilty because we need to go shopping.

[...]

14.	Butterfly:	We did live at his mom's in the basement too and
15.		she didn't want me to do the clothes in the washer and dryer either.
16.		The kids had to sleep on beds, just their toddler bed mattresses or

17.	on the couch or on the floor in the living room.
18.	There was rooms all throughout the house.
19.	There's a mother-in-law house, and
20.	he'd keep on giving me false promises saying,
21.	"Oh, they can maybe have the rooms,"
22.	just like at his dad's,
23.	that they'd set up a bunk bed in the room upstairs and it just never happened.

Butterfly experienced terrible living conditions, suffered humiliations, isolation, and intimidation just for needing to buy groceries, basic human necessities. Immersed in coercive control, Butterfly was essentially stripped of basic human rights and made to feel unworthy when she had basic human needs. She was harangued for needing foodstuffs. Her time was structured and controlled using household tasks associated with women's work, and then she was made to feel bad and inferior for completing the work she had been assigned. Her four children and herself were denied basic living space and adequate sleeping arrangements for no reason, except to demean and humiliate. Abuse structured the everyday environment for Butterfly such that she could never let her guard down, never rest, and never live. Her abuse was patriarchally structured; she was controlled and intimidated at every turn by a man who thought that his access to her was his right.

Nothing that Butterfly describes in Extract 1.4 is considered criminal, though it is clearly domestic violence. She did not have recourse to call the police for being forced to do dishes in humiliating conditions, chastened at every turn. The law is a patriarchal construct, as I described it earlier, and so it can and does function in tandem with other institutions, such as the family. Both law and family favor a masculine way of doing things, and so they work together in male privilege. For Butterfly, this meant that she was kept in that small room.

Coercive control has a complicated relationship to law enforcement. If there is no assault to go along with the coercive tactics, then often times, there is no crime. In the region in which this research was completed, no physical assault equals no crime (destruction of property can lead to arrest). Noncriminal domestics may not be treated with urgency or crisis, directly linked to the fact that psychological, emotional, and verbal forms of abuse are not criminal and so dismissed. This distinction between criminal and noncriminal domestics is not uncommon across the United States. As such, coercive control, damaging and pervasive as it is, runs absolutely under the radar. Compare this with Trinch's (2003) research, which investigates the process of filling out protective order applications. When women came into the office with stories about broad structures of abusive tactics – when they came with stories about coercive control – they were helped to orient their narratives around identifiable, individual events of abuse. According to her research, the law prefers narratives about events of physical abuse, not narratives about the everyday of domestic violence, which includes *both* physical and psychological forms of abuse (Trinch, 2003).

1.5 Seeing Emotional and Physical Violence as Working Together

Both coercive control and patriarchal terrorism are constructed in ways that exclude the other, even though they are most often functioning, knotted together. Coercive control excludes, to varying degrees, physical violence, while patriarchal terrorism is theorized to exclude emotional/verbal forms of violence. Exclusions aside, they share so much in common. They both take a feminist perspective, sharing a political viewpoint that highlights heterosexual violence that impacts female victims more than male victims. Both consider domestic violence a patriarchal issue of power and domination. Here, I argue, there is more the same than different between these two conceptual formations, especially if we see violence as violence rather than differentiating between types of violence. That is, violence can be done to a person in a variety of ways; focusing on the differences simply creates theoretical silos, dismissing the actual experiences of violence that victims/survivors narrate. If we move away from organizing domestic violence into types of violence and instead focus on violence, these two concepts, patriarchal terrorism and coercive control, are two ways of saying the same thing: Men structure the lives of their abused partners using a variety of violent tactics that are intended to control, undermine, and dominate women. As the earlier discussion shows, patriarchal terrorism and coercive control are both involved in domestic violence; they are part and parcel of the same problem: patriarchal control, male privilege, and discourses of power. Importantly, when victims/survivors of domestic violence narrate domestic violence, they give accounts of coercive control and patriarchal terrorism. Indeed, in these stories, they are co-processes that together fuel and bolster domestic violence.

In the story told in Extract 1.5, Melissa narrates coercive control alongside patriarchal terrorism. Like most of the participants, she does not separate emotional harms from physical, and her stories often include elements of each. Melissa's story is about structured abuses and harms that include physical abuse that is steeped in patriarchal control.

Extract 1.5 Melissa

1.	*Melissa:*	I'd put Christmas presents under the—from him.
2.		I'd put one under for myself, because he never bought me a Christmas present.
3.		We were married for 24 years. I bought myself five wedding rings.
4.		They would always get pawned.
5.		There was never any—
6.		all of my pregnancies, while I was in labor,
7.		he was sitting there at the side going,
8.		"C'mon. I don't think you're really in labor. Let's go."
9.		I broke my arm. I broke my fingers from fights, and he wouldn't even take—
10.		he would be like, "Oh, it's just okay to like—" and
11.		literally had me slam my crushed arm into a wall, believing that.

[...]

12.	*Melissa:*	Because he would always put my hands behind me.
13.		He would always tie me up in a shirt, or sit on me—somehow make me immobile.
14.		He would always hold me down, and
15.		we were fighting, and
16.		he held my arms behind me and pushed me,
17.		so I fell, and
18.		I fell on my shoulder, and
19.		I just crushed it.
20.		It was poking out of my arm and everything.

Though this is primarily a story about a physical assault, Melissa introduces it by describing her husband's sustained inattention and emotional cruelty. Her estranged husband has never bought her a Christmas present, nor a wedding ring, a fact made all the worse by the fact that he consistently pawned the wedding rings that she bought for herself. He was nasty to her. He mocked her while she was in labor with their children. These are all indicators that her estranged husband did not care for her, a point that brings Melissa significant pain. She uses such details as a way of establishing a system of abuse, a set of ongoing, recurring processes intended to keep Melissa in her place, willing to take the more extreme forms of abuse that she also describes.

After establishing her estranged husband as a bad husband, the type of guy who has never purchased a gift for his wife and bullies his wife while she is in labor, Melissa introduces information about physical assault in a sort of list: "I broke my arm. I broke my fingers from fights…" (line 11). This list-making discursive move establishes the relationship as having ongoing abuse. But also notice that it owns responsibility "I broke" not "he broke." This segment of discourse establishes a violent life structure with the use of the term "always," to indicate that abuse was ongoing: "he would always put my hands behind me. He would always tie me up in a shirt" (line 15). These were things that happened regularly, in order to control Melissa and maintain physical and emotional power over her. These details indicate that the event she is about to narrate is not isolated. It is structured into everyday life, and it is motivated by power and control – physical and emotional control over Melissa. It is an event that we could call patriarchal terrorism wedded with the ongoing nature of coercive control.

Finally, Melissa tells a small story about a single event, a time when her ex-husband crushed her shoulder so badly that bones were sticking out. Adding layer upon layer of injury, he would not believe that she was hurt, claiming that they can fix the shoulder at home, by "slam[ming] [her] crushed arm into a wall" (line 13). The image is horrifying. Melissa expresses significant pain and anguish over the memory. This story brings patriarchal terrorism and coercive control together. This is control, mistreatment, and violence, all in the name of controlling a female intimate partner.

In Extract 1.6, we return to Killingsworth to look at the story she tells about her breaking point. The event that led her to leave.

Extract 1.6 Killingsworth

1.	*Killingsworth:*	I know when I came back from the wedding
2.		there was garbage all over the back porch that was full of maggots.
3.		And, um, that was kind of, like, what he had left for me to clean up.
4.		And, uh, so I remember cleaning that up and being like, "This is it."
5.		"This is just – this is – this is clearly, like, I'm not allowed to do things, uh,
6.		and this is bad."
7.		And I remember, um,

8.	I think I must have been having back pain, or cramps, or something.
9.	And he used to – he was a huge pill popper and
10.	would feed me as many pills as I wanted that he got from his dad.
11.	So I think I remember I had – I had asked for a muscle relaxer or a pain pill
12.	and I was lying on my back in the entryway and
13.	he sat on top of me so that his crotch was on my chest.
14.	And his – his knees were on my biceps, so he had pinned me down that way.
15.	And he had the pill and he was shoving it in my mouth.
16.	And mocking – and laughing and
17.	I was resisting and saying, "Stop it. Stop it. Stop it."
18.	And he started slapping my face.
19.	And I was so immobile – and that's, like, when I –
20.	that was kinda, like, that moment where I was like,
21.	"Oh my god. This has – this has never been to this degree before."
22.	"And, um, I can't move, and this is serious."
23.	And when he got up off of me I said to him, "You're breaking my heart."
24.	And he said, "Shut the fuck up." And he kicked me in the vagina.

Killingsworth lived under a regime of control and violence in which her every move was monitored, assessed, and punished, in which punishment came in the form of messes full of maggots that were left for her to clean up. This is a story of how that looked for her; how she was required to live. Killingsworth begins with a commentary on her ex-husband's expectation that she should clean the house. Upping the abusive ante, he went so far as to spread garbage on the back porch, where it rotted and became maggoty. This abusive event of control founded in stereotypes about women's work was a response to Killingsworth's defiance – she had gone out of town to see a friend against his wishes. Killingsworth's husband controlled with punishments that were themselves situated in stereotypes about women's labor. He made a disgusting mess for Killingsworth to clean up. As a woman, it was her job to clean. He created a situation in which she had to clean as a condition of abuse.

This play with garbage and maggots is just an opening gambit for the ever-intensifying moments of domestic violence that connect physical and emotional abuses. This episode is embedded within a systemic lifestyle of dominance in which Killingsworth was asked to submit implicitly and explicitly all day long. Killingsworth was consistently physically and psychologically assaulted, in combined attacks against her person and her freedom. In this instantiation of the larger system of abuse, she is humiliated, slapped, sat upon, name-called, force-fed drugs, and kicked. This event is not isolated, but it does provide insight into the styles of abuse that were combined in order to control and harm Killingsworth. Her every choice was dependent on the kinds of punishment she would endure if she strayed from the path established for her by her ex-husband. This is domination, and it is masculinely performed and motivated. Elsewhere, Killingsworth reports her abuser saying, "I'm your husband. I'm not a stranger. I'm not hurting you. You have to submit." This sentiment followed Killingsworth through every moment of her day.

Killingsworth and Melissa both teach us that coercive control and patriarchal terrorism function together in an overlapping style. They underpin and support each other. They are intertwined so closely in victim/survivor's stories of abuse that they cannot be untangled. They make up the knot that is domestic violence.

1.6 Domestic Violence, Law Enforcement, and Verbal/Emotional Violence

The distinctions and overlaps between patriarchal terrorism and coercive control are especially important in the context of law enforcement. In the region in which this study took place, there is a separation between patriarchal terrorism and coercive control at the level of law. It is against the law to beat, hit, kick, and otherwise physically assault your partner. In this region, such behavior would constitute simple assault. Emotional/verbal forms of violence fall outside of the limits of simple assault. Intimidation, isolation, control, name-calling, and screaming are not against the law. Thus, we are in a situation in which patriarchal terrorism is against the law while coercive control is not, even though they are knotted together and do damage together.

Law enforcement officers operate along the lines authorized by law. They have no choice but to treat simple assault – criminal domestics – differently than they treat verbal and emotional assault – noncriminal domestics/verbals. This division effectively makes the violence of noncriminal domestics invisible to law enforcement, who already have a fraught history with domestic violence. Arrests have now become likely, especially with the introduction of highly controversial mandatory arrest policies. Changes still need to be made, however. For example, if domestic violence itself was against the law, instead of lumping it in with simple assault, it would be easier to see the harms done by coercive control on par with those done by physical assault. If domestic violence itself were illegal, we would be able to have a conversation about other types of violence, those that get passed over and dismissed by police officers working within the criminal domestic/noncriminal domestic divide. Police officers trained on coercive control would have the vocabulary necessary to understand the depths of control in a relationship and the way that control manifests as fear in the victim. Police officers need to begin viewing domestic violence as an intricate knot of power, control, misogyny, and domination. Seeing domestic violence as a structure of domination and control would reframe verbal arguments for police officers. Seen as a feature of power, control, and domination, verbal arguments and name-calling become dangerous indicators of violence. A domestic violence perspective would change what is seeable as domestic violence for law enforcement, in important ways, getting more people resources they need to safely exit their relationship.

Seeing emotional and psychological forms of domestic violence as illegal would help abuse victims by making psychological patterns of abuse legally recognizable. Little Bird comments on this when she explains that psychological abuse was terrible. The primary form of emotional/psychological abuse in Little Bird's life was being forced to stay in her home for years. "He wasn't a wizard about insulting me. That wasn't his game. His wizardly, psychology, was somehow imprisoning me. Okay? That has been the hardest thing to get over besides the sexual stuff." The forced "imprisonment" and sexual assault were the most difficult things with which to cope. She goes on to say (Extract 1.7).

Extract 1.7 Little Bird

1.	*Little Bird:*	I can't go into Costco or other big stores.
2.		If I get feeling this way I can only shop at really small markets.
3.		Cause sometimes it feels better to be enclosed like I was for years.
4.		The psychological stuff is way more intense than the broken bones.
5.		Even the strangulation.
6.		Everybody thinks the strangulation is gonna be what's so tough.

7.		It's the imprisonment.
8.		It's the "I didn't drive for three years."
9.		All of the sudden you're driving, and sometimes—
10.	*Jenny:*	It's weird.
11.	*Little Bird:*	It's a weird thing.
12.		People don't get it.
13.		It's like, "hey, he didn't even get charged for any of that."
14.		I was with the cop that worked the case.
15.		We were having coffee with this journalist.
16.		I was pretty in a—because of the EMDR, a little bit unraveling a little.
17.		Then I looked over at him and I said,
18.		"Hey, I have to ask you something.
19.		Why didn't you charge him with false imprisonment?"
20.		I'm pretty annoyed about it right now in this moment."
21.		He's like, "Little Bird, that would've been so hard to prove."
22.	*Jenny:*	Yeah.
23.	*Little Bird:*	I'm like, "I didn't have a car, though."
24.		We got into a little back-and-forth,
25.		because I trust him now because we're friends now.
26.		It's just amazing to me these charges don't exist.
27.		I can understand it intellectually, because then how do you find a line for that?

Leaving an abusive relationship is complicated and difficult, as I explain later, and it does not automatically lead to safety. Leaving is dangerous. We need discourses that connect physical and emotional/psychological/verbal forms of violence so that we can start to see seemingly banal activities, events, and behaviors for what they are. Violent.

1.7 Same-Sex Relationships

I have gestured to same-sex relationships a number of times in this chapter. Research shows that same-sex partnerships have rates of domestic violence that are equal to or higher than those of heterosexual couples (Stiles-Sheilds & Carroll, 2015, p. 638). Murray et al. (2007) found that 22–46 percent of lesbians and 22 percent of gay men have experienced some form of domestic violence in their lifetimes (Stiles-Sheilds & Carroll, 2015, p. 638). The statistics may be similar, but some of the issues are in some ways different, though many can be seen to be motivated by patriarchal concerns, power, and domination. Whatever the different constraints are for same-sex couples, the factors of control and authority persist in same-sex domestic violence. Abusers use intimate terrorism in sync with coercive control to exercise power over their partners.

Some of the unique characteristics of same-sex domestic violence have to do with heteronormative discourses and discrimination. Experiences of bias and heterosexual privilege in social networks may negatively impact same-sex relationships (Stiles-Sheilds & Carroll, 2015, p. 641). That is, prejudicial discourses regarding homosexuality can create stress that may lead to domestic violence and aggravate the experience of abuse. "Sexual minority status may [...] exacerbate the feelings of isolation and helplessness frequently experienced by victims of domestic violence" (Stiles-Sheilds & Carroll, 2015, p. 641). Domestic violence in same-sex relationships still involves tactics that isolate the victim/survivor, which may be made more acute when combined with social factors and patterns of discrimination experienced by same-sex couples. Domestic violence in same-sex couples has been described as a "double closet," because in order to come forward and get resources and services one has to admit not only to being a victim of domestic violence but also to being LGBTQ. Renzetti's (1992) research shows that threats of outing, playing off of the homophobia of the social world are common in abusive, lesbian relationships.

Lesbian couples experience combined intimate (otherwise called patriarchal) terrorism and coercive control. Renzetti's (1992) groundbreaking research concludes that abusive lesbian relationships, like abusive heterosexual relationships, are grounded in structures of power, control, and domination. According to Renzetti (1992), lesbian couples engage in psychological abuse such as abuse, control, and extreme jealousy, "and that power and control were major sources of conflict" (quoted in Johnson & Ferraro, 2000, p. 951). Thus, Johnson and Ferraro conclude that lesbian relationships that are abusive include some features of intimate terrorism. These behaviors are well within a coercive control paradigm, in which a structural regime of abuse consistently haunts the victim/survivor.

Extract 1.8 demonstrates how coercive control and physical violence work together in a lesbian relationship. The extract is made up of two stories. The first is a general account of everyday abuse. It is an account of a type of event, coercive control, that Sasha says would happen regularly. The second story is about a physically violent episode that is a picture of intimate terrorism.

Extract 1.8 Sasha

1.	*Sasha:*	Um, a lot of – like, I would make a mistake.
2.		would, you know, maybe not pay a bill on time,
3.		and – and then she would call and accuse me of ruining our lives financially –
4.		like, you know, she was gonna leave me.
5.		She – I ruined her credit, all of this stuff.
6.		I would spend the day spinning and try to fix it, and then –
7.		I would go home, and she would be like, "what's wrong with you? I wasn't actually mad."

[…]

8.	*Sasha:*	- and all of that. I was like, I can't – I can't do that.
9.		Um, but then it –you know, by the – by the end of the relationship,
10.		it had escalated into physical violence – and – and – and threats –
11.		– where, um, you know, we had one night – where she
12.		– she punched me and choked me and tried to break my nose –
13.		– and had called a friend over, and a friend – sh –
14.		earlier in that night, she had called – the friend to come and said, you know,
15.		that she was gonna kill me if that friend didn't come over –
16.		– and the friend came, and she told the friend that she better take all the knives out of the house.
17.		And – then sh – she left, my – my partner at the time, left the house,
18.		so my friend felt like it was safe to leave –
19.		– and she left. And then she came back, and that's when she beat me up
20.		and stabbed the knife into the wall.

In Extract 1.8, Sasha tells two small stories. In the first story Sasha tells, she is emotionally controlled and manipulated. Her partner is represented as behaving angrily toward Sasha, making Sasha worry about the fate of the relationship, but then acting like Sasha was crazy for worrying – that everything has been and continues to be ok. The use of such tactics made Sasha feel like she was going crazy. The story is told such that we understand these events to be typical, every day. As such, Sasha's abusive partner used coercive control to create a systematic administration of control and domination in which Sasha could not win. Her partner picked small fights, escalated them until they were huge, and then let them drop, acting like now upset Sasha was overreacting and crazy. This is coercive control.

The second story in Extract 1.8 is about physical violence at the hands of her abusive partner. In this story, we see both coercive control and intimate terrorism. Sasha was manipulated through argument and physical escalations into giving her partner what she wanted. Her partner threatened to kill Sasha. She even called a friend over, claiming that if the friend did not come, she would kill Sasha. The friend came over, but finally left when she thought things were calmed down. After the friend left, however, Sasha was attacked. Sasha's abusive partner beat her, choked her, and stabbed a knife into the wall next to her. This is the very picture of both coercive control and intimate terrorism – physical violence motivated by power and control and fueled by intimidation and fear.

The example from Sasha shows many similarities between different-sex partners and same-sex partners. Both coercive control and intimate terrorism show up, and they are both still motivated by power and control, though with a different valence of patriarchy and male privilege. There is also some patriarchal backlash. There exists the notion that lesbians can't be abusive because they are not men. Such a belief negatively impacts lesbians in abusive relationships. Renzetti found that "battered lesbians are evidently less likely to be supported by friends, who often refuse to believe that a lesbian can be an abuser" (quoted in Johnson & Ferraro, 2000, p. 951). Moreover, when they have involved law enforcement and asked for social services, they have historically been less likely to receive warranted social services, though that issue is diminishing somewhat (Johnson & Ferraro, 2000).

Gay male domestic violence is also complex. When abusive, these relationships can be volatile and dangerous. "Gay men were more likely to require medical attention and suffer injuries as a result of intimate partner violence" (NCADV, 2018). LGBTQ men make up 47.6 percent of domestic violence homicides (NCADV, 2018). That is a striking figure.

There are differences between lesbian and gay male domestic violence. For example, Murray and Mobley (2009) suggest that domestic violence in lesbian couples is still motivated by sexism and patriarchy. Compare this to a masculine paradigm in which a man is considered "weak" if he cannot defend himself (Murray & Mobley, 2009). This point may lead to the fact that more gay domestic violence is bidirectional (Stiles-Shields & Carroll, 2015, p. 642). According to Murray et al. (2007):

> The dual identity as perpetrator and victim in bidirectionality of violence may reflect the violation of stereotypical gender norms assumed by the heterosexual paradigm involved in domestic violence: if a man cannot defend himself against another man, he is weak; if he fights back, he is no longer a victim but may be viewed as a perpetrator. (quoted in Stiles-Shields & Carroll, 2015, p. 642)

Stereotypical gender norms that are steeped in patriarchy impact the formation of domestic violence in gay male relationships that involve domestic violence.

1.8 Why Doesn't She Just Leave?

With all of these accounts of abuse, and the many that are to come, perhaps the reader is wondering why victims/survivors do not leave, or do not leave sooner. One answer is that there is no place to go. Little Bird explains it this way: "and nobody else would take us in *[crying]*. I had this little [child] that's not talking, the other one is just totally in distress, and I have a newborn baby *[crying]*." Butterfly puts it this way: "I had nowhere to go, and I didn't know what to do, and I have too many kids, so that's what would stop me. Nobody would help me, so I was literally stuck." Both Butterfly and Little Bird comment on wanting to leave yet feeling trapped because of children and circumstances. Such emotions are punctuated and exacerbated by the fact that nobody would/could take them in. They literally had nowhere to go, until they learned about the shelter system, received resources, and got out.

In addition to a general lack of resources, it is important to remember that leaving is dangerous and that the dangers of an abusive relationship do not go away when the victim leaves. "Abuse victims are aggressive help seekers and are as likely to be assaulted and even entrapped when they are physically separated as when married or living together" (Stark, 2007, p. 12). Leaving is very dangerous, and it is an insecure solution. It may not lead to the results desired. Abuse often continues, even after leaving. "It is estimated that 73% of emergency room visits and up to 75% of calls to the police for domestic violence incidents occur after separation" (Berry, 2000, p. 7). It is often presumed that leaving is the fix to an abusive relationship, but leaving is easier said than done. First of all, discourses of romantic, heterosexual love and relationship put heavy pressure on staying, on working things out. They also support a "stand by your man" rhetoric, in which a good woman stays with her man and helps him improve. Second of all, and this is key, leaving is dangerous. Nobody knows this better than I do. When I told my abusive ex-husband that I wanted a divorce, there was trouble. In short, he tried to kill me, but he took the long way to that end. He held me hostage for hours, pistol whipped me, beat me, kicked me, sexually assaulted me, and shot me multiple times – in both legs, my left arm, and my head.

Leaving can make a precarious situation worse. And still, many men and women do it every day. It takes bravery, stamina, and planning, and it should be applauded. However, it is important to treat those who have not yet figured out a way to leave safely with respect and support. It is easier to leave when social resources are made available. As a society, we need to be thinking about ways to identify abusers and facilitate their changed behavior. As a society, we need to be identifying the structural and institutional components that keep abuse at bay. Things like strong, dense, multifaceted support networks, family planning resources, emotional health resources, education, and work, are all things that reduce domestic violence.

1.9 Conclusions

I want to return to a definition of domestic violence used by the NCADV:

> Domestic violence is the willful intimidation, physical assault, battery, sexual assault, and/or other abusive behavior as part of a systematic pattern of power and control perpetrated by one intimate partner against another. It includes physical violence, sexual violence, threats, and emotional/psychological abuse. (NCADV, 2018)

Domestic violence is about power, control, domination, and intimidation enacted via tactics of physical violence (beatings, choking, pushing, hair pulling, etc.) and emotional/psychological/verbal violence (yelling, name-calling, gaslighting, location monitoring, etc.). Domestic violence is performed with overlays of patriarchy. Developed out of a legal history that supported wife beating, the current model of domestic violence maintains many of the same valences of battery. That is, as long as the culture is sexist, there will be heterosexual domestic violence with female victims.

I have used two concepts to explore the patriarchal flavor of heterosexual domestic violence involving a female victim: intimate/patriarchal terrorism (physical violence) and coercive control (emotional/psychological/verbal violence). Both take a patriarchal perspective to think about violence against women. Domestic violence is about both intimate/patriarchal terrorism and coercive control, which work together. Indeed, they are so knotted together in the stories of victims/survivors that one cannot see where one process stops and the other begins. Domestic violence will not be thoroughly dealt with until we begin creating integrative models that combine patriarchal terrorism and coercive control. Indeed, law enforcement, especially, must be trained such that they recognize the effects of coercive control and have the vocabulary to address it and see it as violent.

Toward the Recreation of a Field of Indexicality
Domestic Violence, Social Meaning, and Ideology

Domestic violence is a social ill that has plagued society for many centuries. Domestic violence is the systematic interpersonal, control, subjugation, and intimidation of another person using physical, emotional, sexual, financial, and other means (National Coalition Against Domestic Violence [NCADV] and National Intimate Partner and Sexual Violence Survey). Domestic violence is a social problem, not only an interpersonal one. Of course, it occurs interpersonally, but that interpersonal interaction occurs within a field of patriarchal discourses that facilitate and bolster individual acts of domestic violence. That is, domestic violence is built into the fabric with which society is made. Issues such as patriarchy that filter through many valences of modern society underpin violence against women. Schneider (2000, p. 5) has shown how "heterosexual intimate violence is part of a larger system of coercive control and subordination." Thus, patriarchy and patriarchal norms create a situation in which domestic violence can flourish. The protections of the public/private distinction keep prying public eyes out of homes, a protection founded in legal precedent (Andrus, 2015; see Chapter 1) that allows the violence that happens at home to stay insidiously behind closed doors. Thus, we find ourselves in a time when the NCADV says that 1 in 4 women and 1 in 9 men will be abused physically and/or emotionally in their lifetimes. These are startling statistics, and they demand address.

In Chapter 1, I discussed some historical discourses that put and keep domestic violence in place, underpinning both emotional and physical violence. In this chapter, I will describe and analyze the current discourses that bolster domestic violence, making domestic violence socially meaningful and reproducible. Much of the discourse is presupposed and forecasted by Detective Sidwell when he says, "[Domestic violence calls are] probably the next dangerous thing next to a traffic stop. [...] It is because for one minute they [a couple] love each other, the next minute they hate each other, but if you take one of them to jail, or not, now they both hate you." Violence, love, and the supposed resistance of victims are all summed up here, in a statement by police that indexes not just the event but also the social discourses that permeate domestic violence and make it meaningful: Domestic calls are dangerous, violent couples love/d each other, and victims are recalcitrant.

The social meaning of events of and surrounding domestic violence are made intelligible and maintainable via indexicality, which according to Silverstein (2003, p. 193) "relate[s] the micro-social and the macro-social" – the personal to the ideological. Indexicality thus relates larger sociocultural practices with on-the-ground communication. Everyday discourses become meaningful in the context of larger social discourses. I argue in this chapter that through indexicality, domestic violence becomes socially meaningful as an event, involving multiple actors, events, and contexts. That is, I do not presume that domestic violence is simply an event that carries its own meaning in itself, but rather, I argue that what it means in a social, interactional sense emerges through indexicality. As Blommaert (2007, p. 115) puts it, "Indexicality connects language to cultural patterns." Indexicality is the linkage between social meaning – what an event means in the social worlds in which it is produced and emerges – and linguistic forms. In terms of domestic violence, what we have is an indexical field (Eckert, 2008) that provides narrative tools that can be used to make sense of and in many ways maintain both the communication events surrounding domestic violence and the acts of violence and policing themselves. In Blommaert's (2005, p. 11) words, "Acts of communication produce indexical meaning: social meaning, interpretive leads between what is said and the social occasion in which it is being produced." This is the connection between what is sayable and the social events in which an utterance can be said, heard, and understood. In this chapter, I analyze narratives that give accounts of domestic violence and police encounters regarding domestic violence in order to understand the relationship between the occasion of saying and what is said.

Indexicality in these data emerges as a field of discourses that are engaged to make sense of the events that make up domestic violence. These discourses are made up of the nth order and the $n + 1$th order indexicality (Silverstein, 2003; see also Johnstone et al., 2006). The nth order indexicality, as Silverstein (2003, p. 194) lays it out, is the "performable execution of an already constituted framework of semiotic value." The nth order of indexicality, then, is that social order that is already available to be performed, using discursive resources at the ready, and in the process, making those resources available for future performances. Johnstone et al.

(2006, p. 82) explain this further, stating, an *n*th-order indexical is "a feature whose use can be correlated with a sociodemographic identity (e.g., region or class) or a semantic function (e.g., number-marking). [...] Occurrence of the feature can only be interpreted with reference to a preexisting partition of social or semantic space." This type of indexicality links social identity with linguistic forms in order to make them meaningful in some already articulated semantic or physical space. "Indexical meanings occur in patterns offering perceptions of similarity and stability that can be perceived as 'types' of semiotic practice with predictable (presupposable/ entailing) directions" (Blommaert, 2007, p. 117). These patterns map out a space in which the semiotic potential for a discourse emerges – what is sayable and hearable within a particular semiotic and semantic space, such as domestic violence.

Within the semantic and semiotic space of domestic violence, a number of topics and narrative potentialities erupt and are exploited in order to make and keep domestic violence meaningful in particular, culturally valid ways. Indexicality functions at a number of levels of awareness, with some studies showing high levels of use and feature performance (cf. Johnstone, 2013). While the participants interviewed for this study may not be fully aware of their linguistic choices and the linkages to social meaning (*n*th-order indexicality), those linkages emerge time and time again in the data.

Indexicality is an un/structured set of discourses that fill and overflow social spaces and discourses. Eckert (2008, p. 454) calls an indexical field "a field of potential meanings." That is, an indexical field is filled with variables that can mean in a number of ways, meanings that can be attached to different variables. An indexical field is fluid, in movement and flux, "a constellation of ideologically related meanings, any one of which can be activated" by a speaker trying to accomplish a sociosemantic task (Eckert, 2008, p. 455). An indexical field contains elements, topics, sounds, words, phrases, and narratives that can be used to interpret and make social sense out of an interactional encounter with a person or group. Indexicality, then, is interactional in as much as it is animated interpersonally. Indexicality is animated when a person talks to another in the hopes that the other will make the correct indexical connections required to make the utterance meaningful. In the interactions analyzed here, the indexical field that emerges is about events of domestic violence and emergent identities in and around domestic violence. This indexical field is peppered with both the *n*th order and the $n + 1$th order indexicality, with participants variously reflective on the semantic work done by/in their stories.

The participants in this study show awareness that they are drawing on and contributing to the social meaning of domestic violence through their stories that are about the same. The awareness, of course, varies by participant. What remains consistent is the story types and indices that are topicalized in narratives about domestic violence told by victims/survivors and police officers and personnel. In these data, a number of themes and topics emerge, topics that make up the indexical field of domestic violence. These topics function as the n + 1th order indexicality (Johnstone et al., 2006; Silverstein, 2003). In the n + 1th order indexicality, speakers start to notice that they speak a certain way, or that a particular form is socially meaningful in a particular way. A term, phrase, or story becomes meaningful "in terms of one or more native ideologies" (Johnstone et al., 2006, p. 82). Thus, it becomes socially meaningful to produce the linguistic Topic selection and narrative formation are present when domestic violence is accounted for via storytelling. A set of common themes, ideas, and values emerge. (1) Nearly every victim/survivor participant talks about family – their own children and their experiences as children. Many of the participants talk about pregnancies and motherhood within the framework of family. (2) All of the participants, both police and victim/survivors, talk about staying in an abusive relationship and the complexities associated with leaving. (3) All of the participants discuss violence in its various forms, with most discussing both physical and emotional violence. (4) Finally, all of the participants talk through issues of policing: occasions when police were called or occasions when they had opted not to call the police. Within each of these groups, subtopics emerge, which will be analyzed and discussed more fully in Section 2.1. Indexicality, thus, functions as a field of discourses that emerge, reemerge, and are animated as participants talk about and make sense of domestic violence.

In what follows, I will show that indexicality emerges in narratives that I treat and analyze as small stories (Bamberg, 2006; Bamberg & Georgakopoulou, 2008). In the indexical field of domestic violence, elements that emerge in and make up the indexical field, which is itself always emergent and fluid, are performed in small stories about family, children, staying/leaving, violence, and police. Small stories here are contrasted to Labovian, "complete," stories. Labov and Waletsky's (1967) framework presents a heuristic for analyzing narratives by looking for relationships between story parts: abstract, orientation, complication, evaluation, resolution, and coda. Analyses using this model are rich and compelling. There are problems, however, with focusing only on narratives that hit all of the notes of a Labovian analysis. It is possible for some narrative information to get left out, ignored, and erased. According to De Fina and Georgakopoulou (2008, p. 380), "Labov's structural definition of narrative has resulted in a tendency to recognize as narratives only texts that appear to be well organized, with a beginning, a middle and an end, that are teller-led and largely monological, and that occur as responses to (an interviewer's) questions." In focusing on one kind of structure and organization that necessarily includes evaluation and all the parts, those narratives that only do some of that work are swept away as deficient. Moreover, as Trinch (2003, p. 28) suggests, "The Labovian definition ignores any other important social and interactional functions narrative might have." Narratives are, after all, interactional and rhetorical, involving people and contexts beyond the teller.

In response to such critiques of the Labovian model, scholars such as Bamberg and Georgakopoulou (2008) have suggested an alternative analytical model that they call "small stories" analysis. The label "small stories" represents the often brief nature of the stories, and it represents "the spirit of a late modern focus on the micro fleeting aspects of lived experience" (Bamberg & Georgakopoulou, 2008, p. 379). A small story model takes into account the late modern idea that identity and lived experience are fragmented, partial, and in flux, just like the stories that represent them.

> Small stories can be about very recent [...] or still unfolding events, thus immediately reworking slivers of experience and arising out of a need to share what has just happened or seemingly uninteresting tidbits. They can be about small incidents that may (or may not) have actually happened, mentioned to back up or elaborate on an argumentative point occurring in an ongoing conversation. (Bamberg & Georgakopoulou, 2008, p. 381)

We tell small stories as we move through our days. They are interactive, rhetorical, strategic, contextual, and sometimes even confabulated. They are everyday stories about life. With a small stories model, "We are able to analyze the way the referential world is constructed with characters in time and space as well as a function of the interactive engagement" (Bamberg & Georgakopoulou, 2008, p. 380). Narrative is a building block for lived experience. It is how we make sense of our social worlds, and as such, in narrative we create indexical links between social and semantic worlds – we make meaning out of experience using the narrative resources available in the field of indexicality.

The data analyzed here include stories that are fragments – pieces of tellings – and other types of small stories, such as general tellings of past and anticipated future events. It also includes longer, more monologic, Labovian style narratives. Rather than place the two types of narratives in a hierarchy and measure them against each other, I use a small stories model to analyze all of the narrative styles encountered. This is because the small stories model allows me to fully engage the interactional and rhetorical elements of the story, without worrying about completeness or fullness. The small stories model allows for a parsing of narrative emergence that takes seriously the rhetorical and semantic work done in the space between teller and interlocutors. In what follows, I show that the indexical field emerges via small stories, just as small stories emerge out of the discursive resources available in the constellation that is the indexical field. The indexical field that emerges through small stories about events of domestic violence, including policing, demonstrates how such events are understood and made meaningful. Indeed, how domestic violence means and means differently for different groups of storytellers is operationalized in the indexical field.

2.1 The Indexical Field

Domestic violence small stories are made up of and reference four types of stories that occur throughout these data: violence (emotional, physical, financial, etc.), staying and leaving, family (children, parents, childhoods, etc.), and policing. Victims/survivors are featured in nearly every story, and abusers are featured in some, but not all. Abusers are especially missing from police officer stories. The indexical field in which these stories emerge, and for which the stories provide the discursive resources, is made up of a number of discursive elements that organize and are organized by the four broad categories. Each category is fitted with discourses, narrative fragments, phrases, and words that make domestic violence meaningful in and for the social worlds in which the police and victims/survivors live and interact. In other words, this indexical field is filled with the nth-order and $n + 1$th order indexicals – indexicals that are being wielded more or less rhetorically and purposefully in the process of performing an ever-emerging group of identities. We will look at each larger category in turn, along with some of the words, phrases, and fragments that feed the indexical field before turning analytical attention toward longer narratives. The statements are organized into topics, and there are similarities between stories in a topical node, but I want to make it very clear that each abused woman's voice and each police officer's discourse is distinct and compelling of its own accord. Even taking into consideration individual speaker's uniqueness, there remain, however, featured elements of the indexical field that form domestic violence. I also want to call attention to the fact that the indexical fields described and analyzed later are by no means comprehensive. These are just some of the indexicals that emerge in the data analyzed here.

2.1.1 Violence Stories

The first portion of the indexical field I want to discuss is stories about violence, which include physical, emotional, sexual, and other forms of violence and abuses. The next set of examples is Examples of Emotional Violence Narratives. It is made up of a number of examples of talk about violence, including narrative descriptions from victims and police personnel. Initially, I have divided the segments into physical and emotional violence, before showing how these two types of violence are more typically described in concert with one another. Some themes emerge from the outset. Emotional violence is described by victims/survivors of domestic violence in terms of isolation, name-calling, controlling, and mistrustful behavior, demonstrated through multiple calls and messages, and criticism of abilities as a mother. These ideas and topics are found in many interviews, with emotional violence being something of a constant in the stories told by victims/survivors. The following examples show the variety, breadth, and depth of emotional, physical, and mixed (emotional and physical) narratives that circulate in these data.

Examples of Emotional Violence Narratives

1. "Isolating from everything I knew, to everything that I knew as myself before, was isolated from everything and anybody, even phone calls, just everything." –Linda
2. Radiance: Call more than 40 times in a row.
    Jenny: Oh yeah.
    Radiance: Leaving messages saying every foul thing you can think of.
    Jenny: Mm-hmm.
    Radiance: Just leaving multiple messages on my phone.
    Jenny: Mm-hmm.
    Radiance: Calling me a bad mother.
    Jenny: Mm-hmm.
    Radiance: Saying I'm unfit and unstable, just anything he can do to basically just bring me down—" –Radiance

3. "Look, it's an argument. Nothin's happened. Nothin' criminally." – Officer McQuaid
4. "Somebody that's never been involved in an argument thinks this is the worst thing that's ever happened to 'em, and to them it is, to them, it really is. It's not realizing to the level of any criminal activity, so that's how we can ask people to leave or do anything like that, which we cannot make, unless we'd have some sort of crimes that's committed, but we can ask." –Detective Jacobs

As these examples show, victim/survivor narratives are quite different from those told by law enforcement officers. Instead of describing the abuses in terms of violence as victims/survivors do, law enforcement downplay so-called noncriminal domestics, that is, emotional and verbal violence, calling them an "argument." Officer McQuaid calls it "nothing" in Example 3 of Emotional Violence Narrative. In that example, notice the parallel construction of "Nothing's happened. Nothing criminally," which positions the only valid happening with criminality. It is as though if it isn't criminal, it doesn't matter, and even further – it didn't happen. Detective Jacobs is somewhat softer when he offers up that it may be the "worst thing ever" (Example 4, Emotional Violence Narratives) for the victim, but still pushes the fact that arguments, emotional abuse, are noncriminal forms of abuse and thus, not within the purview of the police. The indexical field of domestic violence, then, is made up of elements that come from a number of directions and polarities, constraining and enabling identity emergence and agency (choices), among other things.

Examples of Physical Violence Narratives

1. "The first time that he ever hit me, he just gave me a black eye, which I shouldn't say just, but—" –Becky
2. "He's literally not emotionally abusive at all. He always actually builds me up not tears me down. We never even argue, which is interesting, but when he drinks and gets drunk to that point, blacked-out, he's— three different times he's beat the living crap out of me. I've ended up in the hospital three times. That's the only time." –Becky
3. "I left my husband. I had a major black eye. That was the first time he ever hit me in the face, but he has pushed me and thrown me around since day one; cheated on me, all sorts of stuff. Mental abuse like no other." –Bubba
4. "And if I bruised, that motherfucker would punch me and blame me for bruising." –Killingsworth

The narrations of physical violence are representative of those in this study. In particular is the surfacing of the black eye – the *sine qua non* of domestic violence. This clear indicator of having been hit is talked about throughout the data, a key item in this indexical field. Interestingly enough, Becky justifies her black eye with "just," "he *just* gave me black eye" (Example 1, Physical Violence Narratives) before describing abuse that she finds more severe – "he beat the living crap out of me" (Becky, Example 2, Physical Violence Narratives). Even in the face of three severe beatings, Becky excuses, validates, and speaks fondly of her abusive partner when she makes claims such as, "He's literally not emotionally abusive at all. He always actually builds me up not tears me down" (Becky, Example 2, Physical Violence Narratives). Becky apparently feels like emotional abuse is worse than the beatings that put her in the hospital. She uses her ex-boyfriend's lack of emotional violence to justify her relationship. Becky's positive sentiments are followed very quickly by a statement that she has been hospitalized three times due to beatings. The indexical field, thus, includes elements one might expect to see, such as traces of physical abuse, like those we see in Bubba's story – pushing, throwing, cheating, hitting – alongside elements that are unexpected, such as excusing and validating abuser behavior (Example 3, Physical Violence Narratives). The majority of the participants discussed physical and emotional violence together, denying the false dichotomy that we find in the police discourse, in which one (physical) is criminal and the other (emotional/verbal) is just an argument.

Examples of Narratives of Mixed Forms of Violence

1. "He would just explode and push me, mostly pushing me. He choked me a lot and he would always say, "I know how not to leave a mark," so he would just for a brief and then let me up and then push me down and hit me on the head right along the head where it's not visible. That's about it, mostly hitting me on the head pulling out my hair, choking so it doesn't leave a mark and then making me have sex when I don't want to." –Kitty

2. "Every type of abuse. He physically abused me. He broke a couple of my ribs. He broke my arm. He broke my wrist. It culminated with him strangling, suffocating me, and beating me up when I was 30 weeks pregnant in front of my 2 children. He raped me. He abused us with food [withheld food]. He held us prisoner for a few years." –Little Bird

3. "Generally, when we're looking at a history, at an address, it will start out with those verbal domestics where we're just going to make sure everybody's safe and then we leave. Then if it starts to escalate––so, I'll go over those. Escalation, if you start to see jealousy, drug-use, alcohol-use, strangulation, lost his job. Where they're starting to have nothing to lose, you'll see it clear as day. What's going on. What's going to happen with that house. It could start out where it's just, "My husband

won't give me any money for groceries. He's very controlling," to where it's very active and volatile and dangerous." –Jo (dispatcher)

4. "[If] two people are just yelling back and forth that's not criminal. People raise their voice at each other all the time when they're upset. It'd be like if there's actual physical contact, or something in the house was broke, they physically hurt the other person, anything like that." –Amy (dispatcher)

Violence resists boundaries, and different functional violences bleed into each other. The first example (Example 1, Narratives of Mixed Forms of Violence), a story told by Kitty, aptly demonstrates the overlapping of violence, while adding important elements to the indexical field, namely "choking" and "not leav[ing] a mark." These are both issues that come up over and over. Choking is considered to be an escalator by police, and it is incredibly scary and violent for the victims/survivors. Getting a beating while being told, "'I know how not to leave a mark'" is emotional and physical violence combined. The statement is simultaneously a threat and a claim that the assailant is untouchable, uncatchable – that he will continue to do as he pleases to Kitty. The statement instills fear while it controls, and the beating does the same. Little Bird's story (Example 2, Narratives of Mixed Forms of Violence) hits many of the same notes, including rape, which Bubba also discusses. Thus, an indexical field emerges around emotional and physical violence, filled with the traces of violence that police and victims/survivors talk about, some of which are traces that only victims/survivors recognize as violent. This indexical field is pictured in Figure 2.1.

The constellation of the indexical field of violence, pictured in Figure 2.1, is added to by police and victim/survivor discourses. As we saw earlier, the distinction between criminal and noncriminal domestic violence that draws a problematic binary between physical and emotional violence is reproduced for police dispatchers, working within the same discourse, the same indexical field. As we see in Example 3 of Narratives of Mixed Forms of Violence, Jo distinguishes between the two when she says, "It could start out where it's just, 'My husband won't give me any money for groceries. He's very controlling,' to where it's very active and volatile and dangerous." Control and withholding grocery money are not criminal, but more importantly for Jo, they are not "active" or "volatile." That is, even though she has just talked through domestic violence escalation, in which she noted that emotional violence can precede physical violence, she still classifies noncriminal domestic violence as not dangerous. Her counterpart, Amy, talks about "just" yelling as noncriminal, using the hedging work "just" to diminish and overlook the effects of emotional violence (Example 4, Narratives of Mixed Forms of Violence).

Figure 2.1 Violence indexical field.

2.1.2 Staying/Leaving Stories

As was the case for violence, the indexical field of staying/leaving is a mixture of expected and unexpected elements, positive and negative elements that stem from all participants in the study, including police personnel. In many ways, the violent stories discussed earlier are staying stories. Those events happen in the course of staying. What I am interested in this section are stories about why the individual stayed and the difficulties associated with leaving.

Examples of Staying/Leaving Narratives

1. "I mean, sometimes people look at, why did you stay so long? Well, you grow attachment, you—it's not easily cut and dry like some people might think that has never been through it." –Linda
2. "Just convincing myself that, okay, this is—I got to get out or I'm not gonna make it." –Linda
3. "Just making it so hard for me to be able to move on—" –Rainbow
4. Rainbow: because they don't understand and
              you won't understand unless you're actually in that
              situation.

It's so hard.

Jenny: What is it that they don't understand?

Rainbow: To just leave.

They don't understand why you're just going through this.

They feel like you're just going through it like

you just want to—

or you need something out of it.

In reality it's really hard.

5.   "Again, I think when they call us they want us to stop the bad that's happening now. When we arrive, and they realize, oh, they're taking someone to jail. Now, they start to realize, what am I gonna do for food? How am I gonna pay the rent, pay for my car? Who's gonna clothe the kids? Then they realize, wait, I didn't want him to go to jail. Again, we're using him as the bad guy most of the time, 'cause that's mostly what we respond on, but both sides of a couple are to blame, or can be to blame, or can be the bad guy. Though we're using 'he' and 'her,' it's interchangeable. They realize that after, oh, I just wanted him to stop tonight. When they start realizing is he gonna be even more mad when he gets out of jail, he's gonna beat me even worse. Those things start to come up in their mind, and now they're second-guessing, well, don't take him to jail, just make him be nice. I don't know if ever, again, every reason on every scene is different." –Detective Sidwell
    "Let him come back" story

6.   "It's hard, because I would let him come back. He would stop drinking, and then sure enough, seven, eight months later, boom." –Becky
    Excusing story

7.   "It's so hard, because he really isn't like that if he would just not drink." –Becky
    "Not going back" story

8.   "I'm not one of those seven timers." –Marlo

At the center of leaving/staying indexical field is the idea that leaving is exceptionally "hard." Many participants couple explanations about leaving and "hard" with explanations of why they stayed. These explanations are typically directed toward people not in violent relationships. For example, Linda (Examples 1 and 2, Staying/Leaving Narratives) says leaving is "not cut and dried," and further that she had to "convince" herself that she had to "get out." That is, leaving is not something one does on a lark. Rainbow takes it further, claiming "they don't understand. [...] In reality it's just really hard" (Example 4, Staying/Leaving Narratives). Unable to articulate what makes it so difficult to leave, these participants work hard to express the struggle of leaving in order to inform the inexperienced masses. Becky says it is hard because her former partner "isn't like that" when he doesn't drink (Example 7, Staying/Leaving Narratives). Becky is looking for the good in her abusive partner, the part of him that doesn't drink and then beat her. She uses the mantra of "hard" to excuse her former partner's violent behavior. Thus, we see "excusing of partner behavior" emergent in this indexical field in the context of staying/leaving stories.

The small stories about how hard it is to leave are coupled with reasons for staying. Detective Sidwell very aptly summarizes the stresses of leaving that may lead to an individual staying in a relationship that isn't safe. He frames the issue from a police officer's perspective. The story told in Example 5 of the Staying/Leaving Narratives is in many ways a story about an abused person who doesn't want her abusive partner jailed. The ramifications of having one's partner taken to jail – of leaving an abusive relationship – are many. As Detective Sidwell explains, there are worries over money, food, clothes, rent, and car. The abused party starts to think they don't want the abuser to go away to jail but only to "stop tonight." Further, there is every possibility, brought up in the data multiple times, that when they gets out of jail, the abuse will be even more severe (cf. Coker, 2004). All these factors mean that "now they're [the victim] second-guessing, well, don't take him to jail, just make him be nice." Detective Sidwell really gets at the heart of the matter at the end of his story. Victims/survivors want the police to "just make him be nice." In other stories, there are a number of victims/survivors who express a desire to fix the relationship or fix their partner – make him be nice – rather than break up. Thus, as Figure 2.2 shows, adjusting behavior of the abuser is an element of this indexical field of staying/leaving. A desire for the abuser to be nice facilitates staying and leaving narratives.

There is also space for hope in the staying/leaving indexical field. All of the victims/survivors were out of abusive relationships when I spoke with them. In their stories of leaving, we find a hope for a better life. We get a glimpse of this when Marlo says, she's not a "seven timer" (Example 8, Staying/Leaving Narratives) or in other words, she's not going back time and time again. She is out for good. This was a sentiment shared by a number of victims/survivors, even those who still openly yearned for their past relationships. You see, romantic love still played an important role in relationship discourses for victims/survivors of domestic violence.

2.1.3 Family Stories

This section of the domestic violence indexical field is about family, or narratives about children, pregnancy, and parents/growing-up. A number

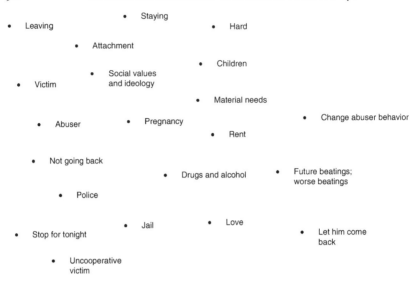

Figure 2.2 Staying/leaving indexical field.

of exemplary extracts about family are in the Family History Narratives Extracts. Difficult childhoods come up a number of times in these data, used as context for stories about tolerance for intimate partner violence. In the story that Rainbow tells, she indicates that her mother was abusive, and that this gave her an "[un]stable foundation" (Example 1, Family History Narratives). According to her story, without a strong foundation, she has been transient more than she would have liked, leading her to try to find stability in a bad relationship. Elsewhere in her interview, Rainbow expresses that it was better to be in a relationship than to be unstable again, and so because of family history, she tried to make the relationship work. We begin, here, to see overlapping between the indexical fields, which I have thus far artificially separated as a way of delving deeper into small stories. Stories about family are supported by stories about staying/leaving, and vice versa.

Examples of Family History Narratives

1. "I was adopted when I was five into a single parent household, it was just me and my brother. I'm 33 years old now. It's been very difficult, me and my mom don't talk. She was very abusive to me growing up, just wasn't there for me at all. She was more there for my brother. Yeah, with that and not really having that stable foundation, I have done a lot of moving around and just trying to figure out life basically on my own and through people around me which was very difficult cause nobody cares." –Rainbow

Examples of Pregnancy Narratives

1. "Just constantly staying pregnant, mainly because he wanted me to."
   –Rainbow
2. "He ended up marrying his side girlfriend on me a few years back—
   after getting me pregnant again. I've placed a couple of our children for
   adoption." –Rainbow
3. "Once I got pregnant, he raised a hand to me, he didn't actually hit me.
   Once he raised his hand to me, it was like instinctual, "Are you serious?"
   There is no line. I thought maybe there would be a line. There'd be a
   growing up or maturing up, evolution, okay. Something's in the past,
   but let's move forward. No, not even now, okay. At that point, I jumped
   out of the car where I was and called the cops." –Kate
4. "He was pressuring me to get pregnant. [...] And he was starting to
   threaten me if I didn't get pregnant." –Killingsworth
5. "Like a bull, I got him out after he strangled me the second time.
   Locked him out, wouldn't let him come back until he—and I didn't
   dare call the police. I administered like I did, because for 10 years, I
   administered first aid or I'd go into the E.R. and I didn't tell them what
   was going on. I made sure the baby was okay. That's all I cared about.
   Was the baby being good." –Little Bird

Example of Children Narratives

1. "I have three kids, and I just learned not to trust anymore." –Violet
2. "It's still recording. You could hear all of this. You can hear him saying
   to me, 'Are you ready to fucking die in front of your kids?' and then him
   strangling me, and me screaming, the whole bit." –Little Bird

Example of Family and Society Narratives

1. "My parents were married for a long time before they divorced, and
   my mom was really big on your wedding vows mean everything. I
   had gotten pregnant shortly after he got back from boot camp. I was
   pregnant and really felt like my child needed a mom and dad." –Zoey

Pregnancy and children are easily the most prevalently emergent indexical
features across the victim/survivor data. What it means to be pregnant
and abused emerges in various formations is discussed by a number of
participants. According to the *Domestic violence sourcebook* (Berry, 2000,
p. 9), "more than one third of pregnant women are abused." Abuse and
pregnancy have many valences. On the one hand, you have victims/
survivors such as Rainbow who were kept pregnant as part of the abuse
and control. She was forced to have children that she couldn't take care of
and/or keep (Example 1, Pregnancy Narratives). Being kept in a vulnerable
position, under control using pregnancy, childbearing was used as an

abusive strategy. Another way that pregnancy plays a role is as an impetus to leave. Kate, for example, leaves when her abusive partner raises a hand to strike her while she is pregnant (Example 3, Pregnancy Narratives). As she puts it, "I thought there was a line," but of course there wasn't. Being pregnant is a dangerous time for a victim/survivor of domestic violence. "25% of all women battered in America are abused while pregnant" (Berry, 2000, p. 9). This figure plays out in the data analyzed here, in which just less than half complained about being beaten and kicked while pregnant. Pregnancy and children also lead some victims/survivors to stay in relationships for longer. As Zoey puts it, "I was pregnant and really felt like my child needed a mom and dad" (Example 1, Family and Society Narratives). This desire to have fathers in the lives of children, a socially validated piece of ideology, is echoed throughout the data, compelling women to stay in abusive relationships. Little Bird's brief narrative adds an interesting note. She describes her ex-husband's abuse in an event in which he indexed their children while he was strangling her, saying, "you ready to fucking die in front of your kids?" (Example 2, Children Narratives). This statement weaponizes the children, using them in a statement that is emotionally abusive. Indeed, the indexical use of "kids" seals the violence of the moment.

The social idea that children need two parents, or that children need a father is a feature of sociocultural ideology. It is a normative discourse in society that, in this case, functions to keep abused people in violent relationships. The "whole family" myth is not the only piece of cultural information circulating in these data (Figure 2.3). Zoey also calls attention to her marriage vows, articulating them as a reason for staying in a violent relationship (Example 1, Family and Society Narratives). Thus, ideology plays a significant role in the indexical field, underpinning and performing family and relationship values that keep people in unsafe relationships. From the "stand by your man" stories of partner improvement in the staying/leaving portion of the indexical field, to the idea of upholding vows, to the idea that children need two parents, we see cultural values play a significant role in articulating, animating, and maintaining violent relationships. To put a finer point on it, sociocultural values and ideology about family, children, and marriage uphold and maintain domestic violence.

2.1.4 Policing

Policing is another important part of the indexical field. This is true for a number of reasons, but it is especially true because domestic violence assault

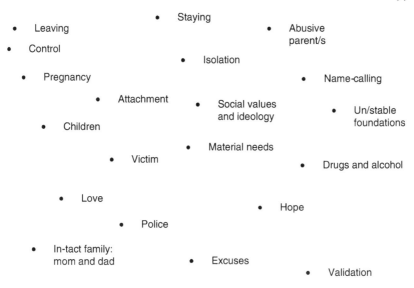

Figure 2.3 Family indexical field.

is a crime, and police/criminal intervention is seen as the only response. Police encounters are discussed in every interview because either the interviewee or the interviewer brought them up. Police can help out when things escalate to a critical point, but when they arrive on scene, things become complicated. While victims might be happy to see the police, because that means safety, they may also lie, as Linda admits, because she loved her abuser and didn't want to see him in trouble (Example 1, "Lied to Protect" Narratives). This sentiment is echoed by Detective Michaels, who says that when victims learn that Western City has a mandatory arrest law, they become less cooperative "because they don't wanna see anything further happen to their partner" (Example 1, Police Work Narratives). Indeed, police describe victims as uncooperative in a number of places. A perceived uncooperative victim who does not want to see their partner arrested becomes an element in the indexical field of policing, as does love. Victims may also be at more risk if their abuser is arrested, a fact they know all too well.

Example of "Lied to Protect" Narratives

1. "There was a few instance where I was scared and had to call for help. Then I also lied when they showed up and didn't say the severity of things at times because of my love for the guy that was abusing me."
   –Linda

Examples of Police Affect Narratives

1. Yeah, [for police it was] just, it was just a day at work. It wasn't, "Oh, my God. I just got kidnapped." –Marlo
2. "To be honest, I felt like it was any other just random situation, [for police]" –Violet

Examples of Police and Domestic Violence Narratives

1. "I think they're good guys. I think they're just—and I understand that they don't like to come to those calls 'cause you never know what you're going into, but I think they need to be more educated about what domestic violence is or isn't, and what it can look like, as well as I don't know, maybe giving resources. There are ways to get out of this." –Crystal
2. "A better maybe understanding of what a victim really looks like. When the police are there, and you're there, and he's there, are you really going to open up right in front of him knowing that there's gonna be consequences later on for you?" –Crystal

Example of "Didn't Call Police" Narratives

1. "Because by the time I picked up my daughter and put her in her bed because she had been asleep the whole time, he was passed out on the bed. I don't know if— now, that I'm thinking about it, part of me is, he's passed out, I don't want to put officers in danger with him just being— getting violent or retaliating against me after they leave. I didn't want him to go to jail. I didn't want to go to any court proceedings. I just wanted it to be over. I went on a ride-a-long about a week or two later and I was like, "Do you think I did the right thing?" I don't know if— because you know you think, what if he does that to somebody else? Type of mentality. He was like, "You know, he hasn't bothered you since. You're out. You're safe. You and your daughter are safe. He can't contact you. He doesn't know where you're at." Within the last year and a half, I don't regret not calling the police, but I had a lot of help with getting out of there without him even being involved. Blocking all communication. Him not knowing where I was. We live in different cities. I don't know." –Jo (dispatcher)

Example of Police Work Narratives

1. "Some victims will be cooperative in the beginning, until you start letting them know more *[unintelligible 8:52]* DV laws in [Western City] then they will shut down, or not cooperate any further because they don't wanna see anything further happen to their partner." –Detective Michaels

In addition to commentary about victims/survivors, this indexical field includes commentary about police. In Police and Domestic Violence Narratives, Example 1, Crystal says, "I think they're good guys," leading with a positive element that the police are not inherently bad, even though she was arrested one time when the police were called regarding a violent attack in which she was choked. She recognizes that police find domestic calls incredibly dangerous. In fact, she is quite generous with police. She goes on to say that they need more education about domestic violence. "I think they need to be more educated about what domestic violence is or isn't, and what it can look like, as well as I don't know [...] A better maybe understanding of what a victim really looks like" (Examples 1 and 2, Police and Domestic Violence Narratives). Crystal very articulately explains the kind of education that police need in order to deal with domestic violence better – they need a sense of victimhood and the complications that go along with that. I describe more on this in Chapter 3. She ends with hope: "There are ways to get out of this." In the face of extreme hardship and difficulty, Crystal finds hope. Figure 2.4

Figure 2.4 Policing indexical field.

shows the indexical field of policing that emerges in these data, with hope emerging alongside police education and caring.

2.2 Mixed Stories: Connecting the Indexical Fields

So far in this section, I have identified some of the key features of the indexical field broken down into smaller categories: violence, leaving/ staying, family, and policing. In fact, most of the discourse and narratives in these data include mixtures of two or more of these indexical fields. The combinations are compelling, with different fields brought into bolster different portions of narrative, and provide evidence for another field, or just parallelly align different portions of a story. Extract 2.1 is a story about the complications that come along with allowing an abusive partner back into the speaker's life.

Extract 2.1 Becky

1.	*Becky*:	My kids will say—
2.		that's what's sad,
3.		my kids really love him.
4.		They adore him, and he adores them.
5.		He's great with them,
6.		but they, especially my boys, because it makes them so angry.
7.		They're like, "Mom, what are you doing?
8.		Why would you even let him come back?
9.		Why would you even"—
10.		even though they like him, and
11.		they get that he's not that way all the time —
12.		they see that end result.
13.		They're like, "Why would you let him come back?"
14.		Even my family, oh, my family—my family won't even help me at all.
15.		Because after last year,
16.		he knocked me out and almost broke my jaw.
17.		I dislocated my jaw.
18.		I ended up unconscious for I don't even know how long.
19.		He sexually assaulted me while I was unconscious.

In Extract 2.1, Becky brings together family and violence in a disturbing story of extreme violence and sexual assault. The narrative opens with a statement that her children really love her estranged, abusive partner. Indeed, they "adore" each other (line 4). This statement establishes the parameters for a loving story that is ironically about violence. This, then, functions as a kind of explanatory discourse that doesn't excuse the abuse but frames it as aberrant in an otherwise loving relationship. The next few lines show the narrative shift. Now we find out that her children are "so angry" (line 6). However, they are not angry at the abuser. They are angry with their mom, Becky, who is telling the story. The "you" in this portion of the story is Becky. The next line goes back to lifting up the abuser, followed by a justification "that he's not that way all the time" (line 11). The story shifts away from a framing of the abuser as good to a story of abuse. It is introduced with another clause about family – her family will no longer help her because she has taken him back too many times. With this introduction of her family, she goes on to list a number of violent abuses, and she does so without framing her abuser as good or decent.

Becky's small story does a lot of narrative work. It sets up her ex-boyfriend as kind, while also establishing him as violent, while also making herself the target for her children's anger, while describing being disowned by her family. She clearly articulates a situation in which relationships are dangerous and can tear a life apart. She also situates herself as loyal to her abusive partner while also trying to rebuild her life. She performs the kinds of complexity involved in leaving an abusive partner and then being expected by society to simply pick up the pieces and move on. Becky teaches us that there is more to it than that.

In Extract 2.2, Crystal tells a small story that involves police, family, and physical violence. In this story, Crystal introduces the fact that her son is ill and that she was managing his care. She was extremely busy.

Extract 2.2 Crystal

1.	*Crystal:*	There was another time that I was going to school fulltime and working.
2.		My little boy had 15 different doctors involved in his care,
3.		so managed all that.
4.		I was in a position where I needed to—
5.		I had this amount of time to get what I needed done.
6.		He was causing problems and wouldn't let me.
7.		He was taking the kids, was trying to get at the kids and
8.		had me pinned up against the wall
9.		so I bit his arm to get away.
10.		He called the cops, and
11.		I got an assault charge because—I did bite him,
12.		but—

Crystal's ex-husband is described as harassing her, bugging her and the kids, and generally not letting her get her work done – anything to stop her from completing her tasks. This is a form of control and emotional abuse, especially coming at her, as he did, through the children. This worked to get her attention and when she attempted to intervene on behalf of her children, she was "pinned up against a wall" (line 8). In order to "get away," Crystal bit her husband's arm, and he called the police (lines 9 and 10). Even though the husband had been the primary aggressor, the police read the details of the altercation incorrectly and cited Crystal. Because there is not legal rubric for emotional violence and coercive control, the police misunderstood the situation and cited Crystal. Moreover, police see themselves as "fact finders," as people who do nothing more than read the facts. Of course, they bring with them culture, ideology, and communication practices. These interactional elements can disrupt a clean reading of the facts, as though such a thing exists. This misreading of the "facts," especially when chronic abusers are good at not leaving marks, as discussed earlier, led to the arrest of the abused party. This was the case for a number of victims/survivors – arrest in the face of abuse literally adding insult to injury. These incorrect findings are often remedied within a few hours. They are troubling nevertheless, and so arrest of victims is an element of the indexical field of domestic violence.

Crystal's story is founded on a concern that police believe the abuser over and above the victim. Nikki has a similar concern. She explains that she would like to tell police to "please believe [her]." She says:

> I'm telling you that he hurt me, and I'm telling you there are visible red marks on my thigh, and he's telling you, "Oh, no, she's just clumsy." *Please just believe me* because I may not have the power or the guts to just walk out of that house, but I called you because I figured, with your help, I could.

This statement to police to believe the victim's story – to read the facts outside of the abuser's editorializing – is punctuated with a staying/leaving statement. She wishes the police realized that they can have the ability to make the victim brave. Leaving is incredibly hard, "I may not have the power or guts to just walk out of that house," and so it requires bolstering from outside parties, the police being one of them. I would add, it may take a number of encounters with police before the victim gets the courage to leave for good, but it will happen, with conscientious support and knowledge about resources.

The last kind of mixed story I want to look at brings together elements of violence, leaving, and family.

Extract 2.3 Katherine

1. *Katherine:*   I just never left because I thought my son needed a dad.

Extract 2.4 Detective Sidwell

1. *Det. Sidwell:*   If an adult chooses to stay with someone who's abusive,
2.   I will do what I can, each time I'm there, to help the situation,
3.   but the children don't often have that choice, and they're stuck there.
4.   That's the one that gets me is,
5.   do this, but look at what you're doin' to the children.
6.   That one's the hardest for me to deal with when it comes to this.

Connecting these two narrative fragments is the idea that children are impacted by their parents. For Katherine, that means that she stayed in an abusive relationship because she thought her "son needed a dad" (line 1; Extract 2.3). Again, we see the social value of an intact family arising in a dangerous way that keeps an abused woman with an abusive man.

Family values are echoed in Detective Sidwell's story (Extract 2.4), but with a different valence. He begins by saying that the victim "chooses to stay," as though that decision was fully in the grasp of the sovereign individual without complication (more on this in Chapter 3). Children, on the other hand, do not have a choice, "they're stuck there." This description of abuse situates the abused on an even playing field with the abuser, thereby blaming the victim, by positioning him/her as equally engaged in hurting their children. Thus, the reason that so many people stay in abusive relationships – children – becomes the discursive resource to criticize and blame victims. That is, people think they are staying to help their children, but others see staying for the children as a mistake that damages the children. This equation forgets, erases, and undermines the lived experiences of violence that abused women live with every day. The indexical field of domestic violence thus includes victim erasure, even as it includes victim hypostatization.What we have in Figure 2.5 is a representation of the indexical field of domestic violence that combines all of the story types and the related indexical features. An indexical field is a set of "potential meanings" (Eckert, 2008), not *the* meaning, and as such it is about possibility, meanings that might and could emerge within and be attached to elements in the field. With a field this full of competing, different, and opposed terms, the meanings that might emerge and the identities that might be performed are diverse and complex. Of note are the terms that come up in more than one indexical field – terms such as emotional violence, family, pregnancy, children, uncooperative victim, and excuses. They provide a structure to the other, more variable features in the indexical field. They act as a set of touchstones around which other ideas, concepts, and values cluster. In the rest of this chapter, I will continue to explore the ways these concepts overlap and come together by analyzing longer, more complex accounts of violence and police interactions with victims/survivors.

2.3 Small Story in an Indexical Field

The narratives told about domestic violence buy into, complicate, and substantiate the indexical field of which they are also a part. Stories about domestic violence emerge within a field of discourse that delimits, defines, and enables the types of stories and features of stories that can be told. These elements are included, denied, excluded, and violated when they are combined and recombined in narrative. Further, because identity also emerges in storytelling, the indexical field of domestic violence also constrains and enables semistable though emergent identity performance

Figure 2.5 Staying/leaving + violence + family + police indexical field.

in important ways. The story and story fragments in Extract 2.5, told by Melissa, demonstrates how the indexical field described earlier enables storytelling about domestic violence, including many of the features of domestic violence indexicality. We also see a complex identity performed that brings together elements of a deep-seated social value of marriage with a strong sense that this victim/survivor is strong. I spoke with this victim/survivor in a women's shelter in Western City, where she had lived for a number of months.

Extract 2.5 Melissa

1.	*Melissa:*	Yeah, and it was never a healthy relationship.
2.		It was always toxic.
3.		Now, I find out—just a couple years ago, I was reading something —,
4.		because I was like, "Something's wrong. Something is not right."
5.		He has no emotional attachment to anybody,
6.		not even his mother,
7.		his other kids, their birthdays
8.		ours—we have five.
9.		Our oldest is 22.
10.		I started researching, and I thought at first he was a sociopath.
11.		I was like, "No. That doesn't all fit."
12.		He's a narcissist. A hundred percent.
13.		If he took a test, he would be clinically diagnosed, on paper, as a narcissist.
14.		They say, "You have to get away from this person.
15.		They're gonna cut you down.
16.		They're gonna just tear you apart.
17.		Everything that comes out of their mouth is a lie.
18.		They can't care about anybody at all."
19.		It just makes perfect sense.
20.		So. It started to make me a little stronger to be able to—
21.		I would listen to the YouTube videos of
22.		the women that have gone through that,
23.		but it's so hard to go, because he- he's so mean.
24.		What helped me is that we have three kids, 17, 19, and 22, and
25.		then we have 2 that are just 2 and 8.
26.		The other three are completely screwed up,
27.		and I know that it's my fault. I know that it is.
28.		I thought that I was doing the right thing, because he was there.
29.		I thought having—.

30.	*Jenny:*	Mm hmm. Keeping the family together.
31.	*Melissa:*	Yeah, I thought having a dad there is better than never knowing one, I thought.

By way of opening her story, Melissa notes that her marriage was always "toxic" (line 2); there was never a good time. She quickly attributes this to the fact that her estranged husband was a narcissist. Narcissist is a common lay diagnosis of abusive partners made by victims/survivors. It is part of the indexical field of domestic violence. Melissa uses the idea that he is a narcissist as a strategy for explaining why she is leaving, which is inspired in part by the fact that others say that she should leave. We see this with the quotation, "They say, 'You have got to get away from this person'" (line 14). Having a group of people in the same boat telling her to leave because "narcissists" aren't safe partners authorizes her leaving. Deciding that he is a narcissist makes him unfixable and intolerable, and so she has to leave him and not go back. There is nothing that Melissa can do. The decision that he was a narcissist and the information about narcissism also "started to make [Melissa] a little stronger" (line 20). She is also authorized to leave by her children – her status as a mother. Like others in the data, Melissa takes the blame for her situation and her children being "completely screwed up" (line 26). As she says, "And I know it's my fault" (line 27). Thus, Melissa takes unwarranted responsibility for staying in the marriage and potentially damaging her children. Children, then, are ultimately something that pushes her out of her abusive marriage.

Melissa follows up her claim of self-blame with an explanation for why she stayed. She explains, "I thought that I was doing the right thing, because he was there. I thought having – […] yeah, having a dad there is better than never knowing one, I thought" (lines 28, 29, and 31). Melissa's story is thus riddled with fidelity to social norms. Melissa wants a family that includes a dad, because she thought it was better for the family, better for the children, and better for her. Of course, as she notes, he still was not a caring father. This is ideology at work, social norms making her story meaningful for herself and others. Thus, there is an indexical link between descriptions of violence and social norms about family completeness and shape. This link is dangerous. It kept her in an unsafe marriage for twenty-four years.

This set of narratives, told by Melissa, call attention not only to the indexical forms that make up the indexical field but also to how they are clustered together. Stories of staying and leaving cluster with stories that include comments about children and the social valuation of a "whole" family that includes a mother, a father, and children. This social value of family, then, puts pressure on, makes difficult, and sometimes facilitates staying in an abusive relationship. Children are also described as reasons for leaving abusive relationships. We also see a cluster around narratives of physical violence, which are told with hedging and hesitancy, and discourses of self-blame on the part of the victim. These are stories that the victim/survivor feels compelled to tell, is willing to tell, but sometimes can't find the words to tell, which Melissa's stories exemplify. The trauma may be too hard to revisit or too hard to put into words. Either way, it often comes with clauses that own the abuse in ways that articulate trauma.

2.4 Small Story: I'm Not a Victim

In Extract 2.6, Kate describes an abusive relationship and interactions with the police, animating a number of elements from the indexical field of domestic violence. Perhaps most notable in this interview is the implicature that she is not a victim, because she "hit back." I interviewed Kate over the phone. She lived in a large metropolitan area at the time of her abuse. Kate introduces her violent relationship, much like Melissa does elsewhere in her interview, with a description of her childhood and mention that she got pregnant by her abusive partner. Kate's mention of childhood is poignant, in that she uses it to explain and justify how she got into a relationship that was "abusive from the beginning." According to Kate, she had learned in her abusive childhood that abuse was "normal" and that "hitting was love" (line 11). She also calls herself "naïve" and "in love" (lines 15 and 16), all features of the indexical field associated with staying stories.

Extract 2.6 Kate

1.	*Kate*:	Yeah. I guess, so the main one that it usually strikes home
2.		is my relationship with my daughter's father.
3.		Umm, and had known each other, um,
4.		just known each other about 18 months
5.		by the time I got pregnant.
6.		So, by the time I had my daughter,
7.		we had known each other less than a couple years,
8.		but our relationship was abusive from the beginning. Um.
9.		I realized later that, uh, I came from a household
10.		where capital- uh, or corporal punishment was normal and things like that.

11.		I thought hitting was love at some point.
12.		So, it took me a while
13.		to understand parts of things, cause as young as I was and as
14.		naïve as I was,
15.		when you're in love with somebody,
16.		I didn't understand, um, what was going on.
17.		So it took me a long time to realize where I was at,
18.		and that things weren't normal.
19.		Um, and, I hit back.
20.		I hit back all the time.
21.		So, because I hit back, do you know what I mean,
22.		I felt like we were all on even playing fields.
23.		I was never one of the abused women.
24.		I was just as much the abuser as he was, um, in that relationship, uh,
25.		which uh I actually ended up trying to leave that relationship.
26.		Um, and, we lived together at the time.
27.		So, I tried to leave- he left for work, and
28.		I basically dropped—left, walked,
29.		took [my daughter] to school, dropped them off,
30.		tried to come back and get in the house so I can get all my things because
31.		I had the day off,
32.		and he switched my key.
33.	*Jenny:*	Oh no.
34.	*Kate:*	So, he switched my keys.
35.		I couldn't get in the house to get my things.
36.		He must have known that I was planning to leave him.
37.	*Jenny:*	Yeah.
38.	*Kate:*	Then he came back around.
39.		Uh he drove porter for a auto dealership. So he came back around to
40.		basically see me sitting on the curb because he knew where I would be,
41.		and then I ended up um—he wouldn't let me in the car, so I could get the keys.
42.		So I ended up like vandalizing the car, yeah
43.		which he called the cops on me in that circumstance.
44.		I had been through a lot of "you don't call the cops on people you love"

45.   training from him.
46.   The whole beginning of our relationship,
47.   until the moment that he needed to call the cops,
48.   in which case he did, and
49.   I went to jail.

[...]

50.   *Jenny:*   Had you called the police in the past?

51.   *Kate:*   I had. More than once, but
52.   there was also like we lived in a neighborhood where he hit me,
                 I hit him, and
53.   if people came around, we hid it.
54.   Nobody, you didn't tell anybody.

As Kate expresses it, because of childhood patterns, it was hard for her to recognize that she was in an abusive relationship, making it hard to leave in the beginning for both personal and community reasons. Indeed, Kate still finds it hard to acknowledge abuse and accept the ideological status of victim. "I felt like we were all on even playing fields. I was never one of those abused women. I was just as much the abuser as he was in that relationship" (lines 22–24). Kate is loath to see herself through the lens of victim, leading her to take some blame for the abuse. Like we saw in Melissa's story, Kate takes partial responsibility for the violence in her relationship, describing herself as an "abuser [...] in that relationship" (line 24). Victimhood is expressed, then, as an intolerable identity, and so it is discursively avoided, put off, ignored, and erased, by both Kate and for Melissa but in different ways. Moreover, Kate's distancing of a victimhood identity is co-occurrent with narratives of staying. As such there is a problematic recognition of blame and fault that facilitates staying in abusive relationships.

This narrative about staying is wrapped up with a narrative of emotional abuse and leaving, in which Kate talks through a regime of control and fear. Indeed, Kate describes coercive control (see Chapter 1). This regime leads to an early but thwarted attempt to leave her abusive situation. In anticipation of Kate's leaving, her abuser had changed her keys and laid in wait for her. She ended up vandalizing the car he was in, leading him to call the police. The next statement is telling: "I had been through a lot of 'you don't call the cops on people you love'" (line 44). Not only does Kate characterize her relationship as loving but she also explains why she didn't call the police all the times she thought about it. She was not allowed, with reference to a manipulation with love. The statement presupposes that she had been told this, ostensibly by her abusive partner, on multiple occasions. Part of a regime of control and emotional abuse. In the next line, Kate frames this view of police not as an interpersonal one, but as a community one. "We lived in a neighborhood where he hit me, I hit him. And if people came around, we hid it. Nobody. You didn't tell anybody" (lines 52–54). Here, Kate is expressing the social value that divides public from private. Private issues should remain private, and this was a value not just discussed in her home as a threat but expressed socially in the neighborhood. As I explained in Chapter 1, the public/private is a social value that underpins and supports domestic violence.

In addition to developing a sense of the public/private divide, Kate also expresses that notifying the police was complicated by the abuse itself. Police intervention would not help, but rather it would lead to an escalation of violence. In Kate's words from elsewhere in her interview, "there were a lot of fearful times when the cops were right there, and I didn't say anything." Kate expresses what many of the victims/survivors echo: It is hard to talk to police because of fear of retribution. Kate is afraid of her abusive partner, community values, and reprisal in general. Abuse is always around the corner for Kate, announcing itself with no elicitation, no warning, and no recourse. Thankfully, Kate decided to leave when she got pregnant, an impetus shared by some of her peers. When her abuser raised his hand to her when she was pregnant, it was the last straw, and she left. She had hoped that the pregnancy would make her abuser grow and "mature." When that was obviously not the case, she got out of the relationship.

2.5 Small Story: I'm Not an Abuser

In my data, all but one of the victims/survivors are female. This is slightly out of line with the national statistic that 15 percent of reported domestic violence victims are male. The one man in the study, Bob, tells stories that are in many ways similar to those of the female participants. Regardless of the gender dynamic, domestic violence is about abuse, control, intimidation, and dominance. Bob's story is no different. Bob was interviewed over the phone. He lives in a major metropolitan area in the United States. In Extract 2.7, we hear him talk about fear, physical violence, and emotional violence. He brings up family situations, and he talks through social expectations and the complications of staying in the relationship after major events of abuse.

Extract 2.7 *Bob*

1. I didn't—you know, I - I, you know, or— or, uh,
2. one time we were driving and she was just— just so irate.
3. I think she just got off the phone with something about her kid—
4. with the dad, and - and she was just—she was going, like, 90 miles an hour,
5. just— just flying down the road. And I was just—I couldn't believe it. I was just—
6. I was really scared at that time. I really was.
7. It was kinda scary.
8. But, I stayed by her side, no matter, I did—
9. I mean, no matter—I was getting that kind of stuff, that treatment and things,
10. and I was— I was scared and nervous.
11. I still, I would just be there.
12. I— I wouldn't, you know, think about harming her back or—
13. — doing anything like that.
14. I just was going through it, basically, just— just going through it.
15. Uh, I mean, she always kinda threatened me with, uh, with, uh, you know,
16. a scene if she didn't get her way, and that's one thing.
17. If she didn't get her way when she was under the influence,
18. she just is the scariest thing ever.
19. But—

Bob hedges his descriptions of abuse with "kinda." He calls his girlfriend "kinda scary" (line 7) and he says that he was "kinda threatened" (line 15). This hedging puts the abuse in abeyance – it wasn't *so* bad – ameliorating the effects of staying. Like other victims/survivors, this might be a mitigating move meant to diminish the violence, make it seem less intense. Given his position as a man in US society, it might also be read as a face-saving strategy, meant to protect his socially dominant position. Given other discursive moves he makes, I suggest that at the same time that he performs "domestic violence victim," Bob is also performing a masculine position. Indeed, the hedging maintains a troubled, vacillating line between Western views of masculinity and his position as a victim/survivor. "Kinda" does this work by acknowledging and off-setting the threats and the scariness of the situation.

On line 3, Bob recalls a time when his girlfriend had received a bad phone call regarding her daughter. She was driving fast and precariously, and Bob recalls feeling "scared" (line 6). As he puts it, he was "getting that kind of stuff, that treatment and things" (line 9). The situation Bob describes of being scared, of being anxious, of being abused is punctuated by his unsolicited claim that he would never hurt his girlfriend back. He says, "I wouldn't, you know, think about harming her back or – doing anything like that" (lines 12 and 13). He makes a strong claim here that he is not an abuser. Where Kate claims she is not a victim, a socially prescribed viewpoint, here Bob claims that he is not an abuser, also a socioculturally charged assertion. Bob understands that the social meaning of domestic violence typically involves heterosexual relationships with a female victim, and he distances himself from that stereotype by making it explicit here and in one other part of his interview that he would never harm a woman. A troubled identity emerges for Bob that is distinctly male and that understands the stereotypes of violence and gender in US society but that also understands that he was being abused. However, he rejects the portions of that identity that would lead to him being actively abusive to a partner.

2.6 Small Story about Policing Victim Behavior

Police officers largely talk about domestic violence in terms of a criminal/ noncriminal distinction and in terms of victim behavior. In Extract 2.8, Detective Jacobs weaves together a number of small stories in order to make a few points about domestic calls, with special attention to interacting with victims. I spoke with Detective Jacobs in his precinct, along with Detectives Sidwell, Michaels, and Johnson. All four are domestic violence detectives.

Extract 2.8 Detective Jacobs

1.	*Det. Jacobs:*	True. Very true, and at that point—
2.		They're so dynamic and so different, each one individually is—
3.		because I don't wanna take you to jail because you're arguing with somebody.
4.		You can argue, we can yell at you, we can even call each other names, and
5.		there's nothing against the law on that.
6.		Maybe you get loud and you can do the disorderly or something like that, but
7.		to argue is okay.
8.		It's when you [start] crossing that line

9.	from starting to break stuff inside the house,
10.	or touch each other, not in a loving way.
11.	That's when things start to change and
12.	it now starts to turn into a criminal case versus a non-criminal case.
13.	The biggest key to have anybody is to either one:
14.	they have to know that you're being genuine, that you're trying to help them.
15.	If anybody can sense—
16.	you don't have to be a police officer to sense that.
17.	If somebody's not being genuine-
18.	they're just kinda like, hey, this is just another call, and
19.	I need to hurry up and get on to the next one,
20.	then they're not as likely to open up to you.
21.	If you can have your victims, or suspects, or
22.	anybody that you come in contact with,
23.	basically give them your undivided attention
24.	while still being aware of your surroundings,
25.	because we're in an unknown area,
26.	to be able to give them that comfort level, for me, seems to work a lot better,
27.	and then that way they can kind of get their minds put at ease, and
28.	we can either discuss options, but
29.	before we even get to that point, it's just to be able to discuss what's happened,
30.	because it could just be an argument.
31.	Somebody that's never been involved in an argument thinks
32.	this is the worst thing that's ever happened to them, and
33.	to them it is, to them, it really is.
34.	It's not realizing to the level of any criminal activity, so
35.	that's how we can ask people to leave or do anything like that,
36.	which we cannot make,
37.	unless we'd have some sort of crimes that's committed,
38.	but we can ask.
39.	Sometimes that's all that's needed to help de-escalate the situation,
40.	then we do that.
41.	On top of all that source, that stuff's documented in case it escalates again.
42.	There's a call log in there.
43.	The reports, you wouldn't be able to see that moment, but

44.   there would be a call log from dispatch saying,
45.   "hey, we were out here probably four hours ago, on the
                       same people,"

Detective Jacobs begins by laying out the distinction between criminal
and noncriminal domestic violence: "I don't wanna take you to jail
because you are arguing with somebody" (line 3). Detective Jacobs
told this story in a group interview with Detective Sidwell (and two
others, Detectives Michaels and Johnson). Earlier in this same interview,
Detective Sidwell uses the word "just" to characterize an argument:
"just an argument." Using the same construction, on line 30, Detective
Jacobs uses this construction: "just an argument." The sense here is that
arguments are simple, typical, nonabusive, not important, and not a big
deal. In fact, cruel fighting is a mainstay of emotional abuse. The violence
and abuse of a fight are downplayed, because they are not criminal. What
is interesting in Detective Jacobs language is his shift of the pronoun
"you" to the pronoun "we," when discussing arguments, rather than "he
or she": "You can argue, we can yell at you, we can even call each other
names, and there's nothing against the law on that" (lines 4 and 5). Not
only does this diminish the importance of and even exonerate verbal
violence, which according to victims/survivors often takes place verbally
in yelling and name-calling, it does so by normalizing such behavior
with the use of "we." "We" includes the speaker and the listeners in the
phrase at the very least, making it seem typically accepted and normal,
not the actions of an active abuser. The use of "we" here shifts to a
characterization and an identity of "every person," reducing the violence
of verbally and emotionally abusive arguing, about which a victim may
call the police for help. This phrasing normalizes the behavior of yelling
and calling names as the regular behavior of anybody. This referencing of
"anybody" indexes social discourses on interpersonal behavior, in which
argument and yelling are merely features of interaction that anybody
might have to deal with. Violence is thus surreptitiously dismissed. Then
with the explanation that this is not against the law, it is expelled from
the realm of violence, from the realm of law enforcement and legality. As
Detective Jacobs puts it in line 7, "But to argue is ok."

As the narrative goes on, Detective Jacobs moves to a discussion of
interacting and listening genuinely. This process links back to distinguishing
between criminal and noncriminal domestic violence. He states, "it's just to
be able to discuss what's happened, because it could just be an argument"
(lines 29 and 30). Again, he drives home the idea that just an argument is

not a police matter, and thus they need to tease out that issue as quickly and correctly as possible. Engaging with both victim and abuser in a sincere way facilitates policing and police behavior. The downplaying of emotional violence and the binary between criminal and noncriminal are active features in the indexical field of domestic violence.

After dismissing verbal/emotional violence, Detective Jacobs describes criminal violence: "break stuff inside the house, or touch each other, not in a loving way" (lines 9 and 10). Here, he uses the vocabulary of love, pulling in the social meaning of a typical relationship in order to make a point about criminal behavior. The criminal abuser breaks the social contracts that are in place, such as love. Violent touching, including breaking things, equals criminal domestic violence, because it breaks the social contract of love.

Detective Jacobs hopes that police involvement will deescalate a situation so that it doesn't turn to violence. He also readily acknowledges that they may get called back to the house "in four hours" (line 45) to deal with a "criminal" event of domestic violence. That is, he recognizes that noncriminal domestic violence, such as arguing, may escalate into physical violence. In the context of thinking about escalation and violence, Detective Jacobs comments on people who know the system (Extract 2.9).

Extract 2.9 Detective Jacobs

1.	*Det. Jacobs:*	there's some people that they know the system,
2.		been in the system, try to work the system, and talk about system,
3.		but we say the law enforcement part of it,
4.		where they look at law enforcement as enemies,
5.		and they're not gonna help in one way or the other,
6.		and so they're not gonna give us anything that they don't have to.

Some people, as Detective Jacobs says, "they know the system, been in the system, try to work the system" (lines 1 and 2). It is unclear whether he is talking about the abuser or the victims/survivors, given his use of "they." While he could be using the plural pronoun to reference all abusers, the use of the plural pronoun often means "the couple" in this interview. If it does refer to both members of the couple, it positions them as a pair against law enforcement, lumping the victim in with the abuser, who both know and try to manipulate the system. It distrusts the motives of the victim. "They look at law enforcement as enemies" (line 4). Positioned against the police in this way, neither member of the couple is going to "help" or give the police "anything that they don't have to" (lines 5 and 6). This positions victims as resistant to police intervention. They are discussed as not being helpful for the investigation, and indeed, they are described as going so far as to support the innocence of the abuser, denying the abuse that was reported. In short, they are represented as recalcitrant. Stories about recalcitrant victims – or victims who support their abusers and disrupt police work – abound in the police officer data. Questions about the motives of the victim, their recalcitrance, are a social discourse that runs throughout the data, and it creates an identity "recalcitrant victim" within the indexical field.

In an interview with a police dispatcher, Jessica, a view about victim behavior is presented in a different way (Extract 2.10). Jessica introduces domestic violence in terms of "screaming" and "frustration," gesturing to the emotional violence that underpins other forms of violence.

Extract 2.10 Jessica

1.	*Jenny:*	Yeah. Um, so you've mentioned domestic violence a couple of times. As you
2.		know, that this is the s—that's the-the focus of my study. What does a domestic
3.		call sound like? What are features?
4.	*Jessica:*	Um, usually, it's a lot of screaming, um, frustration.
5.		If it's one that we've responded to multiple times—
6.		— it's—you can hear the sighing and the exaggerated,
7.		"Uh, just get out here already. You've been out here."
8.		"You know us. The officers know us."
9.		So, you can tell that it's something they've been dealing with.
10.		Um, they've called before.
11.		Um, and the ones that are scary are the ones that they haven't called before.
12.		And, um—
13.		You don't know what to expect.
14.		You don't know how severe it is because
15.		I think they go through the moment of—
16.		especially if it's physical and dangerous—
17.		— they go through the moment of they're in fear for their lives—
18.		— or their children's lives.
19.		So, they're calling just to get help.
20.		And then, as it sinks in, or as the threat isn't as eminent—

21.   — they start to realize, "Oh, but I don't want them to get in
              trouble."
22.   And so, they kind of back pedal or, maybe, try to—
23.   — change the facts a little bit.

Jessica starts out by characterizing domestic calls as full of "screaming"
and "frustration" (line 4). The people she talks to are often afraid and
calling to get help. She uses this characterization of domestic violence
in order to comment on homes "that [they]'ve responded to multiple
times" (line 5). There are more data on such homes. The victims on this
type of call are characterized as exasperated, as "sighing" (line 8). Jessica
uses two quotations to emphasize this point: "just get out here, already"
(line 7). "The officers know us" (line 8). Domestic violence is presented
as normal, everyday. The victim here is positioned as impatient and
aware of the fact that they are known to police officers – aware that
domestic violence is common in their homes. Jessica then says, "So, you
can tell that it's something they've been dealing with" (line 9). The direct
antecedent for the pronoun "they" is police officers. However, given the
structure of the story in which the victim and the assailant are typically
the subjects in the story – the people who the story is about – this vague
pronoun could just as easily be the victim and thier abusive partner. If it
is the police officers, then the phrase "been dealing with" indicates both
an ongoing issue in the home and also a fed-upness with the ongoing
situation at that address. If it is the couple in an abusive relationship, it
indicates a longevity to the abuse by which the victim has already been
exasperated (sighing). Combined, we get a sense of an everydayness to
the situation, a sort of normal form of operation. This exchange, in other
words, normalizes violence for some residences and couples, and it shows
police officer frustration with victims, especially those that do not leave
– those that continually call the police.

   After talking through those calls at residences with multiple calls, Jessica
discusses the "scar[ier]" calls, of first-time callers (line 11). To be clear, it is
more dangerous for the police, who do not know what they are walking
into. Many of the police note that they get as much information as possible
before going into a domestic call because they are so dangerous (Detectives
Sidwell, Michaels, and Jacobs). Officer safety is, of course, paramount. It
is an incredibly dangerous job. When Jessica is thinking about dangerous
calls, she is explicitly talking about physical violence. She says, "You don't
know what to expect. You don't know how severe it is because I think they
go through the moment of—especially if it's physical and dangerous—"

(lines 13–16). Here, Jessica equates physical with dangerous, which ignores the very real dangers of emotional violence, which have lasting effects and can escalate quickly and erratically. Again, this reinforces a physical/emotional binary that doesn't play out in victim/survivor stories, where physical and emotional violence very often go hand-in-hand.

In addition to undermining the damaging effects of emotional abuse, Jessica also acknowledges the role that the victim/survivor's emotional state plays in a domestic call. She states, "they go through the moment of they're in fear for their lives—or their children's lives. So, they're calling just to get help" (lines 17–19). Jessica recognizes the distress, panic, and fear for one's life and one's children's lives that underpins domestic violence. This recognition of the emotional experience of domestic violence is immediately undercut when she says, "And then, as it sinks in, or as the threat isn't as eminent – they start to realize, 'Oh, but I don't want them to get in trouble.' And so, they kind of back pedal or, maybe, try to— change the facts a little bit" (lines 20–23). Here, we see Jessica move into a description of a recalcitrant victim, very similar to that which we saw in Detective Jacobs' story. This victim, who is presented as typical, normal, and regular with the group pronoun "they," takes back what they said and lies to protect their violent partner. Using a quotation, she puts words into this victim's mouth, "'but I don't want them to get in trouble'" (line 21). Jessica makes presumptions about a typical victim's motivations and relationship. She positions the victim's "back-peddling" as a move of protection for an abusive partner (line 22). This is a socially resonant view of domestic violence victims – they won't leave, and they will protect their abuser. With this move, then, we see Jessica index the social discourse that abused people do not leave and that they lie to protect their partners.

Throughout this story, Jessica uses quotations to give the story color and a sense of realism, and the group she chooses to quote from is the victims. These internal quotations do not position the victims/survivors in a positive light. The pseudoquotations are used to normalize a particular view into what it means to be a victim of domestic violence – a viewpoint that is socially sanctioned. Victims of domestic violence call the police over and over rather than leaving their abusive partners. Victims want police to just hurry up and get there already, with a sort of bored affect – sighing rather than panicking affect – even though they do not plan on leaving. They do not want their partners to get into trouble, and so they lie to officers who answer their calls. Combined with Detective Jacobs' narrative, police do not paint a particularly flattering picture of victims of domestic violence. Because they have social and institutional power, police discourse is effective, it creates filters with which to understand domestic violence and its victims. Police discourse adds a powerful set of variables to the indexical field of domestic violence: recalcitrant victim, untrustworthy speaker, victim of physical violence, and dismissal of emotional violence. I will discuss this further on that in Chapter 3.

2.7 Conclusions

Domestic violence is saturated with, maintains, and is made meaningful by the social discourses that underpin it and are reinforced by it. That is, domestic violence is a product of ideological and sociocultural discourses. These processes of creating and maintaining domestic violence happen in the discourses that are available to talk about domestic violence. In the stories about domestic violence told by police and victims/survivors we find cultural discourses about love, relationships, and family. We find a value system. Therefore, it is essential that we pay attention to discursive structures when we analyze the ways that domestic violence is a sociocultural formation – an indexical field. As Fairclough (2001, p. 21) sees it:

> In seeing language as discourse and as social practice, one is committing oneself not just to analyzing text, nor just to analyzing processes of production and interpretation, but to analyzing the relationship between the texts, processes, and their social conditions, both the immediate condition of the situational context and the more remote conditions of institutional social structures.

Thus, in order to understand the relationship between texts, utterances, and the world, we must look at and parse issues of representation and interpretation from the local to the global, from the detail to the theory, and from the specific to the ideological. Social discourses find instantiation in everyday talk about social issues such as domestic violence, and in so doing access, maintain, and reproduce the indexical field. Those social discourses of love, family, gender, and public/private are scattered in and across the indexical field on which domestic violence is meaningful as a sociocultural artifact.

In addition to noticing how sociocultural discourses maintain the indexical field of domestic violence, maintaining it as a fairly stable, discursive formation, police officers and domestic violence victims/ survivors relate to that indexical field in different, sometimes competing ways. Indeed, I believe that I have shown that "domestic violence" is something different for police and victims/survivors. For police, domestic violence indexical field is a narrow thing that involves fists, choking, hairpulling, and the like. Domestic violence is limited to that which is against the law. For victims/survivors of domestic violence, the indexical field is much broader, including emotional and verbal violence to be sure, but also extending beyond legal discourses. The indexical field of domestic violence includes reasoning, justification, explanations, hard work, leaving, love, and fear, just to get the list started. For victims/survivors, domestic violence is a way of life – part of every moment, awake or asleep. For police officers, domestic violence is isolated events that either are or are not criminal. The entire indexical formation is different for each, overlapping where the two groups physically overlap. Together these two groups make up a large portion of the indexical formation of domestic violence for the larger sociocultural milieu. What domestic violence can and does mean in most discursive venues will draw on the work that these two groups do and put into circulation, indexically speaking.

   In this chapter, I have discussed some of the elements that keep domestic violence stable in our communities. Social values associated with love, family, gender, and public/private all keep domestic violence in place. Other elements in the indexical field inform and facilitate domestic violence. What is concerning and compelling is the fact that the identity of domestic violence victims/survivors emerges within these fields of indexicality. This is a problem. The constraints and enablers on victim/survivor identity are positive, largely stemming from victim/survivors' own stories of strength and hope. However, they are also negative, facilitating feelings untrustworthiness (police), of self-blame (victims/survivors), and ultimately the hypostatization of victimhood. Identities of leaving, of hope, of love, and more emerge within this field as victims work against the social norms, status quos, and damaging discourses at work in the field of indexicality, that is, domestic violence.

3

Storying the Victim/Survivor
Identity, Domestic Violence, and Discourses of Agency

Language is social and interactional. It happens in real situations between people who are trying to accomplish authentic goals that are motivated by histories and contexts that are both brief and ongoing. Though it does not do so necessarily or always, ideology can impact, affect, and generally be a part of indexicality and a socially meaningful utterance. Institutional values, for example, can run through and operationalize sets of social meanings, as can ideologies and social values. Ideology is made up of the social and institutional values that infiltrate and impact social interactions and the meanings that emerge therein. The ideologies that manage the social meaning and indexical links analyzed in this chapter have to do with competing conceptions of agency in a particular context – domestic violence. Police and victims/survivors have different conceptions, formations, and performances of agency. Presupposition manages the competing forms of agency displayed in police officer and victim/survivor discourses and identity performances and constraints. Police officers make presuppositions about what victims/survivors of domestic violence say and how they behave, assigning identities to victims/survivors that do not necessarily align with those performed by victims/survivors themselves. In this chapter, I argue that law enforcement assumptions about agency allow police to misunderstand and in some cases do damage to those agencies that victims/survivors perform themselves.

At the core, this chapter is about agency and its relationship to identity. Police presuppositions about agency enact, constrain, and expect particular agentive and identity performances. Such constraints and expectations regarding agency are effectual in the lived realities of victims/survivors. A useful starting definition for agency can be found in Ahearn (2001, p. 112): "Agency refers to a socioculturally mediated capacity to act." For Ahearn, agency is not unconstrained "free will," but rather, agency is located in a social space, which constrains and enables action. That is, people do not act of their own "free will," to use Ahearn's term. Instead they act in ways that conform to, inhabit, comport with, and sometimes trouble the expectations of the social contexts in which they are situated. Individuals act with constrained, situated agency; they do not act with what I will call full sovereign agency. I develop the concept of sovereign agency out of Foucault's definition of the sovereign. The sovereign is the monarch, allowed to act in any fashion at his (/her) own discretion. "Sovereignty [involves] the necessarily spectacular manifestations of power" (Foucault, 1975, p. 217). That is, the sovereign has a kind of obvious, external, unquestioned/able power that is exercised in the community, primarily via punishments; these are "ostentatious signs of sovereignty" (Foucault, 1975, p. 220). By full sovereign agency, then, I mean the agency of the sovereign: a kind of unconstrained, uncontestable power that is available to the fully autonomous individual who can and always could act at will, in a way that transcends situation and constraint. Of course, according to Foucault, this kind of power has been superseded by discipline, a discursive form of agency in which the individual internalizes the policies of the sovereign and polices themselves. I will continue with the concept of sovereign agency here, because it better matches the views of agency presented and discussed by the police. Thus, here I will make an argument for the claim that discursive and sovereign agencies intermingle in police discourse. Police believe in and operate from a perspective of full sovereign agency, a belief that itself functions as a discursive agency, policing individual's behaviors, and asking them to police themselves accordingly.

What is negotiated in the narratives that follow are three models of agency, held and performed by different groups, and functioning alongside and in conflict with each other; the first is a kind of agency that is unimpeded, full sovereign agency (police), the second is more measured and self-conscious, constrained agency (victims/survivors), and the third is a discursive agency that provides the discursive resources to understand and make sense of the ideologies of agency that both groups hold. Circulating in police discourse, we see an ideology of agency as full sovereign agency. This viewpoint, in the end, functions as a discursive formation, impacting those who come into contact with law enforcement. Police officers present this viewpoint when they presume that victims have the full sovereign agency to spontaneously leave a violent relationship, if only they would do it. Not leaving, according to the police ideology of agency, is a performance of damaged sovereign agency.

Victims/survivors have a different ideology of agency. They see agency as situationally constrained, rhetorically purposeful, and in accordance with their lived experiences and goals. Their performances of agency are, therefore, rhetorical, driven by their life experience, and constrained by contextual forces. There is power asymmetry between the two groups – police and victims/survivors – leading to trouble around agency. Police officers are endowed with institutional power – the ability to incarcerate (Officer Roscoe). "Unequal power relations can result in – and be the result of – symbolic violence" (Ahearn, 2001, p. 111). Power asymmetry can lead to a situation in which discursive resources that do violence are created, maintained, and distributed. We see the potential for this when we notice the effects to the victims/survivors done by the agency ideologies held by police. These effects are highlighted when we contrast police views about agency with victim views on the same topics.

In this chapter, I argue that identity and agency do not emerge in a vacuum, but rather they emerge in situations that come stocked with a host of ideologies, values, and discourses, some of which are endowed with institutional power. In this case, those institutionally powerful discourses are produced by the police who believe in full sovereign agency. Their model of agency becomes a filter that erases the complex, constrained agency of real victims and, along with it, their identity work. This pared down, iconic version of victim agency and identity itself functions as a filter, simplifying, ignoring, and erasing emotional and physical violence. Ultimately, then, my argument is that victims of domestic violence are told that they should be able to leave at will, but they are also contradictorily assumed to have a defunct agency that makes them stay in abusive situations – a hypostatized identity/agency that is facilitated and underpinned by policing discourses, and that is dismissive of emotional and at times even physical violence. Thus, I argue that a construction of agency that I call agented nonagency, is attributed to domestic violence victims/survivors, and works to ignore emotional and physical forms of violence.

3.1 Iconization, Erasure, and Agented Nonagency

According to Foucault, disciplinary power that functions via discourse has superseded sovereign power. Disciplinary power runs on discourses that constrain and enable the production of objects, utterance, and ideas within that discourse (Foucault, 1972). I suggest that police discourse works this way. It is a field of knowledges and discourses that presuppose what utterances and behaviors may be produced and recognized as legitimate in that field. Police discourses about agency are constraining and enabling in just this way. That is, the belief in sovereign agency is itself a discourse that has disciplinary power because it is discursively and materially productive.

In addressing the victim/survivor within and from the perspective of police discourse, the victim/survivor is produced in a particular way (Butler, 1997; Foucault, 1972, 1975) – as a victim, full stop. This productive function creates an iconic victim that erases and ignores identities that matter to and emerge in victim narratives. Thus, these data demonstrate just how complex agency is, with a number of versions of agency emerging alongside identity formation and performance. I will show that the institutionally sanctioned version of agency that we find in police discourse iconicizes victims through storytelling and the ideologies operationalized therein.

In the data analyzed here, agency emerges in narrative, primarily (but not only) in small stories. The small stories are about violence: staying in violent relationships and leaving violent relationships. I analyze narratives about victimhood that victims/survivors tell and those that police officers tell. The analyses show the emergence of semiotic processes that Irvine and Gal (2000) call "iconization" and "erasure," which together act on and inform conceptions and performances of agency. Iconization is the process of making links between a social group and a linguistic form, such that the link seems essential or the form seems natural to the group with whom it is associated. Erasure is the process of limiting a semantic field such that objects in that field are reduced, overlooked, ignored/ignorable, and generally less nuanced than they may appear elsewhere. Irvine and Gal (2000) develop these concepts to understand language ideology, or the ways that ideas about language are linked to and index ideas about populations and groups of people. In this chapter, I import these two concepts into a paradigm of victim ideology, or ideas about victim behavior, motives, and speech, in order to understand how iconization and erasure work at the level of identity performance, emergence, and constraint.

Iconization and erasure occur in these data in police discourse, especially in discourses that are ultimately about agency. Police discussions of victims iconicize an ideal victim such that other performances of "victim" are unrecognizable or ignored. Because of power asymmetry, police discourses can affect victims in ways that victim discourses cannot affect police. Therefore, it matters that police create an iconic version of victims that limits, ignores, erases, and/or dismisses many of the complicating factors of abuse – complicating factors that victims/survivors present as key elements of their identities in their own narratives. Further, this iconic victim is caught in a double bind of agented nonagency, or the expectation that everybody has full sovereign agency (in this case agency to leave at will), but that at the same time assumes deficient agency, or nonagency, when the victim/survivor chooses to stay. Iconic victims are essentialized as having both, in police discourse; they are assigned agented nonagency or a defunct form of full sovereign agency. The iconized victim's actual, constrained, but active victim/survivor agency is thereby placed under erasure. The choices they really make are ignored and overlooked. Agency is not the only thing that is erased. Interestingly, in the process of erasing active agency, emotional and physical violence are also ignored and dismissed in police discourse. In the stories they tell, police discourse tends to focus on victim/survivor behavior more than either the violence of the situation or the abuser.

Though police and victims/survivors use similar narrative strategies for recounting abuse – a combination of full and fragmented narratives – a number of key differences emerge, differences that lead to iconization, erasure, and what I refer to as troubling, typically performed by a victim/survivor. When police story victimhood, they may begin with a narrative about a particular victim, but that quickly slips into general victim talk, especially focusing on discussions of victims staying and diatribes about why victims should leave abusive situations, in which victim agency is critiqued. That is, for police, narratives about victimhood slip into leaving/staying stories. Police accounting of victimhood ignores some of the contexts, situations, and abuses that are storied by victims/survivors that constrain and complicate leaving. These accounts also ignore or downplay emotional and physical violence. We get a sense of these issues when we pay attention to the discursive details in the narratives produced in the victim/survivor interviews, details that trouble the iconic victim. Instead of beginning with stories about why they stayed or why they eventually left – and all of the victims/survivors interviewed for this project did leave – victims/survivors nearly always begin with a story about emotional abuse, though a few begin with stories of physical abuse. Victims/survivors use these carefully formulated narratives of violence to move into a discussion of staying/leaving that emphasizes the scariness of the relationship, the fear involved in staying and in leaving, and their strategic decision-making regarding both staying and leaving. In the iconic representation of victimhood that emerges in the police stories, these details of violence and fear are erased. That is, the iconization of victims of domestic violence as having agented nonagency creates the erasure of not only their real if constrained agency, but also the violence and fear with which domestic violence is saturated. Essentialized agency that presumes sovereignty becomes a filter that erases other forms of agency and violence.

3.2 Staying/Leaving Stories of Violence

The narratives I focus on are the staying/leaving stories produced by both victims/survivors and police officers and the stories about emotional violence told by victims/survivors. Emotional violence is stated by many of the victims/survivors to be one of the worst parts of abuse. As Radiance puts it, "the part that really broke me down the most was the mental and emotional." Of course, physical and emotional violence are intertwined with each other, as many of the victim/survivor stories demonstrate. I do not intend to draw a false binary between emotional and physical violence. Nevertheless, victims/survivors sometimes divide the two and produce arguments that mental/emotional/verbal violence is worse and that it has staying power. One explanation for why emotional and verbal violence might be so negatively effective for victims of domestic violence comes from Butler (1997, p. 5), who writes, "Certain words or certain forms of address not only operate as threats to one's physical well-being, but there is a strong sense in which the body is alternately sustained and threatened through modes of address." That is, the body comes into being and is sustained in and through discourse when it is addressed by an/other. Sustaining and producing bodies and identities can also threaten, and put the body at risk.

In order to understand the production of dominant police discourse and processes of iconization and erasure and their relationship to agency, I analyze two story types: staying/leaving and emotional violence stories. When told by police officers, both types of stories tend to focus on the victims/survivors' status as a victim – they story their victimhood. (Police use the term victim, and so when I represent police discourses and perspectives, I will also use that term.) When victims/survivors tell the staying/leaving stories, the stories are often coupled with stories about emotional violence that lay out a history of abusive strategies and give detailed descriptions of events of victimization. These narratives, then, point to moments of inauguration into victimhood, with attendant notions about agency, for example, assumptions that victim agency is defective. Importantly, for the victims/survivors, this inaugural moment is partial and complicated. The identity category of "victim" for victim/survivor is not permanent, stable, or unified, but rather it emerges, sometimes strategically, in fleeting ways that reveal partial and multiple identities in any given situation. For victims/survivors, "victim" is only one of these identities. For police, on the other hand, the identity category of "victim" is much more durable and static, functioning, as I will show, via processes of iconization.

Before moving on, two quick notes. The first is a note on vocabulary usage in this chapter. When referring to victims from the perspective of policing and police discourse, I will use the term "victim." I will continue to use the term "victim/survivor" when talking from the perspective of the author and book. The term victim is not sufficient to account for the experiences or identities that emerge when the victims/survivors give accounts of situations in which they were victims. That is, when victims/survivors story their own victimness, the identity of victim does not emerge on its own, in toto. When used monolithically and in a totalizing way, the term victim is part of the indexical apparatus that iconizes victims of domestic violence only, a positional identity that the victims/survivors themselves trouble.

As a second note, in some parts of this chapter, I critique the idea in police discourse that victims should simply leave, not because I think victims/survivors should stay, but because the police discourse overlooks victims/survivors' reasoning for staying, as well as their contextual, sociocultural, and institutional constraints. Victims are essentialized in police discourse as unable to extricate themselves from abusive relationships. Though it may take a few attempts to leave, this idea is patently false. Not only do victims/survivors eventually leave, when they do, they do so thoughtfully, with safety and sustainability in mind. This is all to say, I never presume that it is good or right or safe for victims of domestic violence to stay in abusive relationships. However, I also do not dismiss victims/survivors' reasoning and emotional responses that play a role when they do stay. I honor their stories and reasoning when they describe staying for the amount of time that they chose to. That is, victims/survivors narrate complicated and compelling stories and reasons that I value. All of the victims were in safe situations at the time I interviewed them.

3.3 Iconization, Erasure, and Agency

When the police talk about victims, they tend to overfocus on certain aspects of victimhood, while ignoring, downplaying, or explaining away other aspects of experience that victims/survivors themselves find relevant and essential to understanding their experience. Police presuppose agency, and in that presupposition, they create an iconic victim. This happens through the metapragmatic co-processes of iconization and erasure. Iconization is when "linguistic features that index social groups or activities appear to be iconic representations of them, as if a linguistic feature somehow depicted or displayed a social groups inherent nature or essence" (Irvine & Gal, 2000,p. 37). In other words, iconization is the process of making an indelible link between a linguistic feature, social meaning, and a social group, such that the linguistic form functions as an icon of the relationship and/or social group. As Milani (2010,p. 120) puts it, "Iconization describes how linguistic phenomena are portrayed as if they flowed 'naturally' from a social group's biological or cultural essence." That is, iconization naturalizes linguistic processes, making them seem essential or innate to the group.

Iconization goes hand in hand with erasure, which, according to Irvine and Gal (2000,p. 38), is the process by which "facts that are inconsistent with the ideological scheme either go unnoticed or get explained away." Erasure functions when some aspects of a linguistic or behavioral interaction appear to be inconsistent with the ideological framework used to read the interaction. When this happens, those aspects will be ejected or overlooked in the process of making meaning of the situation—placed under erasure.

Together, these processes of iconization and erasure have been studied and analyzed in the context of language ideology, or "the ideas with which participants and observers frame their understanding of linguistic varieties and map those understandings onto people, events, and activities that are significant to them" (Irvine & Gal, 2000,p. 35). Language ideologies are the ideas and values about people and language that are brought to bear when making sense out of a linguistic interaction. Iconization and erasure play important roles in mapping and maintaining the parameters of a language ideology. This has been well studied by Irvine and Gal (2000) and others. For example, Gagné (2008, pp. 143–144) has shown how ideas about "women's language" are used to define, naturalize, and iconicize a static account of Japanese Gothic/Lolita youth, who are used iconically to stand in for all "counter publics." Milani (2010) uses the concepts of iconization and erasure to understand how a controversial debate regarding language and education in Sweden leads to the iconic link between a particular population and the phrase, "our new Swedes," erasing other aspects of identity and culture. Milroy (2012) uses the concepts to show how myths and stories told about languages are intimately and essentially linked to ideas about culture and the people who use the language.

In the present study, I am not using a language ideology framework, looking at how talk about and ideologies of language impact the people who use the language. The victims/survivors and police officers who were interviewed did not talk explicitly about or narrate instances of speech or linguistic usage. Instead, I am importing these ideas into a victim ideology framework, looking to understand how iconization and erasure function at an identity level, enacted in talk about victims and agency. That is, rather than considering the metapragmatic effects of talk about talk, I am interested in the identity work that occurs in talk about victims and talk about agency. Victims/survivors discuss and narrate instances of victimness, including expectations of behavior and motives. Police narrations of staying/leaving stories create an iconic victim that is monolithic, general, and two-dimensional. The behaviors that are naturalized and made to seem essential in victims are (1) a type of agency that presumes fully autonomous action and (2) a presumption that victims cannot leave violent relationships. That is, one presupposes agency, while the other presupposes nonagency. This is a classic double bind. Victims should and could leave if they wanted to, but it is anticipated that they will stay for a litany of reasons that are not articulated. The iconic victim would be able to leave an abusive situation, just as anybody would, because they have sovereign agency to leave at will. The iconic victim also stays and stays and stays, because abuse has made their agency nonoperational. In this discourse, this indexical formation, victims are essentialized as both having agency and nonagency at the same time, putting them in a position that I call agented nonagency.

In many ways working in opposition to police discourse, victims/survivors see themselves as empowered agents of their own change, but their agency is expressed in complex, situation-rich decision-making, in what Ahearn (2001) might call practice agency or a "practice theory" approach to agency. In purporting a practice theory, Ahearn (2001,p. 112) "emphasize[s] how individuals, including scholars, actively construct and constrain – rather than passively receive – interpretations that are both socially mediated and intertextually situated within a bounded universe of discourse." Translated to think about agency, this means that agency is actively situated in a discourse that bounds, constrains, and enables action at any given time. Agency is mediated socioculturally and actively produced. Agency, after all, is a complicated thing, both theoretically and practically. Sovereign agency is uncomplicated, autonomous, unconstrained action, like that of the sovereign who performs inviolable agency (cf. Butler, 1997; Foucault, 1975) – the power to do what one wills. This view of agency allows police to hold criminals accountable for crimes committed. Individuals must act with intention and knowledge, in order to be held accountable for many, if not most, crimes. The assumptions of agency by police point to a version of uncomplicated, self-actualized, action.

Police discourses presuppose that victims can leave, thereby creating space to critique them when they do not leave. "There are also the ugly situations that it's like, why did you get him from jail again?" (Det. Jacobs). This statement presupposes that the victim is staying in the life of her assailant by picking him up from jail, and it critiques the victim's behavior as "ugly." No move is made to understand the victim's reasoning or circumstance. She is simply given as an example of a type of victim – one who won't leave. Detective Jacobs presupposes both the correct thing for the victim to do, and that the victim has sovereign agency to leave, ignoring, contributing, and constraining factors that do not neatly fit into the iconic schema of victim. Presupposition thus functions to create the iconic victim and erase the "extra" factors that do not fit with the presupposition. In the same interview, another detective, Detective Sidwell, stories an abused woman who has continued to stay with her husband while calling the police on multiple occassions. Detective Sidwell suggests in Extract 3.1 that she is "playing games" (line 3).

Extract 3.1 Detective Sidwell

1.	*Det. Sidwell*:	That's kind of the words I had with her.
2.		I said, "Look, we wanna help you out. We'll be here, but
3.		you gotta help us out and quit playing these games, because
4.		all you're doing is you're hurting yourself and your cases, and
5.		you're saying all this is going on."
6.		You've already got, I don't know, it was a four or five-year-old kid,
7.		now you're pregnant with his kid.
8.		You really wanna be with somebody this much longer,
9.		that's still causing all this grief for you?

Not only does this detective assume what the victim *should* do, he presupposes a sovereign style of agency when he asks the rhetorical question, "you really want to be with somebody this much longer?" (line 8). This statement-question presupposes both that she should leave, and that she stays because she "wants" to. Any other factors that may circulate in her world and her actually performed agency are erased as unimportant, and ignored. Also, recall from Chapter 1, leaving is dangerous.

Police discourses like those briefly analyzed earlier iconicize victims through presupposition, creating a stable, iconic victim that is presumed to match the experiences, performances, and identities of those who are and have been the victims of domestic violence. Through iconization and erasure, especially with regard to agency, the resources for an iconic victim are established for agented nonagency. This is the double bind of agency in which victims/survivors are situated and which they contest in their narrations of leaving and staying in abusive relationships. As it is created and performed in police discourse, this iconic linkage presumes that if this victim does not leave, it is her/his fault; that she is complicit in the violence in some way; and/or that they are mentally/emotionally deficient. This essentialized version of full sovereign agency (rather than partial, constrained agency) works as a filter for violence, occluding the violence by overfocusing on victim behavior. The iconic representation of victimhood and victim agency is troubled by the accounts of victimhood by the victims/survivors themselves. They complicate this picture with detailed accounts of emotional and physical violence. However, these complications function under erasure, subverted from the public sphere by the institutionally empowered police discourses, which are, coincidentally, supported and buoyed by public discourses about domestic violence that also presume sovereign agency with regard to leaving.

3.4 Leaving and Staying: Policing Victim Identity

One of the most common and important story types is staying/leaving stories. Issues of staying/leaving appear in every single interview, whether it was police, police staff and personnel, or victim/survivor. These stories and explanations do different discursive identity work, however, depending on whether they are told by victims/survivors or police officers. When victims/survivors story leaving and staying, they talk through the reasons they had for staying, and then they narrate the event that caused them to leave and the related emotions and danger. Leaving stories are nearly always stories of emotional and physical violence – events or homelife situations that pushed them out the door.

Functioning differently for police officers, these stories of staying/leaving are not typically personal – about the self – as they are for victims/survivors, but instead they are distant – about the other. The lack of personal detail and experience necessarily changes the shape, scope, and function of these narratives. For police, staying/leaving stories focus on the fact that the victim stayed, presuming full sovereign agency with regard to leaving and defunct agency with regard to staying. This leads to two things. First, police stories can lean toward critique of those who stay, especially in those homes that the officers are called to more than once. Second, without being coupled with stories about emotional and physical violence, these stories assume that leaving is a simple process of standing up and walking out the door, forgetting and/or ignoring other complicating factors, factors that are articulated by victims/survivors. Take, for example, Officer McQuaid who states, "We get some people we go on numerous times. The guy won't leave the girl. The girl won't leave the guy. They have that relationship. They keep it going." Here, the police officer lays out a situation for those people who call the police out many times without leaving, and he presents the situation as simple, and perhaps even more problematically, as equal. The use of "they," which positions the couple together in culpability and more, is telling. "They," the dysfunctional couple, should choose to desist together, just as they choose to "keep it going" together. It is the couple that is articulated as unhealthy, not the abuser, reiterating an old notion often held by police that domestic violence is simply an unhealthy relationship, in which both parties are equally culpable. There is no comment on the fact of dominance or power differentials in abusive relationships. Officer McQuaid assumes that it is the equal responsibility of both parties to end the relationship, eliding the fact that the relationship is violent and abusive. The type of couple described here "have that relationship," a phrase which suggests that violence is a part of this type of relationship and that both parties are responsible for nurturing the violence. This is ultimately a staying/leaving story that critiques the victim for staying and that presents leaving as the only way to end the violence. Of course, this view forgets that 75 percent of police calls, nationally, were made after the victim left (Berry, 2000). Leaving does not always, or even usually, end abuse.

Victim discourses about leaving/staying look different and more complicated than that presented by Officer McQuaid. Take, for example, Butterfly's statement in Extract 3.2.

Extract 3.2 Butterfly

1.	*Butterfly:*	Everybody's like, "You're not gonna go back, right?
2.		You do realize that if you go back, you're gonna die, or
3.		you're gonna get your kids taken away,"
4.		I'm like, "I'm not gonna go back."
5.	*Jenny:*	It's good to have that idea in mind.
6.	*Butterfly:*	Yeah, I know that he thinks that he wants me to, in a way. I can feel it.

Butterfly has in her mind that she won't go back, but that many people – "Everybody's like" (line 1) – have questioned her on the topic. She can feel the pull of the relationship, but she actively resists it. She does not see herself as a victim, and she understands that staying away from an abusive partner is sometimes difficult.

In what follows, I will first show how police discourses create an iconic victim to whom a problematic agented nonagency is attributed before turning my attention to the intricate stories about leaving/staying that victims/survivors tell.

3.5 Police Iconization of Agented Nonagency

When police story victimhood, they make a strong pitch for agency, seeing all parties as equally agented in every way, and in many ways ignoring the power asymmetry of a violent relationship, as we saw earlier with Officer McQuaid's statements. This leads to discourses that (1) position the victim on equal footing with their abuser and (2) presume agency in relationship to staying and leaving, which leads to an assumption of a willingness to be abused. In saying this, I am not presuming that the agency of the victim is deficit in some way. On the contrary, I find the assertion of agency by police officers problematic across the board. All agency is partial and context bound, constrained in every way. What I am arguing is that many of the police officers interviewed believe in a sort of internal, powerful agency that should authorize anybody to make their own individual choices, and that only one logical choice exists for the victim – leaving. If the victim doesn't leave, then it must mean that their agency has been damaged in some way. This belief in agency is an indexical resource that leads to the iconization of the victim as static, monolithic, and two-dimensional. In the following extract, we see Officer McQuaid, story a strong expectation to leave coupled with an assumption of equal footing.

Extract 3.3 Officer McQuaid

1.	*Off. McQuaid:*	You go to these domestics, and they say, "Look, we've been married 10 years.
2.		The last three years have been hell."
3.		They're both saying the same thing. You're talking to both of 'em,
4.		"It's been hell." "We don't get along, blah, blah, blah."
5.		You're thinking to yourself, "Okay. Go your separate ways."

6.	*Jenny:*	Right.

7.	*Off. McQuaid:*	Right. I know there's kids involved.
8.		I get that, but this is to the point where we've been here a couple times now, and
9.		"Go your separate ways"—for whatever reason,
10.		whether it be financially, which I get to a point,
11.		but they won't go or because of kids they won't go.
12.		They don't want them—"I want to show the kids that we're still happily married."
13.		The kids see that you're not. Trust me, they know more than you know.
14.		They stick around each other.
15.		You just wanna say to them, "Are you stupid?"

16.	*Jenny:*	Mm hmm.

17.	*Off. McQuaid:*	You know what I mean?
18.		"You're gonna wind up on this path where this is gonna go down a
19.		road where one or both of you are gonna end up in jail or seriously hurt or
20.		the kids are gonna end up hurt." You know what I mean?

21.	*Jenny:*	Yeah.

22.	*Off. McQuaid:*	They don't see that aspect. They don't see that—
23.		they think that, "Oh, we can try to work our way.
24.		The status quo is good. We'll just hang together."

25.	*Jenny:*	It's hard to disrupt your whole life even when you should.

26.	*Off. McQuaid:*	Well, but yeah, they'll take the disruption of calling the cop and
27.		going off to jail or tearing up the house or breaking things.
28.		You know what I mean?

In Extract 3.3, we hear Officer McQuaid articulate a view of abusive relationships in which the relationship is merely unhealthy rather than abusive. There is no gesture of blame nor any kind of agency attributed to the abuser. Instead, what we hear him say, more than once, is that they should both simply choose to part – "go [their] separate ways" (lines 5 and 9). The grammatical construction here situates individuals in a relationship that simply doesn't work with nobody at fault. This linguistic construction assumes that leaving is a process equally divided between the parties, ignoring the power asymmetry and ignoring abuse. Here, there is an equal sharing of fault, the forgetting of abuse, and the assertion of an equal relationship to leaving. This elision of abuse and fault is punctuated by the claim that "one or both of you are gonna end up in jail or seriously hurt," which further distributes the fault of the abuse to the victim himself/herself. That is, there is equal likelihood that the victim and the abuser may himself/herself end up in jail (and I have plenty of stories of this happening) and that the abuser and the victim may be injured in the relationship. Both parties in the relationship are situated in problematic equilibrium that works to place abuse under erasure. There is a strong belief, in this passage, that abusive relationships are really just unhealthy relationships, and thus that both parties are responsible for changing the status quo of the relationship (cf. Ferraro, 1995).

Detective Michaels echoes the sentiments of Officer McQuaid. He puts the blame on the victim even more directly saying: "When they get into relationships, if this guy's not beating me, I must not have the right man. If she's not screaming at me, I must not have the right girl." The assumption here is that the victim enjoys the abuse, understands it as part of love. In other words, Detective Michaels claims that abuse can be equated with love for some people. This statement assumes more than just equal footing; it presupposes a desire to be in the violent relationship.

In Extract 3.3, Officer McQuaid asserts quite strongly that victims of domestic violence should just leave. Victims understand that police feel this way. One victim/survivor, Rainbow, told me that when she has dealt with police, they have acted like the solution to the violent altercation was all on her and her ability to just leave. Police acted like, "'[Y]ou have to handle it now. We're not going to do anything about it. Why don't you pack your stuff and leave?'" That is, the police see leaving as the only solution to end a brawl that resulted in a call to police. They also believe that she has the full sovereign agency to leave at that moment. Not leaving is presumed to be a deficit of her agency. Rainbow knows that police want victims to pack up and leave instead of calling the police over and over. She feels the weight of their critique. Victims feel the power of the police discourse; they recognize it.

In Extract 3.4, Officer McQuaid goes on to develop the indexical linkage between the victim and a double bind of agency: agented nonangency.

Extract 3.4 Officer McQuaid

1.	*Off. McQuaid*:	I just want to say to people, "You just need to go your separate ways.
2.		Just go. Just stop."
3.		What I usually end up saying to the aggressor is,
4.		"Look, it's an argument. Nothin's happened. Nothin' criminally."
5.		Now at my age, I'm like I treat the damned juvenile kids.
6.		I'll tell 'em, "Guess what? If I come to this house again, I am gonna kick your ass."
7.		They're usually, "You can't do that."
8.		"Yeah, I can because if you're—" I'll explain the laws to 'em.
9.		"Verbally fighting. There's no kids here. You're lucky.
10.		Had there been kids here, I'd be charging you right now, but there's not."
11.		I go, "I get it. Hey, everybody argues. It's how you do it. Right?
12.		Me and my wife, we have little arguments, but we don't fight."

[...]

13.	*Off. McQuaid*:	"Look, we're comin' back here because you can't control yourself.
14.		You're a 35-year-old or a 42-year-old or a 27-year-old."
15.		I make them feel stupid.

In Extract 3.4, Officer McQuaid speaks quite directly, without hiding his feelings or sugarcoating his comments. According to Officer McQuaid, victims who stay for a day, a month, or a year are, according to him, "stupid" (line 15). Officer McQuaid reiterates again the idea of just "go[ing] separate ways" (line 1) as a way of jumping into a comment on verbal violence, which he dismisses with "Nothing's happened" (line 4). He then threatens that if he returns to the residence, he is "gonna kick your ass" (line 6). It is unclear whether this "your" is plural or singular – directed at the victim, the abuser, or both. Given the context, the rest of the invective in which he addresses the abused and the assailant in one breath, it makes sense to treat the "your" as plural or at least as either the victim or the abuser, indicating a further sense of victim blame or of shared blame. If the victim returns, doesn't leave, he will kick their ass. This point is driven home at the end of the extract where he says one of his tactics in dealing with a domestic call is to "make them feel stupid," which echoes the rhetorical questions, "Are you stupid?" from Extract 3.3. In Extract 3.3, "stupid" is directly and unquestionably directed at the victim. The iconic identity of the victim that emerges in this interview is one in which the victim has sovereign agency to leave, and so if they stay, they are stupid. Staying for any amount of time, shows that she has a deficit of agency, broken agency, or nonagency, according to police discourse. This is a classic double bind. Under the rubric of the iconic victim, she should, nay *does*, have the agency to leave, and so if she does not leave, it must be because that agency has been damaged somewhere along the line.

Elsewhere in the data, we find another way of explaining why victims might stay in abusive relationships. Officer Roscoe, who has about five years of experience on the force, explains, "There's a litany of reasons, right, but ultimately they're bad excuses or reasons it results in violence, or child abuse or criminal behavior." He calls the real, contextually rich, compelling reasons of victims/survivors "bad excuses," dismissing them out of hand as incorrect without even trying to articulate what those complex reasons may be. Still another way the police officers explain victims who stay is to presume a violent life in which these violent episodes with an abusive partner are naturalized. Officer Oliver puts it this way, "They used to be common callers. This is exactly how their life has always gone. It's sad because you can't save someone that doesn't want to be saved. You and I both know this." In this statement, Officer Oliver pathologizes victims, assuming that their entire lives are saturated with violence, such that it has become normalized. Additionally, she apparently sees herself as having a double role, that of police officer and of savior. This officer is frustrated that she cannot "save" people because they resist her efforts, both from the perspective of her identity as police officer and as savior. Indeed, Officer Oliver performs these two identities as one and the same.

More criticism of victims occurs in a group interview with Officers Roscoe and Oliver and two others, Officers Angel and Winters, who narrate an abuse victim story about a violent relationship. Extract 3.5 is a story about a woman who had police at her house for a violent incident between herself and her boyfriend. While police were there, she revealed earlier assaults, including one with a gun. In the story, the officers focus on her victimhood with critical commentary about victims who stay and the fact that she did not always report her abuse. Of course, as we discussed earlier, if she had called multiple times, she would also have been criticized. In this extract, officers work together in a way that fundamentally misunderstands domestic violence.

Extract 3.5 Officers Roscoe, Oliver, Angel, Winters

1.	*Off. Angel:*	We had, yeah, actually, so two months ago. Whose case was it?
2.		It was [Winter's] case. [Winter.] [Winter's] case?
3.		The man had shot his gun at her from six feet away in their bedroom,
4.		around her body into the wall.
5.		Didn't even report it.
6.		She did not even report it until we were there the next day for some other reason
7.		and this came out during the investigation.
8.		Oh, he was drunk, mind you, probably again, and
9.		his friend called on his drunk friend.
10.		Then while we were there, wife tells us yeah, by the way, yesterday.
11.		You know? See what I mean? That's just crazy. Crazy thinking.
12.		She was terrified, though. Right? Terrified.
13.	*Jenny:*	Mm hmm.
14.	*Off. Oliver:*	That is crazy.
15.	*Off. Angel:*	Yeah, yeah.
16.	*Off. Oliver:*	You're describing a […]
17.	*Off. Angel:*	I know, I had to call him out.
18.	*Off. Oliver:*	Wow, that's totally […]
19.	*Off. Angel:*	I'm sure these guys have something on the tip of their tongue,
20.		but um-- Wasn't that your case?
21.		That the guy shot at the girl into the bedroom into the wall and she didn't report it?
22.	*Off. Winters:*	Yeah. It wasn't my case but I was there helping with it.
23.		She told me about it and
24.		we went down and found the—found the bullet holes. […]

[…]

25.	*Officer Roscoe:*	training in domestics.
26.		She gets mad finally at boyfriend.
27.		She's had enough of the arguing and
28.		then she reports two weeks later that oh,
29.		the last time he was mad, he started punching holes in the wall.
30.	*Jenny:*	Mm hmm. Mm hmm.
31.	*Off. Angel:*	Yeah, this was last week, right?
32.	*Off. Roscoe:*	He has a fractured hand from it.
33.	*Off. Angel:*	She's pregnant with his kid. Yeah.
34.	*Off. Winters:*	That's how we went.
35.		It was just an assault and then it turned into an ag [aggravated] assault
36.		because he had been drinking.
37.		I think she was scared to say anything she knew then.
38.	*Off. Angel:*	The shooting one?
39.	*Off. Winters:*	Yeah. Immediately I calm her down.
40.		"It's fine. It doesn't give anyone permission."
41.		Then come to find out a gun was involved.
42.		That's what he hit her with.
43.		Then it came down to well, he shot at me three days ago, and
44.		then, oh yeah, by the way, I'm three months pregnant.
45.		It felt like it just kept going and going and going.
46.		I was like oh my gosh.
47.	*Off. Angel:*	The staples of DVs, which response, is always
48.		a DV packet,
49.		separating the involved people,
50.		determining if a crime happened,
51.		but we don't follow up with these people.
52.		It's literally not our job.
53.		Of course, I've thought people need more follow up.
54.		There needs to be more programs and outreach. There just needs to be.
55.		That's beyond me, though.

The crux of the story in Extract 3.5 is that a victim/survivor did not report abuse. She had been shot at by her boyfriend and had not called the police, much to their dismay. As the story is told, the mistake that is made is not that the man shot at his girlfriend, but rather that the victim did not call the police. The officers fundamentally ignore the fact that the victim did eventually report to the police what had happened, during a different interaction with them. However, instead of focusing on her reporting, they instead critique her for remaining in the violent relationship – a point that they find impossible to understand. As an agent like any other, she should have called the police, and then she should have swiftly pulled herself out of the relationship, pregnant or not. Agency is tricky in this extract, however, because the woman they are telling the story about is also interactionally constructed as "crazy" (lines 11 and 14). The fact that she didn't call about such a violent event means that she is not rational; she is characterized as having "crazy thinking" (line 11). This presumes that she isn't fully agented, but rather that the agency that she should have is deficit in some fashion – "crazy thinking." The victim is described as terrified, but she is also willing to stay – "crazy thinking." This combination of terrified and crazy thinking positions the victim outside of agency. In the authoritative discourse, there is no authorized link between the victim's terror, exacerbated by her pregnancy, and possible reasons she is finding it hard to leave at this point. Context is ejected by the police officers' co-construction of the narrative, and all that remains is acontextual ridicule and criticism. The assumption that regular people have full agency to leave, but that this victim is not leaving, blames the victim by questioning her ability to make good choices for herself and her unborn child. The story culminates in Officer Roscoe excusing himself from following up with victims. "It's literally not our job" (line 52). Working with victims should be somebody's job, but it does not fall under the purview of the police.

Taken together with other portions of police discourse that position the victim as fully able to extract herself from a terrifying situation, these discourses create an iconic victim that has a problematic relationship with agency. They are in a double bind of agented nonagency: either a sovereign agent who chooses to stay, or outside of agency, crazy and unreasonable. Discourse is effectual; it creates the things it names (Foucault, 1972). Police discourses construct victims as having agented nonagency by presupposing both that the victim should be fully agented like anybody and that their agency has been voided by the violent situation. From this, an iconic identity for the victim emerges that is limited and deficit, ignoring many of the facets of experience and relationship to agency that the victim brings to the table. This identity is then blanket applied to victims of domestic violence, erasing, dismissing, and undermining the contextually rich pieces of experience that victims bring with them when they consider leaving and in their productions of identity. These complications, these victims' troublings, are in many ways ineffable.

3.6 Victim/Survivor Accounts of Staying/Leaving

For victims/survivors, a multifaceted identity that sometimes includes that of "victim" emerges in the process of storying staying/leaving, emotional violence, and agency. Their stories of staying and eventually leaving are rich with context, reasoning, and strategic choices. The first set of extracts we will look at comes from Radiance (pseudonym selected by the participant). Radiance was a young woman in my study who had a young infant and had left an abusive husband a year or so before the interview. She was living in a residential women's shelter in Western City when I spoke with her. In the following extracts, she emerges neither as a victim nor as without any agency, but as a strong woman making the best choices possible for herself and her infant under terrible circumstances. She emerges as having a practical agency, constrained though it may be.

Though Radiance stories victimhood, she doesn't occupy that identity only. Along with it, an identity closer to survivor emerges and is occupied by this forthright and powerful storyteller. She begins by explaining why it is hard to leave an abusive relationship. Notice that she does not blame "crazy thinking" nor does she give "bad excuses." Rather, she is strategic and caring in her explanations of staying.

Extract 3.6 Radiance

1.	*Jenny:*	Yeah, it's so complicated.
2.		That actually gets to my next question.
3.		People often say, "Why doesn't she just leave?"
4.		What's your response to that?
5.	*Radiance:*	Because it's scary and sometimes you don't know where you're gonna go.
6.		Money is a issue for a lot of women.
7.		For me he was the sole provider financially.
8.		It was just not really feasible in my mind.
9.		"Where am I gonna go? I don't have family or friends here in Western State."
10.		"So where am I gonna go?"

11.	I used that as a threat sometimes, I'd be like, "I'm leaving."
12.	He would just be like, "Yeah, cool. Yeah, do that."
13.	"Yeah, you should do that."
14.	"Lose my number, don't y'all call me."
15.	He would say all these things,
16.	but the moment that I left it was just like, "How could you do this?" You know?

In Extract 3.6, Radiance explains factors that make it hard to leave, with money and no place to go topping the list. She was coercively controlled (Stark, 2007; see Chapter 1). Radiance had been moved to a new city, and her abuser had made it impossible for her to make new friends. Isolation is a key factor in coercive control. In this passage, Radiance is thinking carefully about how to take care of herself and her infant daughter. She gives a number of infixed narratives about an exchange, or a number of exchanges, between her and her abusive partner throughout the story. In these exchanges, she describes a situation in which her abusive partner used his knowledge of her situational constraints, constraints such as isolation that he helped put in place, to dismiss her desire to leave as ridiculous and impossible. He is reported by Radiance as mocking her gestures to leave by saying things like, "Yeah, cool. Yeah, do that" (line 12). In mocking her, he operationalizes his knowledge that she has nowhere to go and that he has isolated her from the outside world – the very picture of coercive control. What Radiance describes is a style of emotional abuse that Stark (2007) calls coercive control: mocking and derision, and isolation. Her abuser is able to downgrade her claims that she will leave, because he knows he has isolated her. He mocks her for being isolated, a fact that was his own doing. Radiance tells this story to demonstrate how emotional abuse functions. Not just what it is, but what its mechanisms look like and how they function. She shows how emotional abuse is itself a factor in staying, a tool used by abusers, that is discursively cruel, dense, and hard to combat. In this brilliant story, Radiance stories context for staying, while representing her desire to leave.

Hard though it may have been, Radiance did leave. She strategized, planned, and left in the safest possible way. Remember, she needed to keep her baby safe. Radiance demonstrates self-control and planning. She did not stay because her agency was broken, but rather she stayed because it was intact, highly functional. In fact, Radiance uses the final small story at the end of Extract 3.6 to jump into a story about the night she left. Extract 3.7 follows directly after the narratives told in Extract 3.6.

Extract 3.7 Radiance

1.	*Radiance:*	It [leaving] was just in the middle of the night like I'd planned it.
2.		Well, I really didn't plan it, but
3.		I feel like it was my guardian angels like, "You need to pack.
4.		You need to get rid of a lot of stuff.
5.		You need to just get it down to a certain amount of stuff.
6.		That's what I did.
7.		One night when he went to work I just was like, "Here's my chance."
8.		I just started packing stuff in the car.
9.		My daughter helped me.
10.		She didn't want to go to sleep and she helped me pack.
11.	*Jenny:*	Mm hmm. And you left?
12.	*Radiance:*	I took that as my sign.
13.		I'm like, "I don't know where we're going. We'll stay in a hotel tonight."
14.		My mom got us a hotel. Yeah.
15.	*Jenny:*	It's very brave.
16.	*Radiance:*	It was brave.
17.	*Jenny:*	It's really hard.
18.	*Radiance:*	She was like my rock. She was the one –
19.		we were experiencing a lot of verbal abuse.
20.		He would do certain things in front of her and she was just like –
21.		I was breastfeeding her and she just looked up at me and she just stopped feeding.
22.		She just gave me this look like, "We're gonna stay here?"
23.		Like, "You're gonna let me witness this and he's gonna talk to you like that?"
24.		It just broke my heart and I was like, "I don't think - I can't do it."
25.	*Jenny:*	Can't do it anymore.
26.	*Radiance:*	Yeah, she was like my motivation to just go. You know?

The identity that emerges interactionally in this story is not one of victim (only), but one of something like planner (among other identities). In her story, she tries to conceive of a way to leave even when all ways seemed blocked, and she finally makes it happen. Note that emotional and verbal abuse is a big part of how Radiance sets up for and accounts for staying/leaving. In this case, verbal abuse is the reason for leaving. This linkage is important in that it gives meaning to leaving with context. Throughout the victim/survivor interviews, leaving is a response to an event that pushes past all of the reasons for staying. Leaving is hard, and it takes planning and courage, which Radiance demonstrates. This leaving story is two smaller stories stitched together with the idea of leaving. She begins with a story about packing her stuff in which her baby daughter figures centrally. The baby was her "rock" (line 18), staying awake in order to "help" pack up the necessities and leave (line 10). Radiance didn't know where she would go, initially. She just knew that that night was her chance to get out of there. As her story continues, she explains that her mom helped by getting them a room at a hotel. Radiance left. While she says it wasn't planned, Extract 3.6 makes it clear that she had been thinking about leaving, mulling over her options. The catalyst for leaving, however, was her infant daughter who with a look, asked that they find a way out of the verbally abusive situation. In response to getting berated while she was nursing her baby, her baby looked at her as if to say, "You're gonna let me witness this and he's gonna talk to you like that" (line 23)? Her answer to the rhetorical question posed by the infant is no, we won't stay and endure this abuse. "I can't do it," said Radiance (line 24). Radiance decided that she would not let her abusive partner talk to her that way any longer.

Radiance tells a set of stories in which her daughter and motherhood figure centrally, and she leaves. She will not ask her infant daughter to witness or withstand the verbal abuse any longer. The identity of "mother" emerges in this telling alongside "fighter" and "planner." Radiance's identity emerges multifaceted and compelling. She shows that she was thinking strategically about leaving a terrible set of circumstances. Radiance does not demonstrate a dearth of agency, but rather, she shows constrained, context-rich agency, decision-making, and planning. Her agency has antecedents, motivations, and interpretations – her infant daughter, for example. Even when she talks about choices and decisions, they are explicitly situated. They are never "mere" choices, but choices that come from experiences in her environment. She knows when the time is right to leave without having to endure further abuse. The decision to leave isn't a "mere" decision: it comes from a complex set of motivations and contexts. She wants to leave safely, and ultimately, she does.

Radiance's stories trouble the police discourses that create an iconic victim with insufficient agency. Addressed with respect rather than assumption, she gives an account of herself that is strong, rich, and agented within the circumstances. It is not that she operates without constraint, but constraint does not mean an absence of agency. She behaves with reason and rhetoricity. Indeed, she is paying attention in extreme ways, looking for her moment – both emotionally and physically – to leave. Though she is ascribed agented nonagency by police discourses when she talks about interactions with police, there are no indications of a voided agency in her account of leaving. Further, Radiance's stories call attention to the discourses and pieces of identity that are cut off through erasure by police discourse – made to seem insignificant. That is, in her stories we get a fuller accounting of what being a victim of domestic violence looks like and even more importantly, what it means to inhabit this space. We get a complex accounting of identity within the constraints of domestic violence.

The next set of stories comes from Butterfly, a young woman who has four children. In Extract 3.8, Butterfly describes mental and physical abuse in order to position her comments about staying/leaving.

Extract 3.8 Butterfly

1.	*Butterfly:*	Yes. He would grab [child], he'll be four this month, and
2.		squeeze him really hard when he was bad.
3.		Then [child], he was rough with her too and would just go attack when he'd get mad.
4.		He was passive aggressive.
5.		Oscar, he would just go running at him too and just grab ahold of him and
6.		stuff like that and
7.		be like, "Listen here," and right up in his face.
8.		Things happened quickly.
9.		When things got bad, it got bad fast, but
10.		he always made it seem like it was my fault, so it was hard.
11.		Even though I would stick up for myself all the time.
12.		It just seemed pointless and I don't know.
13.		I just kept going through it because I thought that I loved him.
14.		I had nowhere to go, and
15.		I didn't know what to do, and
16.		I have too many kids,
17.		so that's what would stop me.

18. Nobody would help me, so I was literally stuck.

19. *Jenny:* A minute ago you said also you loved him.

20. *Butterfly:* Yeah.

21. *Jenny:* How did that play—what part did that play? How did that complicate it more?

22. *Butterfly:* Because I have a kid with him and
23. then I know he wants to see him.
24. If I just stay with him, then we can just share [child].
25. I can try to make sense to him what he's doing wrong and get it through to him,
26. but it wasn't.
27. I knew it wasn't, but I thought maybe it would.
28. It was just up and down, up and down.
29. The next day I'd be like, "Oh, it's gonna be okay tomorrow," and
30. it would be for a short amount of time, but
31. then it'd go back to him talking crap and
32. not being able to deal with me and the kids.

Butterfly does a lot of discursive, indexical work in this extract. Like Radiance did, Butterfly reframes leaving and staying to coordinate with and take account of emotional abuse that, in this case, correlates with physical violence. Butterfly uses a narrative about violence to springboard into a story about staying. Two things about the strategies used in Butterfly's staying/leaving story are interestingly different to the strategies we found in Radiance's stories. First, rather than describing material conditions, Butterfly, like other participants, describes mental and emotional states. She comes back to the emotional state in two places. First, when she says that she "kept going through it because [she] thought that [she] loved him" (line 13). Butterfly is very candid in stating that she stayed initially out of love. Second, she stayed because she wanted to help him. As she puts it, "I can try to make sense to him what he's doing wrong and get it through to him, but it wasn't. I knew it wasn't, but I thought maybe it would" (lines 25–27). Here, she expresses a desire to help her husband see his wrongdoing. She sees her role in the marriage as one of managing his strong emotional responses; she is doing the emotional work for her husband to try to make him a better man. She explains this goal in an absolutely reasonable way, as she does her continuing affection for him.

That is, Butterfly rationally describes her reasons for staying; they are neither slapdash nor accidental. She is not acting out of a defunct sense of agency, but in fact, she is strategically attempting to get the life she wants with the partner she has chosen.

The sense of love and support for her spouse that Butterfly expresses correlates with the other difference between her story and Radiance's, namely, the role that parenthood plays in this narrative. Where parenthood drives Radiance to leave, for Butterfly, it provides a reason to stay. In her explanation of wanting to "get through" to her abuser, she says, "Because I have a kid with him and then I know he wants to see him" (lines 22 and 23). That is to say, staying with and teaching her abusive husband to be a better person, repairing his injurious behavior, all of this would make it possible for him to still be a father to his son and for her child to know his father. Butterfly wants this. Butterfly is working hard to make the life she wants in a challenging situation. Butterfly is not telling stories that comport with the iconic representation of victim and agented nonagency produced in police discourse. Indeed, that discourse occludes the strategic agency and identities that she is performing. An identity emerges for Butterfly that pays attention to the emotional details of family life. She is thoughtful and caring, trying to make decisions for her family, under the most impossible circumstances.

Because the discursive and personal resources were different, because the circumstances were different, even though there was overlap in that they were both in abusive relationships – both are technically "victims" – different, multifaceted identity/ies emerge for Radiance and Butterfly as they story their reasons for staying and ultimately leaving. Both perform and inhabit an identity of victim, but with other identities emerging alongside. Butterfly performs an identity of hopefulness and helpmate. She hopes that things will improve, and she sees herself as central to the improvement of her spouse. Radiance performs an identity of strategic survivor. Both worked hard to achieve the life they wanted, eventually leaving in order to get it. The different performances of identity are important, especially when seen in light of the police version of staying/leaving that identifies one monolithic identity for victims of domestic violence. When we look at actual victim speech, we can see complications to the iconization established in the police discourse. Importantly, we get insight into the facets of victimhood that are erased in that iconization. If we pay attention to what victims/survivors themselves say, we can see that victim/survivor agency, constrained though it may be, is at work. This agency is effectively erased unless we pay attention to the stories that victims/survivors tell.

Indeed, Butterfly gives a number of significant accounts of violence that matter to her partial identity as a victim, and further, that complicate iconic notions about victimhood and agency. In some places, she describes emotional torture, kept in a small room with four children, where she was expected to take care of all of the cooking and other household chores. She describes absolute fear and terror. She describes a lifelong fear of police, combined with fear of her abusive husband's certain retribution. In Extract 3.9, Butterfly describes the event that finally caused her to leave her abusive situation.

Extract 3.9 Butterfly

1.	*Butterfly:*	I was just afraid of all of that because
2.		I'm scared of cops because
3.		my mom taught me that way.
4.		I try to stay away from authority.
5.		I know they're there to help, but
6.		I get scared.
7.		I have anxiety and I'm on medication.
8.		I know I should have got on it a long time ago, but
9.		I didn't want cops involved.
10.		I knew that cops weren't gonna get involved,
11.		unless somebody was dying or bleeding, and
12.		I'm not even the one that called the cops that night.
13.	*Jenny:*	Tell me about that night.
14.	*Butterfly:*	We were all sleeping in the basement. [child], [child] and [child] were—no—
15.		[child] and [child] were at the head of the bed.
16.		We only had one bed in the room and two toddler beds
17.		and then a cushion bed for [child].
18.		Then me and [child] were at the foot of the bed and
19.		we were sleeping.
20.		Then [child] was on his [cushion] bed near [ex-husband].
21.	*Jenny:*	Uh huh.
22.	*Butterfly:*	He [ex-husband] was up until 2:30 am playing video games, like always.
23.		He has two TV screens on and hooked up and stuff,
24.		so [child] [young toddler] went to go wake up and
25.		I says, "No, lay back down," and
26.		he told him like, "Come here. Let me see him."

27.	I was like, "No."
28.	I told him he was a piece of shit and that,
29.	if he doesn't turn his stuff off, I'm gonna cut the cords or something
30.	because I was so mad.
31.	He called me a rotten bitch or something.
32.	My son, my oldest, woke up and says, "She's rotten? Who's rotten?"
33.	Or something like that,
34.	He [ex-husband] responded, and he threw the heaviest computer chair on my son child
35.	[child] was screaming, and
36.	I got up quickly and I took it off of [child].
37.	I went up to his neck, and I pushed him, and
38.	I was talking crap like, "Don't ever do that again," and
39.	he just grabbed ahold of my neck and was choking me really hard and
40.	hitting me in my head, and
41.	I was biting on my tongue.
42.	He was saying, "Are you gonna stop? Are you gonna stop?"
43.	I wasn't even doing nothing.
44.	I didn't even attack him or anything.
45.	I was trying to tell him I would stop so he'd get off of me.
46.	I was biting on my tongue and going *[gurgling noise]* like that,
47.	and my son was hitting him in his head and
48.	that's why he let go.

In Extract 3.9, Butterfly clearly articulates the material conditions of abuse, conditions in which we see constrained and practical agency. What Butterfly describes is nothing short of horrifying. She poignantly stories the physical ramifications of emotional and physical abuses. Keeping the family awake in a small room while he played video games into the night, expecting his young wife to keep the kids asleep and quiet, this all amounts to emotional abuse and coercive control. The physical violence to his stepson and wife is extreme and brutal. Strangulation is an escalator that police and other police staff watch for and take seriously. When he strangled his wife, she fought, as did her young son. In response to these defensive gestures, the abusive husband called the police himself, which also gave Butterfly the opportunity to speak to the police, even though she was afraid of them. Even with all of this violence, the situation was treated like he-said-she-said and no arrest was made. Only the next day, when detectives interviewed the children individually, was the abusive husband arrested.

What is notable in this extract is how Butterfly presents herself as an agent. She defended herself and her children. She does not express an identity of cowering to an abusive husband. Recall in Extract 3.8, Butterfly stated, "I would stick up for myself all the time" (line 11). She sees herself as a fighter and as able to fight. When we take both extracts from Butterfly together, we get a sense of a woman who against all odds, has courage. Toward the end of the interview, Butterfly avowed: "I know I'm not gonna go back." She is making explicit decisions. Butterfly is a person who suffered under an abusive structure of coercive control, but she is not and was not devoid of agency. At the same time that she performs an agented identity, she does not articulate the kind of full sovereign agency that the police presume. This is a practical, rhetorical, situation-specific model of agency that emerges in response to circumstances, such as being fed up with being kept in a tiny room; being forced to take care of all of the household duties; enduring late-night video gaming in the room where the entire family slept; and, physical assault. Butterfly articulates her fear, her emotional abuse, her physical abuse, all of it, without losing a sense of self. Remarkable.

3.7 Accounting for Violence

Along with victim agency, violence is also placed under erasure when police officers story domestic violence. That is, violence is oddly absent when police officers talk about domestic violence. When the police story violence, they do so with a point – a point that is clearly different from victims/survivors and thus is associated with different emergent identities. As we discussed earlier, when victims/survivors narrate violence, they do so as a way of providing context for stories of staying/leaving. Police narrations of violence toward victims/survivors, on the other hand, tend to slip into critiques of victims that reify them as victims. In addition to the erasure of agency, the *violence* described by victims such as Butterfly and Radiance is placed under erasure in police discourses about domestic violence. That is, both physical and emotional violence are underrepresented in police discourse about victims and domestic violence. Police give problematic accounts of violence that either ignore or downplay the violence and focus on the behavior of the victim rather than the assailant. When they describe the gunshot through the wall in Extract 3.5, for example, they problematically describe the victim. They focus on the fact that she didn't call police earlier and her pregnancy, but they only occasionally mention violence in a sort of off-hand way. Violence is an afterthought. One officer, Office Winters, does finally chime in, "I think she was scared to say anything" about the gun out of fear, we would assume, of her abuser. This idea is dropped in by Officer Winters, but it is not taken up by the others in the conversation – a tidbit that they all let fall away as minor in order to continue discussing the victim's behavior. Overall, little attention is paid to the violent act itself, the fear it would instill in the victim, and the consequences of the violence.

Police focus on the fact that the victim had not reported; they are affronted by this fact: "The man had shot his gun at her from six feet away in their bedroom around her body into the wall. Didn't even report it! She did not even report it until we were there the next day!" Officer Angel's tone of voice showed dismay, disgust, and disbelief that somebody would not report being shot at to police. They cannot believe that she would not call the police when she was shot at. With the focus on the motivations and lack of action by the victim, the abusive event itself receives little attention. That is, the victim is evaluated, but the violence and the perpetrator are not. Thus, the victim is characterized in negative terms – staying when she *should* leave; acting "crazy" – but the act of violence against her is not. The act is presented in an almost neutral, matter of fact way. "Then come to find out a gun was involved. That's what he hit her with. Then it came down to well, he shot at me three days ago, and then, oh yeah, by the way, I'm three months pregnant." This reads like a list of doings, but there is no evaluation of them, no exclamation of how terrible this event is. Instead, the crime is just one of a number of things in a list. Moreover, this list of doings is presented in order to underline the ridiculousness of the victim's behavior. Emotional violence is dealt with even more poorly.

Because it is not illegal, officers tend to find emotional violence calls less important, and often frustrating, to go on. Take, for example, Extract 3.10, in which emotional violence is described and, in many ways, dismissed. The correlation between overall fear and emotional violence is misunderstood. Emotional violence is treated as benign – producing no fear. This process of misunderstanding and ignoring, I suggest, is facilitated by the fact that emotional violence is not against the law.

Extract 3.10 Officer McQuaid

1.	*Off. McQuaid:*	Nowadays, it's more a lot of arguing,
2.		a lot of doin' things psychological to each other.
3.	*Jenny:*	Right. Emotional abuse stuff?
4.	*Off. McQuaid:*	Emotional kind of stuff.

5.		Seriously, there has been a distinction where I've seen— in the calls—
6.		and I don't go on every domestic call—
7.		but distinction of when I first started, I can tell you,
8.		all the domestics seemed like there was blood, bruises, and broken stuff in the house.
9.		Almost all of them.
10.		Now, that's part of the thing, too, people call the cops for—
11.		which I'm not dismissing domestics—for everything nowadays.
12.	*Jenny*:	Mm hmm.
13.	*Off. McQuaid*:	Like I said, they could Google it. You know what I mean?
14.		Half the stuff they call us for. You go on these domestics.
15.		This person, "It's a violent domestic."
16.		You get there, "What's the violence?"
17.		"He's calling me names."
18.		"Did he threaten you?"
19.		"No, he's calling me names."
20.		"Okay. It's not violent. It's mean and mean-spirited. That's not very nice, but
21.		him telling you 'you're no good' is not a criminal offense."
22.	*Jenny*:	The weird thing about that is that when you're getting yelled at in that fashion,
23.		you know, the victim knows,
24.		that the next thing that's gonna happen is getting hit.
25.		She called just before she got hit because she didn't wanna get hit. It's that mentality.
26.	*Off. McQuaid*:	Yeah. Some of these calls, they've never been hit.
27.		They call just every time there's a,
28.		"I think I have-- to fear him. I think he's gonna do something."
29.		I said, "You need to go--
30.		"I can't."
31.		"Okay. I can't hang out at your house 24/7. I can't—"
32.		"I think he's gonna do something." "Has he ever done anything to you before?"

33.   "No, never."

34. *Jenny:*   Yeah. But the amount of fear that emotional abusers
                     inspire—

35. *Off. McQuaid:* But they won't leave him.

Extract 3.10 is about emotional violence, which Officer McQuaid equates with fights, with "doing things psychological to each other" (line 2), again attributing equal blame to both parties of what he sees as a simple altercation. Officer McQuaid describes emotional and verbal violence as nonviolence. "What's the violence?" (line 16) he asks, indicating that in such situations there is not violence only disagreement. Officer McQuaid creates a fake conversation with an "any-victim," in which he presents a typical conversation with an emotional abuse victim. He characterizes the general, any-victim as saying, "He's calling me names" (line 19) to which he replies, "Okay. It's not violent" (line 20). He acknowledges that it is not nice, but because it is not criminal, he cannot see it as violent. Officer McQuaid further characterizes the victim as saying, "'I think he's gonna do something'" (line 28) to which he responds that he cannot stay at the house indefinitely in order to ensure that the abusive party will avoid physical contact. When I, as the interviewer, attempt to provide context for verbal violence and just how scary it can be, Officer McQuaid simply states, "But they won't leave" (line 35), presuming not only that the victim can simply leave but that they do not leave, for all the wrong reasons. The assumption here is that leaving is easy, obvious, and nondangerous. This is an assertion of agented nonagency presented in a narrative that places emotional violence under erasure – not criminal and not violent. Further, the idea is presented that leaving is the solution, not police intervention. Police, remember, deal with criminal not civil issues, and emotional violence is merely a civil issue. The sense is created that calls for emotional and verbal violence are a waste of the time of busy police officers because they are not real violence.

The downplaying of emotional and verbal violence creates an indexical link between emotional violence and not violent, not a crime, and not important. This cluster of language enacts erasure of the types of emotional violence that the victims themselves claim are at the heart of feared, long-lasting violence. This all culminates in the statement in Extract 3.10 that "it's not a criminal offense" (line 21). Violence, here is equated with a criminal offense; in order for it to be one, it must also be the other.

There is a similar notion about how criminal domestic violence functions in Extract 3.11. They start out with a statement about staying/leaving that presumes that good victims must immediately leave their abusers.

Extract 3.11 *Officers Angel, Roscoe, Oliver*

1.	*Off. Angel:*	The knack is how do you convince the person that's in the middle of it to
2.		either recognize it and or get out [of] it, right?
3.		We're not a multi-tool, the police.
4.	*Jenny:*	What do you mean by that?
5.	*Off. Angel:*	We don't have all the resources and our function is criminal. It's not

[…]

6.	*Off. Roscoe:*	It's not specifically social, right?
7.		We deal with mental issues a lot on other types of calls and domestics.
8.		We're not counselors either.
9.		We do our best and give out the resources that we have available to us
10.		about mental health, etc., speak to the DV kit, but
11.		then we're on to the next thing, and
12.		who knows what kind of call it is.
13.		While we're there we try to give them as many resources as we have.
14.		Continued separation of course, is ideal.
15.		If it's a non-criminal, we can't make he or she leave and go to brother's house
16.		or sister's house or whatever for a handful of hours so this doesn't reignite.
17.		We always advise it.
18.		We look for a solution rather than just leaving the problem alone.
19.		Again, we're only there for a little bit of time.
20.		The problem is bigger than the police, or it's other than the police.

Here, officer Angel starts out by saying that the trick is to convince the victim that they are in an abusive relationship – a fact the victim likely knows – and to convince them that they must leave. Leaving is the focus, even though leaving is itself very dangerous and hardly an end to abuse, issues the police officers either do not know or do not consider relevant. As a way of punctuating his comments on leaving, Officer Angel states that the police are "not a multi-tool" (line 3), by which he appears to mean that they should not be used for, and that they can't fix every problem associated with domestic violence, especially emotional and verbal abuses. He directly states "We don't have all the resources and our function is criminal" on line 5. Criminal is contrasted to emotional/verbal forms of violence that Officer McQuaid talked about. As Officer Angel indicates, they do not have training for emotionally violent encounters because their stated goals as law enforcement are to deal with criminal offenses. Thus, dealing with abusive fights and trying to convince people to leave abusive relationships are not his job. When these issues are treated like they are his job, he responds with frustration. Officer Roscoe extends Officer Angel's sentiment when he says his job is "not specifically social" (line 6) and further, "[police] are not counselors" (line 8). That is, domestic violence victims of emotional abuse, and in general, are in need of therapy and mental help, more than just police intervention. This officer is seeing emotional violence entirely in terms of psychological issues on the part of the victim, rather than in terms of violence. There is no recognition that a violent verbal assault might inspire fear, that it might precede a beating, or that it might lead a person to call for the police. We see domestic violence and victims of domestic violence pathologized as a psychological problem, thereby blaming the victim while avoiding any discussion of violence or criticism of the abuser.

The police only have so many resources to cope with these problems. The presupposition is that these limited resources would be sufficient if only the victims were more compliant. Seeing the issue as a sociopsychological problem, domestic violence, both physical and emotional, is framed as "bigger than the police" (line 20), that is, beyond the purview of the police. Indeed, Officer Roscoe urges that domestic violence is "other than the police" (line 20). This is a major dismissal of domestic violence, making it unequivocally not a problem for police.

When narrations of violence get more physical and more specific, by comparison, they also get more contextual and place the burden of violence on the abuser. Take, for example, this small story told by Officer McQuaid.

Extract 3.12 *Officer McQuaid*

| 1. | *Off. McQuaid:* | It's way worse. It's bad now. |
| 2. | | call that I had, was it last year? |

3.   Wife wanted him to stop playing his stupid video games.
4.   She kept bugging him, kept bugging him.
5.   He assaulted her.
6.   In his mind, she kept bugging him.
7.   "Dude, doesn't mean—" You know what I mean?

In Extract 3.12, we see Officer McQuaid tells a story about a man who assaults his wife after she bugged him too many times about playing video games. This story is not punctuated with a statement of how the victim should leave. Instead, it ends by pointing a finger in the direction of the abuser – nearly the only time in these data – and says, "Dude, doesn't mea— " (line 7). While Officer McQuaid trails off at the end of the sentence, the implicature is that the storyteller is admonishing the abuser that he does not get to assault his wife just because she is bugging him. This small fragment does gesture to the fact that police officers understand the larger issues to some degree.

3.8 Conclusions

Victims/survivors are operating with practical agency, constructing and performing identities that comport with their lived experiences and social interactions. By and large, they recognize constraints on what they can do and when they can do it. This is not the same thing as saying they are forced to stay in abusive relationships by their circumstances, but rather to say that they are strategic about surviving abusive relationships and making decisions about leaving. They know when it is safest to leave, an inherently dangerous operation. They see themselves as making real, practical decisions, and in fact, domestic violence victims/survivors do leave, in time and with practice. They neither see themselves as having full nor absent agency. That is to say, they recognize that agency emerges in each daily interaction that they have, and they operate with a situated agency that is true of most of us. They do see the extremeness of their situations as curtailing their agency, but they also recognize that abuse is one factor that gives their agency shape.

Police see agency in a different way. They presume that victims/survivors have the agency to leave at will, at the same time that they presume that victims will stay in their violent relationships because that agency has been curtailed. Police thus position victims/survivors in a space of agented nonagency, and victims feel it. As Rainbow indicates, she knows that police ultimately want and expect her to just pack her stuff and go and that they blame her if she does not. This expectation, this discourse of agented nonagency, creates a discourse that constrains identity formation and anoints a particular kind of faulty agency. This discourse itself wields a sort agency that Butler calls discursive agency. The discourse itself operates with agency, creating effects and realities as it moves through a situation. Thus, because of institutionally performed power asymmetry between victims/survivors and police, the police discourse is situated to do damage to the agency and identity formations of the victims/survivors. This is because, as Butler (1997, p. 3) puts it, some utterances are effective in the act of utterance: "by saying something, a certain effect follows." The effect is in the saying. Situating victims/survivors of domestic violence, as a class, in a position of agented nonagency produces and reproduces, propagates agented nonagency – makes it a reality. By operationalizing the node of agented nonagency in interactions with victims/survivors, police find agented nonagency where they expect to find it. This matters because police are in a position of power, and thus, what they understand to be true about the people with whom they talk is effectual – it proves itself to be true, in a kind of self-fulfilling prophecy. Thus, in recognizing victims/survivors as having agented nonagency, they find it. Discourses give rise to the "possibility for social existence, initiated into a temporal life of language that exceeds the prior purposes that animate that call" (Butler, 1997, p. 2). That is, discourses create and constrain identity performances that are recognizable within discourse, regardless of the intentions and motives of the speaker. "The contemporary address recalls and reenacts the formative ones that gave and give existence" (Butler, 1997, p. 5). Prior instances of enunciation that have formed identity and agency create the potential for contemporary and future such identities and agencies. This is because "one 'exists' not only by virtue of being recognized, but, in a prior sense by being *recognizable*" (Butler, 1997, p. 5, emphasis in original). In police discourses, the victim is recognizable as such, and in that way, in that moment, agented nonagency is reenacted, reanimated, and made available for other uses and performances.

Discourse can in this way be injurious (Butler, 1997); discourses can harm those on whom they act – those whom they make recognizable in ways that conscript the ineffable. In the situation discussed here, victims of domestic violence are made recognizable in iconic form as victims who should have agency but who do not operationalize that agency. The discourses that make victims/survivors recognizable in this way strip away context, situational knowledge, violence, and the identities that victims/survivors themselves perform. Thus, "to be injured by speech is to suffer a loss of context, that is, not to know where you are" (Butler, 1997, p. 4). Victims/survivors of domestic violence suffer precisely this loss, stripped of the complicating factors and contexts that constrain and enable their real lives. Thus, this iconic discourse of victim creates a loss of agency – it erases agency, swallowing it up in discourses of agented nonagency.

In addition to jettisoning agency, police discourse also copes with emotional and physical violence in problematic ways. Physical violence is accounted for in neutral terms with very little evaluation or discussion. It just is something that happens. It is not critiqued, but victims are. Amidst descriptions of violence, the fact that victims sometimes stay for whatever amount of time they stay for is an affront to police who are flabbergasted by the choice. They attempt to account for that choice in some places by pathologizing the victim, a move that immediately matches the assumptions of nonagency. They cannot leave because they lack the agency to do so, and they lack the agency because of "mental issues." Emotional violence is even more thoroughly rejected, because it is not even part of the job, according to the police officers I spoke with. Emotional and verbal violence are not crimes. Indeed, according to Officer McQuaid they are not even violent. Police do not feel like they should have to or need to answer these calls, and so they are dismissed, out of hand.

What we see, then, is a powerful discourse internalized, operationalized, and enacted by police who see victims of abuse in deficit terms and that downplays violence. The abuser him or herself as the purveyor of violence is given even less attention. This discourse is constructive – it works to fashion and perform a worldview that blames and misunderstands victim agency and identity, identities that are fascinating and multifaceted.

4

Storying Policing
Identities of Police and Domestic Violence

When police officers and victims/survivors tell stories, they are not only about themselves but they are also about others, characters in the story who do things, with whom the storyteller interacts, and with whom the teller positions themselves, relationally. In the story, the storyteller creates relationships between the characters in the "story world." In their 2011 article, De Fina and Perrino (2) recapitulate Young's (1987) tripartite theory of narrative, writing that "narratives always involve the discursive production and coordination of distinct domains: (a) the domain of the communicative event (in this case, the interview), (b) the domain of the storytelling world, and (c) the domain of the storyworld." Via De Fina and Perrino, Young articulates that storytelling involves communication, during which a story is told about a world that is constructed in the story itself – the "story world." This chapter is partly about the communicative interaction of telling a story in the course of an interview, but it is primarily about the discursive work done in building the story world and the process of articulating relationships between characters within that world. The interview itself necessarily affects the construction of the story world. In the interview:

- A story is created
- in response to questions from the interlocutor or interviewer
- in which the interviewee answers the question and
- communicates what they think the interviewer knows and wants to hear. Additionally, there are
- contextual features, such as
- location,
- table setup,
- visible audio recorder, and the like.

The interview setting affects the story constructed. For example, the resultant narrative is constructed for me, with the storyteller fully aware of my research agenda. Identity emerges in this level of interaction. Indeed, identity emerges and is performed at both levels of interaction, in the interview and in the story world; or more precisely, identity emerges at the point of intersection between these two levels of interaction when the story world is constructed as part of the interview interaction. Identity in the telling interaction is accomplished by constructing, assigning, and performing identities in the story world, a recapitulated set of events and characters.

In the narratives I discuss here, these on-the-ground identities are often the result of positioning self in relationship to other in the story being told. Police do this when they story victims/survivors, and victims/survivors do this when they story police. More than analyzing the interview interaction, however, this chapter digs into the ways story worlds are constructed and made meaningful by the teller for the listener. At the center of the analysis are the identities that are created, performed, assigned, and affixed to police officers when police tell stories about their work. In the following pages, I argue that police officer identities emerge within an institutional field that marries stories about procedure with stories about domestic violence victims/survivors. Police officer identities also emerge/are performed in relationship to and negotiation with conceptions of victims/survivors in the stories that they tell.

In their stories about policing domestic violence, we see police doing compelling identity work. "Identity work is a highly politicized process in which social actors claim, contest, and negotiate power and authority" (Bucholtz & Hall, 2008, p. 154). Identity work is political because it is ideological and interpersonal. Individuals must negotiate relationships, how they are understood by another, and what they hope to accomplish with their identity performances. The relationship between police and victims/survivors is a contest over authority in domestic violence encounters, or what police call domestic calls, and a contest over appropriate behavior for victims/survivors. In the process, I argue that semi-stable, re-performable identities emerge for police officers that are related to and draw from policing discourses. To be sure, identity emerges anew with each encounter. Nevertheless, there are striking similarities between different police officer identities and between performances by the same officer in different stories. I argue that policing discourses provide resources for identity formation, performance, and re/performance, which provide some, but not totalizing, structure for police identity.

Though here I acknowledge the partialness and transience of identity (Bucholtz & Hall, 2005, 2008; Ochs & Capps, 2001; Stokoe & Edwards, 2007), I primarily argue that police officer identities are re/performable by different individuals and the same individuals across time, borrowing from seemingly resilient and adoptable identities that can be animated in the indexical field of domestic violence for police officers. In addition to such semi-stable identity features, there are also more nuanced, partial, emergent identities available in the ways they story themselves and others. That is, police officers tend to present quite similar and seemingly stable identities. However, we also find multifaceted, partial, emergent identities arise alongside those that are semi-stable. Police officer identity is complex. Such a complex identity formation constructs, performs, and borrows from discourses that also impact, constrain, and enable interactional identity formation, emergence, and performance. Policing discourses that surround the interactional contexts of both policing and storytelling about policing play a role in the performance and construction of identities. Discourses are "used to construct identity positions" (Bucholtz & Hall, 2005, p. 594). Discourses are resources for identity emergence and performance, even as those performances alter and compel change within those discourses.

Identity is not only discursive, but it is also indexical, created and performed via discursive, ideological, and social linkages that make identity socially meaningful in any given performance. The domestic violence field of indexicality provides the resources for police officer identity formation, even as each performance feeds values, beliefs, and terms into the indexical field that are available for future performances (see Chapter 1). Identities that emerge in storytelling are performed positionally in relationship to others and society, and they are also positioned within and through discourse/s. Identities that emerge are not solely in the control of the teller, but the constraints of discourses and the interpretations of listeners will necessarily play a part. Nevertheless, when the police tell stories, policing discourse provides a fairly stable set of endeavors, values, and behaviors as identity building blocks.

Discourses, in particular, ideas and indexical linkages that are already circulating in the discourse, shape the production and uptake of a narrative. Through storytelling, "speakers adopt, resist and offer 'subject positions' that are made available in discourses" (Benwell & Stokoe, 2006, p. 43). In other words, a performance of identity may be shaped by discourse and the storyteller may readily adopt that shaping, or they may also contest and challenge it. Discourses constrain and enable identities that people may accept, reject, or confer on others, using the available discourses and indexical meaning-making strategies. In this way, identity is indexical. It emerges in a field that links language to social meaning. Further, "Ideology mediates between the interactional stances taken by speakers and the indexical relationships to identity that are thereby produced" (Bucholtz & Hall, 2008, p. 154). As Bucholtz and Hall contend, ideology plays an integral role in creating linkages, relationships, and ultimately meaning for speakers. Prior discourses and indexical forms mediate and put pressure on any performance and emergence of identity.

Indexicality is closely linked to "positionality," which pays attention to the micro and local ways by which identity emerges and is performed. People draw on, contest, and operationalize social meaning in their storytelling as a way of performing a particular identity that makes sense within the indexical field. In their stories, police tend to position against and around their conception of what and who a victim is and how they behave, while also drawing on social and policing discourses about domestic violence in the context of police work. Identity is performed and emerges relationally in the stories analyzed here, in relationship with those being interacted with and the requirements of context and situation. It also emerges relationally within the narrative, as the storyteller positions their character in the story world against those of other people presented in the story. Police officers do this when they story domestic violence and position against the victims that are characters in the stories, often accomplished through evaluation of their behaviors and imagined motivations.

Perhaps there is so much consistency among police officers' narratives, ideologies, identities, and discourses because of training that officers go through regarding police work in general and domestic violence specifically. I'm sure this plays a role. However, it is likely that such consistency and similarity have more to do with interactions and discussions between police. After all, they form and comprise a discourse community. There is a typified vocabulary and typical ways of explaining and narrating experiences within the community that are learned from each other. Most of the interviews with the police were done in groups, so officers were talking to each other as much as or more than to me. As they spoke, their ideas were ratified with nods, "mm hmms," and conjoining, supportive narratives from others in the room. The ideas about victims/survivors expressed in this chapter and elsewhere in this book were not surprising to the other people in the room, but rather they were points of relationality – regularized ways of discussing domestic violence and victims/survivors of domestic violence.

In this chapter, I propose that this positioning of identity between self and other occurs at least partly in the story world of the narrative. As police officers narrate some prior interaction, they also narrate the relationality between themselves and others – primarily victims/survivors, in a recapitulated, narrated event. I argue that when narrators perform for a local audience, they are talking about a cast of characters that they position against as a way of performing an identity with which they are comfortable, which aligns with policing discourses, and which comports with their larger sense of self. In other words, police officers cast those they story in a particular light, during which a particular identity for themselves emerges. Relationality here occurs at two levels: the interaction of the interview and the interaction of the story world. The identity that emerges relies heavily on the presence of the person or group for whom the narrative is performed, but it relies equally heavily on the people accounted for in the narrative and how they are characterized for the present listener in the narrative. Both interactional levels come together in order to make a particular, rhetorical point in the interview interaction, drawing, of course, on the indexical field within which their identities and utterances are meaningful. When speaking about "victims" – victim is the term used by police – they are sometimes individuals (a victim), but at other times they are a generalized group (victims). When representing police discourse, I will momentarily adopt their use of "victim," rather than "victim/survivor." As I will show, the relationship between prior and current interactions, and this shifting between individual and general group constitute a policing perception of the social world for victims in general, and in the process, identities for the police officer emerge positioned against "the victim."

The procedural/legal identity – what police officers have to do according to police procedure and law – informs and intersects with the identity formation that positions against and in relationship to victims/survivors. This is a truly interactional identity, always working in relationship to an/ other, positioned within the story being told. What the police performances and attributions of identity reveal is the relationship between emergent identities and semi-stable identities structured in the discourse of policing, and beyond that, the ways in which police identities are invested in and structured against a view of who victims/survivors are and how they behave. The semi-structured identities are not windows into the souls of the officers, but rather they are situated performances meant to accomplish particular identity-related tasks, namely, to demonstrate to me the competence, authority, and, in some cases, caring of the officers. Thus, I argue that the ways in which other people are accounted for, described, and cast become the resources for identity construction, emergence, and performance of the storyteller. This is true for both the ways that police story victims/survivors and the ways victims/survivors story police.

4.1 Interaction and Identity

Storytellers build worlds that come with worldviews that are intimately linked with, conform to, and build the social worlds and discourses to which they are related. As Schiffrin (1996, p. 170) articulately explains, "telling a story allows us to create a 'story world' in which we can represent ourselves against a backdrop of cultural expectations about a typical course of action." Police officers tell stories that represent, build, and in many ways adopt ideological values and beliefs about domestic violence and victimhood that align with cultural expectations and, more specifically, those circulating in police discourse. Thus, as Schiffrin (1996, p. 170) goes on to say, "our identities as social beings emerge as we construct our own individual experiences as a way to position ourselves in relation to social and cultural expectations." Not only do we position ourselves in relation to social and cultural expectation but also to other groups, individuals, and institutional values. "As varied and inventively distinct as [stories] are, they are stories 'disciplined by the diverse social circumstances and practices that produce them all' (Gubrium & Holstein, 2003, p. 3)" (quoted in Benwell & Stokoe, 2006, p. 41). Stories in this formulation are both distinctly individual and social, and institutional and ideological at the same time. They manage the range of contexts that are indexed and drawn upon in any given narration, and thus they constrain and enable the identities that will emerge in those stories.

Identity emerges in real time, meeting situational demands, but that doesn't mean storytellers do not also draw on previous interactions and identities in social interaction and identity performance. "Identity work in any given situation may derive from resources developed in earlier interactions" (Bucholtz & Hall, 2005, p. 588). This is not to say that identity is indelible and stable, but it is to say that speakers and storytellers remember prior interactions that were successful and draw on the resource offered by those prior interactions. To put it another way, identity emerges anew each time, but it is also linked to earlier identities, performances, and meaning-making/identity-making practices that have been ratified in earlier interactions. Thus, one thing that this chapter shows is that a hard-line distinction between emergent identity and semi-stable, reperformed identity is a false binary. Depending on the discourses and the situational demands, an identity can emerge that is both emergent and reproduced/reproducible. Indeed, here I am arguing that prior interactions recapitulated in narrative offer important resources for the construction, deployment, and performance of identities, which may be very similar to other performances, and even to other people's identity performances in the same subject category, such as police officer or domestic violence victim. In other words, when people tell stories of prior interactions and identities, those prior interactions and identities become identity resources for the current interaction and identity emergence. Police tell stories about procedure, policy, and law, and they also tell stories about interactions with victims/survivors of domestic violence. Storying interactions between police and victims/survivors by both groups leads to the emergence of complex identities in the interview context as well as rich identities described in the story world.

4.2 Policing Identity

Police officers perform identity in the process of constructing a story world. One key way that police officers construct their identities is relationally, in relationship to "victims." Police descriptions of victims are on a continuum, with them expressing caring at one end and "frustration" at the other. Indeed, performances of caring infiltrate and inform performances of frustration and vice versa. Police work in extreme conditions. They try to remain neutral, and they work hard to control their emotional responses. The job is taxing, and they want to "make a difference" (Det. Tyler). With regard to this, Detective Tyler states, "remember, officers are working on skeleton crews. We don't have a lot of time to waste, and I think if an officer feels like they're going to a call where they're not being able to make a difference or do their job because of somebody else's choice, then it's frustrating." This discussion of the demands of the job quickly slips into a commentary on victims, who do not cooperate, do not allow police to "make a difference," and who waste the time of police officers. This leads to frustration. Police are frustrated when they cannot "do their job" because of the choices made by others – in this case the choice made by victims not to leave their abusive partners.

Police use stories such as the small one above about interactions with victims to perform a range of identities. "Frustrated officer trying to do their job" is just one of them. As an example of a competing identity, in a group interview with officers Angel, Roscoe, and Summer, Officer Oliver, a victim/survivor herself, says the following about leaving a violent relationship: "Even when you know it's for the best. It's scary and it's hard." In this statement, Officer Oliver brings together her identity as a police officer and a correlating identity that she is also a victim/survivor of domestic violence. On the one hand, it would be for the best for victims to leave immediately, a common police sentiment, but on the other, leaving is dangerous and, as many of the victims/survivors put it, so very "hard." This officer is seeing herself reflected in victim/survivor behavior, in particular of staying in a violent relationship that her police officer self finds less than ideal. This statement is even more interactionally relevant, because it comes in a conversation with other officers that is quite negative about people who stay in violent relationships, leading Officer Oliver to interject with explanatory discourse on the part of victims. A dual identity emerges that works to explain leaving and staying behavior to other police officers, but that also sees and shares the perspective of her peers, complicating the conversation in important ways.

Where Officer Oliver makes moves to validate victims/survivors' staying behavior, it is far more common in these data to see victims/survivors critiqued. Detective Jacobs finds victim/survivor interactions with police more frustrating, a word that is used often by police officers. Like Detective Tyler, Detective Jacobs is frustrated by answering multiple calls at the same residence, with returning functioning as an indication that the abused party hasn't left their abuser. Detective Jacobs says:

Extract 4.1 Detective Jacobs

1.	Det. Jacobs:	It's kind of the boy who cried wolf.
2.		We try to be sensitive to not be jaded to that kind of thing,
3.		but when you go and go, and go, and go, and go, and
4.		you find out that you're being used to manipulate,
5.		now who's the victim?
6.		That can be difficult to keep an open mind about.
7.		Look, I'm gonna find the evidence of a crime, and that's what I'm gonna act on, and
8.		try to take the emotion and the frustration out of it.

This short extract, Extract 4.1, raises a number of questions. Who is the "we," the "you," and the "I" that are referenced? Who is the victim and what does it mean to be a victim? What are the characteristics that make one a victim? Where does the emotion and frustration stem from? What identity emerges and what is the identity positioned against? What is the interactional situation represented and how does identity emerge in relationship to that interaction? These are questions that run throughout the police interviews and discourses. Detective Jacobs begins by talking about victims, a group against which his own identity emerges, interactionally. He calls people, victims, who call police over and over "manipulate[ive]" (line 4) and "boy[s] who cr[y] wolf" (line 1). Victims, according to Detective Jacobs, are just using police to get something – to manipulate the situation – if they do not immediately take the next step and leave. Leaving is the only logical result from a call to police for help, for this officer and others. Leaving an abusive relationship is a contextually rich decision, and it takes time and practice. As one victim put it, "leaving is not an event. It's a process" (Penelope). Note also that Detective Jacobs ascribes no culpability to the perpetrator of the assault. The perpetrator is not urged to stop abusing as a way of ending calls to the police. The abuser's actions receive no scrutiny. In response to his framing of the victim as both unwilling to leave and manipulative, he poses a rhetorical question: "now who's the victim?" (line 5). He could be implying that the abuser is not only being victimized by the constant threat of police intervention, but he could also be insinuating that the police are the victims here, victims of being manipulated by victims to end regular, everyday arguments; victims of people who make multiple calls to the police without taking the proper action.

After establishing the victim as a foil against which his identity can emerge, Detective Jacobs then makes a number of identity statements that comport with policing:

- "That can be difficult to keep an open mind about," (line 6)
- "I'm gonna find the evidence of a crime," (line 7)
- "that's what I'm gonna act on," (line 7)
- "try to take the emotion and," (line 8)
- "the frustration out of it" (line 8).

Each of these statements that follow the initial story of the extract presents a component of policing identity for Detective Jacobs. First, he reminds officers to "keep an open mind," to put off judgment in the process of doing the job. The goal is to keep the focus on procedure. The second point he makes is about fact finding and looking for evidence, a point that most police present as the main part of their job. The third point is about taking action, taking control, and following the law. This central component of police identity has to do with authority – the ability to control a situation and arrest if warranted by the facts. Next is an adage about leaving emotion out of it, which hearkens back to the first point about putting off judgment. Finally, Detective Jacobs ends with a claim that he is frustrated, frustration being the primary emotion that needs to be controlled in the service of fact finding and controlling the heat of the situation. Frustration, though it may exist, should be ignored. Such a statement presupposes not only that frustration with the situation and victims exists but also that the speaker is trying to keep that frustration at bay in the service of doing the job correctly, according to procedure. Frustration with the victim coordinates with police procedure.

Some of Detective Jacob's sentiments are echoed in the same interview by Detective Sidwell who says, "We have to try to figure out what's really going on, and not what we're just hearing, and try to keep our emotion out of it." In both speakers' speech, we see a desire to find the "facts," evidence, with which to understand the situation, and to suppress emotional response. The idea is that "what [police] are hearing" from the victim and the assailant are just stories spun to blame the other. This surreptitiously evicts the victim's story from the realm of fact, and with it, domestic violence as the root of the call. Instead, she is framed as engaging in a game of he-said-she-said. The victim's account of violence is merely a story, motivated by placing blame on the other party and protecting the self. In this short statement, we also see Detective Sidwell's desire to remain neutral and unemotional in an emotionally charged situation, but in a way that distrusts the victim. The detective's procedural, calm identity emerges against the victims' frustrating behavior and their stories about what happened. Similar identity points emerge in the field of indexicality of domestic violence for other police officers.

As the analyses discussed earlier show, police operationalize a number of complex, but in some ways consistent and institutional, identities that relate to victims/survivors and their behavior. In particular, police identities emerge and are expressed in relationship with the fact that victims are assumed to endlessly stay in abusive relationships, calling police multiple times, and leading to police officer frustration. That is, the construction of a particular kind of victim/survivor leads to the emergence of police officer identity. In the following analyses, we continue to see this trend. Police officer identity emerges against a backdrop of discussions about procedure/policy and victims/survivors. In both ways that police identity is formed and emerges, we see a group identity performed.

4.3 Procedural Identity

Perhaps because of the way questions were organized by the interviewer, or perhaps because of the way police officers think about their jobs, the first things police officers talked about in nearly all of the interviews were procedure and law. Indeed, as we will see, many of them came back to legal and procedural constraints on interactions at the scene of a domestic call more than one time. The interview with Detectives Jacobs, Sidwell,

Michaels, and Johnson was exemplary in this regard. In Extract 4.2 Detective Jacobs explains procedure in a domestic call to me, an explanation that is endorsed by his peers. This bit of story comes back around to police group identity many times.

Extract 4.2 Detective Jacobs

1.	*Det. Jacobs*:	Any information we can get from dispatch, or from witnesses, or
2.		from whoever's calling in, is a bonus to us.
3.		We try not to have any kind of preconceived ideas of what we're gonna do,
4.		because we don't know what is actually happening until we arrive.
5.		The history of the household is vital to us, we can kinda—
6.		okay, this is a violent house, maybe 3 officers is better.
7.		Previous history of weapons,
8.		let's approach from a different direction, or
9.		have them come out to us,
10.		so when we get there, we start, we'll try to separate the parties involved,
11.		so we can get a better idea from them,
12.		while we're interviewing them,
13.		of what is occurring.

Detective Jacobs uses the group pronouns "we" and "us" exclusively, gesturing from the start to a group identity – indeed, physically gesturing to the other detectives in the room. This group identity is associated with constraints stemming from social expectations, workplace training, and policing discourses. From the orientation of this group identity, he walks us through procedure and best practices. For example, one best practice seems to be to get any and all information relevant to the location of the call before entering the premises. Using group pronouns, "we" and "us," Detective Jacobs presents ideas about gathering facts and information. He says, "Any information we can get" (line 1), and "the history of the household is vital to us" (line 5) because information directs officer behavior and ensures officer safety. If the situation warrants it, they'll get more officers, or make contact in a different way. Thus, they try not to have "preconceived ideas" (line 3) about what they are going to do upon arrival, because they need to be able to respond to the situation on the ground. Finally, they separate parties for questioning, yet another form of collecting information that is framed using group pronouns.

This is a fairly typical narrative description of going on a domestic call. The identity that emerges is one of groupness. Using only plural pronouns that reference police in general, these procedures and strategies are presented as typical operating procedure that everybody does. As it is presented in Extract 4.2, this isn't just the procedure that Detective Jacobs uses. It is *the* procedure and best practices that everybody uses. In addition to being a group identity, an identity of carefulness emerges. Because domestic calls are widely recognized as dangerous and volatile, officers behave carefully, using procedural knowledge and safety protocols. Finally, in Detective Jacob's speech, we see a group identity of information gatherers emerge.

Detective Jacobs explains that fact finding in a domestic call involves separating the parties and talking to them individually, to get information and stories about what happened: "if that means to separate them, whether it's just by room, or having them sit down and be able to talk to them as we figure out what's happening, that would be our first step on what's going on." These parties, the domestic violence victim and the perpetrator, provide information, evidence, and facts that satisfy the important element of police identity – fact finding, neutrality, and not taking sides. Police identity relies heavily on evidence and information and on their ability to discover the "truth" of a situation – what *actually* happened. This links to an ideological underpinning that there is a reality of a case like this; that the "facts" just lie in the situation waiting to be found (see Brooks & Gewirtz, 1996); and that they are transparent and carry their own meaning in themselves, regardless of interpretation, interaction, or ideology. In these extracts, semi-stable group identity emerges around fact finding and doing the job that police are sworn to do. It is apparently available to officers, who draw on discursive resources, procedural knowledge, and current contexts to develop, deploy, and perform an identity that is institutionally and ideologically sound.

4.3.1 Positioning in Relationship to Domestic Violence Victims: Frustration and Caring

The procedural identity operationalized by police and emergent in their storytelling coordinates with a relational identity, in which officers position in relationship to domestic violence victims/survivors in stories about domestic calls. We saw the beginnings of this analysis in the previous section. In the next two extracts, we see police officers telling stories about victims, or interactions with victims on domestic calls as a way of doing identity work. In what follows, police either only talk about victims in a general way, or they introduce general views about victims before telling a story about a specific victim. Their identities emerge against the backdrop of the characterization of the victim. Take for example, Detective Sidwell's account of victim behavior in Extract 4.3, in which he articulates a police view of victims, while also doing identity work.

As has been the case across police interviews, the pronouns tell an interesting story, and Detective Sidwell's is no different in Extract 4.3. He uses "we" for the police in general, and "they" for victims and abusers, grouped together and generalized.

Extract 4.3 Detective Sidwell

1.	*Det. Sidwell*:	And we get that.
2.	*Jenny*:	Yeah, yeah.
3.	*Det. Sidwell*:	They felt a bad moment, whatever, alcohol, something involved, high emotion, stressful situation.
4.		In someone's head, they still love each other.
5.		And a lot of them will work beyond that and live happily ever after, and
6.		we hope so.
7.		There are also the ugly situations that it's like,
8.		why did you get him from jail again?
9.		You know, and that's where it goes back to—
10.		and you hate to have this feeling.
11.		And again, we try to do everything right based on policy and procedure and state law,
12.		but it's like, don't call me if you don't want us to do something.
13.		But on the other hand that doesn't really help the situation.
14.		And so, being human, officers sometimes get that feeling,
15.		and it's horrible to say, but it can be super frustrating
16.		when you're trying to help somebody, and
17.		they continue to shun you away, and
18.		bring the problem back that you then have to deal with again.
19.		Because Domestic Violences are very dangerous.
20.		And, you know, we don't know if we're going into an ambush or going to a
21.		problem and that they're super emotional.
22.		They're— they're an ugly case to have to respond on, especially blind.
23.		Going into it and not knowing what you're— what's really going on.

This extract begins with a phrase that uses "we," immediately indexing groupness: "we get that," in line 1. This statement is a showing of affinity and understanding, and it is the first move Detective Sidwell makes in this narrative. His way of getting the floor. Right off the bat, we see an identity of understanding in police work beginning to form. This is further punctuated when he says, "And a lot of them will work beyond that and live happily ever after, and we hope so" in lines 5 and 6. Though hyperbolic in its phrasing, this statement hopes for a bright future for the couples he meets on the job. This cheery attitude is used to imagine people as coupled in his discussion, allowing him to group the victim and the abuser into a pair, which has the added effect of holding them equally culpable. This coupling discourse has the unintended effects of downgrading violence to a regular argument and of including the victim in the blame for the violence – the couple performs the violence together as a unit. This blames the victim for the violent situation as much as the abuser.

While his hopefulness that violent relationships will suddenly and completely turn around and become nonabusive relationships is somewhat misplaced, statistically speaking, it clearly articulates Detective Sidwell's belief in relationships. He makes a number of other similar statements throughout the interview, performing caring, hopefulness, and a deep trust in relationships. His hope and caring are underpinned by stereotypical, social myths about relationships, namely, that fixing relationships is always possible and that the goal is a fairy tale ending rather than therapy and honest hard work.

Where the pronoun "we" is used to do positive identity work for police, the pronoun "they" accomplishes something a bit more complicated. "They" creates a group other than and excluding the speaker, often including both the victim and the abuser, against which the police identity is positioned. When used by Detective Sidwell, "they" very often groups together the abused party with the abuser, followed by discursive moves that focus on un/healthy relationships, thereby blaming the relationship and both parties in the relationship for the violence. We see this in the first statement about domestic violence in lines 3 and 4 of Extract 4.3: "They felt a bad moment, whatever, alcohol, something involved, high emotion, stressful situation. In someone's head, they still love each other." The plural pronoun "they" clusters together the victim and the abuser, as if both parties are equally responsible for the "bad moment," the "high emotion," or the "stressful situation." This phrasing also downplays violence, diminishing it to a "bad moment" while blaming alcohol, emotion, and stress without indexing domestic violence or the abusiveness of the assailant. "Bad moment" chalks violence up to a bad day, an isolated event, and a single choice, not the regime of violence that makes up domestic violence. Domestic violence is jettisoned with the use of "they," ignored in the service of believing in a whole relationship. This is a breathtaking elision.

This omission of violence is followed by a claim that the couple are "still [in] love [with] each other" (line 4). The use of "they" combined with the allusion to a loving relationship overlooks domestic violence and the fact that police are on call because of interpersonal, intimate partner violence. The claim of love is not framed about an "any person," but rather it seems to denote an individual person with the use of "someone," "in someone's head" (line 4). This clause clearly references an individual, but it is not a specific individual. It is any anybody – a victim who is still in love and therefore problematically staying in an abusive relationship. This claim comes up a number of times. We will discuss a more direct version of this inference later in this chapter.

Lines 5 and 7 of Extract 4.3 set off a contrast between good and bad domestic violence and victims. The first point of contrast on line 5 imagines a repaired relationship, while lines 7 and 8 begin to introduce a recalcitrant victim, a victim who does not cooperate with police and doesn't leave. Rather than talking about fairy tale endings, as he did above, Detective Sidwell moves into a discussion of "ugly situations" (line 7) after which he poses the question, "why did you get him from jail again?" (line 8). This combination of statements calls the victim and their choices ugly. It blames the ugliness of the situation, not on the abuser and the violent situation, but on the victim, who chooses to stay. The entire weight of fixing the violent relationship is placed on the victim's leaving. There is a pronoun shift in line 9 from "they" to "you," which isolates the victim out of the relationship and targets them accusatorily. With this statement, we see a narrative in circulation in police discourse in which victims return to their partners, fight police intervention, and take the side of their abuser. These behaviors are treated as the problem for police; how problematic the violence is goes undiscussed. This stereotyped, iconicized version of victims may represent the broader social stereotype that abuse victims always return to their abusers, but it certainly represents policing discourse views of victims. Police ability to do their jobs correctly, identity as a police officer, hinges, in Detective Sidwell's characterization of victims' behavior and choices, on eliding domestic violence as the systematic abuse of an intimate partner nearly entirely.

As the narrative about victims continues, Detective Sidwell introduces the concept and identity of frustration. An identity that emerges carefully, with many hedges and explanations preceding the assertion on line 15, "It can be super frustrating." Let's back up and look at how he builds to this claim. First, he introduces the problem that he wants to have fixed: that is the fact that abused people come to the jail to pick their abuser, over and over. On line 9 of Extract 4.3, Detective Sidwell says, "that's where it goes back to," gesturing back to the claim-question that victims pick up their abusers from jail. Then he says, "you hate having this feeling" (line 10). This move is presented to offset the negativity and judgment that is coming. It is unpleasant to feel frustrated, the feeling to which he is building. With the pronoun "you" used in the general, plural sense as a synonym for "one," Detective Sidwell presents himself as speaking for anybody – anybody would have this feeling – but they would also dislike having the feeling. With this general use of "you," he presupposes that any person would take issue with a victim returning to her abusive partner over and over again, and this claim is made in a context void of consideration of the lived experiences of individual victims, their reasons for staying, their reasons for returning, and their reasons for eventually leaving.

On line 11, another evasion, using the procedural identity discussed earlier. "We try to do everything right based on policy and procedure and state law." This is another exonerational statement, back in the "we," police officer voice. What police do, their decision-making, is not individual; it is prescribed by policy, procedure, and state law. Police procedure and attendant identity protect this speaker from the ramifications of decisions made under the auspices of policies, procedures, and laws. They also make this detective, and those that fall under "we" good officers, who know how to do their jobs. Finally, all of this exemption and hedging ends in the first true evaluation of victims of domestic violence. "Don't call me, if you don't want us to *do* something" (line 12). Detective Sidwell even moves into a "me" voice to make this claim, truly owning it. This is a warning to victims: Victims, do not call the police if you are not prepared to have them follow their procedure and if you are not prepared to leave.

The buildup to the first evaluation of victim behavior comes after much justification:

- "they felt a bad moment," (line 3)
- "why did you get him from jail, again?" (line 8)
- "you hate having this feeling," (line 10)
- Follow "policy and procedure and state law," (line 11)
- "Don't call me if you don't want us to do something," (line 12)
- "It can be super frustrating when you are trying to help somebody, and" (lines 15 and 16)
- "they continue to shun you away" (line 17).

This crescendo shifts from "we" to "you" and moves through a distancing effort that references policy and procedure, thereby shedding any individual, personal, or in this case even group responsibility. This process makes the negative views about domestic violence victims seem typical and expected – what any person would think and feel – rather than personal, individual, or even generally held by the group of police officers.

"You" is an interesting pronoun in Extract 4.3. It is both used to accuse the general-victim, and it is used to reference the any-person. We see the first use of "you" on lines 8 and 12, where "you" is a generalized victim. In both uses of "you," victims are critiqued for staying with abusive partners without a corollary critique of abusers. This "you" is critical. In lines 19–21, "you" becomes any person, a general "you" that both captures the speaker, the listener, and people in general. We see the second use of "you" in this sentence: "You're trying to help somebody, and they continue to shun you away, and bring the problem back that you then have to deal with again." Instead of using "me" or "I," which would personalize the statement, Detective Sidwell uses plural, general "you" – "you're trying to help" – which adds distance and makes the process of shunning away law enforcement seem like it happens to all police officers and like it is normal and typical for most victims – "they." This then brings the problem back to the general "you," police officers, who have to deal again with the "problem." Is the problem the victim or domestic violence? I suggest it is both, with the blame for domestic violence falling on the victim who refuses to leave. No culpability lies with the abuser. This is a representation of a group identity positioned against and performed through a critique of victims, especially those who are oppositional, recalcitrant, or stay in abusive situations.

After creating an antagonistic relationship between police and victims, Detective Sidwell makes the justificatory, explanatory declaration of identity, "being human" (line 14), as a way to set up for the next victim critique that "it can be super frustrating when you're trying to help somebody, and they continue to shun you away, and bring the problem back that you then have to deal with again" (lines 15–18). "Being human" is an identity claim to regular human weakness. It is also a claim to being a regular person – not always an arm of/for law enforcement. As regular people, not as police officers, this speaker is frustrated with a recurrent situation that he can neither stop nor control, forgetting the fact that 75 percent of intimate partners continue to experience abuse after they have left their abusive partners (NCADV, 2018).

What we have here is an identity of policing that is complex. It involves many components, all of which emerge in a telling of a generalized prior interaction and in relationship to an/other, in this case, victims of domestic violence. This identity is multiple, fragmented, and partial, including the indexical notes: regular guy, human, frustration, rejected, problem solver, in control, and caring. The identity that emerges in this extract is a multifaceted and compelling account of policing and police identity. Some of the elements are apparently semi-stable identity formations in police discourse that can be animated and performed, creating a group identity that binds police officers together and makes them recognizable.

In Extract 4.4, we return to Detective Jacobs, who topicalizes officer safety, a point that comes up on multiple occasions in this extract, as well as in every other interview with a police officer.

Extract 4.4 Detective Jacobs

1.	*Det. Jacobs*:	Domestic calls are, are, are quite frequent,
2.		and obviously they first start off with a patrol level where
3.		everyone's here started off with.
4.		They go from ten, I guess you could say, all the way down
5.		to trying to figure out what it is.
6.		We're pretty lucky that our dispatch is trying to get us as
7.		much information as they can,
8.		Whether there is history on that area, or on the complainants,
9.		or who's calling in, or who the witness is, or anything like that,
10.		as we're going through the case.
11.		And that's more to give us more of an officer safety issue,
12.		so other than to have any preconceived ideas about what's going on.
13.		Although, if we have been to the house, 4, 5, 6, 7, 8, 9, 10, 20 times,
14.		then obviously we kinda have a—
15.		not a preconceived idea about what's going on,
16.		But, uh uh, knowledge of the house, the residents, and
17.		possibly what's happening on there.
18.		But, your first, your first thing is— we try to, officer safety.
19.		We don't wanna add more drama, or more confusion, or more uh, bad
20.		elements, I guess, to the crime.
21.		We'll start off basically with officer safety
22.		and ensure that there's at least 2 officers at this thing, because they're very volatile.
23.		It's probably the next dangerous thing next to a traffic stop.

24.	\<aside to group\> It was just funny that we've all done motors [motorcycle/traffic patrol].
25.	It is. Because for one minute they love each other,
26.	the next minute they hate each other,
27.	but if you take one of them to jail, or not, now they both hate you.
28.	Officer safety is paramount, for us to be able to make sure that we do that.
29.	We don't park in front of the house.
30.	We make sure we have at least two officers in the room, and
31.	then we take a situation as it goes, right?
32.	At that moment in time, we're just fact finders.
33.	But we're trying to find out what's going on,
34.	but we're trying to do it as safely as possible.
35.	If that means to separate them, whether it's just by room, or
36.	having them sit down and be able to talk to them,
37.	as, as we figure out what's happening,
38.	that would be our first step on what's going on.

As Detective Jacobs says on line 28, "Officer safety is paramount," as it should be. Indeed, he indexes officer safety and the dangerous nature of domestic calls five times total, on lines 11, 18, 21, 22, and 34. This is clearly an issue of importance. Because of how dangerous domestic violence calls are, a fact that is well documented, officer safety affects procedure: how many people answer the call, where they park their cars, how they approach the residence, and the like. Thus, procedure emerges as an identity point alongside officer's acknowledgment of their own danger and the importance of safety protocols. Identities of safety and of fact-finder emerges in lines 33 and 34, together with safety procedure, structured with two subordinating conjunctions, "but." "At that moment in time, we're just fact finders, but we're trying to find out what's going on, but we're trying to do it as safely as possible" (lines 31–33). The use of "but" implies that the next clause will contest some aspect of the preceding clause, and it is an interesting choice for the linking together of these specific clauses. This sentence breaks down to this: We are looking for evidence, but more than that, we are investigating the situation, but more than that, we need to stay safe. That is, collecting evidence is presented as the most important aspect of police work, an idea that is complicated using "but" to present the idea of investigating the situation. Finally, using "but" again, officer safety is presented as the most important aspect of police work. The string of subordinating conjunctions creates a sort of cascading effect, where the final clause is the most important, which has the effect of positioning officer safety as the highest value on a domestic call.

Identity emerges in this talk about procedure and officer safety – a group self that is cautious and that follows the rules and the law. In the middle of this procedural narrative about protocol and procedure that focuses on fact finding and officer safety, Detective Jacobs inserts a statement about abuse victims/survivors and perpetrators. That is, as he performs a policing procedural identity, he also chooses to position against domestic violence victims. He positions in relation to domestic violence, abusers, and especially victims. This statement is sandwiched between a comment on how dangerous domestic calls are and police safety:

> It's probably the next dangerous thing next to a traffic stop. […] It is because for one minute they love each other, the next minute they hate each other, but if you take one of them to jail, or not, now they both hate you […] Officer safety is paramount for us to be able to make sure that we do that. (lines 29, 32–34, 36)

In this statement, we see a positioning against victims that occurs in the context of officer safety identity emergence. Here, we see Detective Jacobs characterize relationships, lumping the abuser and the abused together with the pronoun "they," characterizing their relationship as merely dysfunctional, and completely jettisoning abuse. That is, instead of talking about the abuse going on in the home leading the victim to call police, which may affect officer safety, he talks about the couple in a shifting relationship that is sometimes loving and sometimes hateful. The phrasing, "they love each other […] they hate each other" (lines 25 and 26) forgets the context of abuse, and in doing so, it situates the victim and the abuser as equals on the same playing field, with the group pronoun "they." Further, it is their fluctuating affection for each other that makes the situation so dangerous. Finally, the real problem is that the victim is participating in the anger against the police for making an arrest. The victim is framed as problematic because or when they continue to support an abusive partner instead of the work of the police. Both points made – the erasure of violence and the characterization of the victim as on equal footing with their abusive partner – creates the backdrop against which the notion of officer safety can emerge. This construction of a fully agented victim is further solidified and iconicized (see Chapter 2) when she is framed as taking the side of her intimate partner against police, "now they both hate you."

In this discussion of domestic calls inserted in a discussion of officer safety, the victim is consistently narrated as part of a relationship, as with her abuser, and as taking his side. Victim decision-making thus emerges as a feature of, and a concern in, officer safety and the related identity formation. To put a finer point on it, victim behavior is positioned as a liability with regard to officer safety. Victims can create dangerous situations or make a dangerous situation worse.

4.4 Recalcitrant Victims

Recalcitrant victims are those victims who are presented in police stories as unreasonable, oppositional, combative, committed to their abuser, and/ or staying in abusive relationships. Extracts 4.5–4.7 all deal with victims who are framed as recalcitrant and uncooperative – a typical feature in a common storyline about domestic violence in stories told by police officers. For each storyteller presented here, the difficult victim provides a backdrop against which a number of different identities emerge for the teller, a police officer. Rather than managing the identity relationship between victim and police officer using pronouns as we saw above, these extracts use quotations and topicalization. Victim opposition to jailing an abusive partner is the point of all three of the police narratives analyzed in this section.

In Extract 4.5, Detective Sidwell tells a story about a victim who will not cooperate with police wishes. Rather than seeing him go to jail, the victim just wants her abusive partner to leave for the night.

Extract 4.5 Detective Sidwell

1.	*Det. Sidwell:*	Yeah, some victims just want us to make him be nice, or her be nice.
2.		They want us to end whatever situation they're in.
3.		Um, and because what we're able to use, as a tool—
4.		Really the only tool we have is incarceration.
5.		Um, and so when that's explained, and a lot of it's like,
6.		"well, I don't wanna cooperate."
7.		"I just want him to leave for the night," or
8.		"wanted her to do this for the day."
9.		So we've had, you know those victims that range—
10.		every call is different, and as he said, from 1 to 10.
11.		You know, sometimes it's like, well, we just argued.
12.		Had a case early on where, as we were walking the- the spouse to the car,
13.		to book him in jail,
14.		because there was evidence to show that he had committed a crime.

15.	Um, the other half did not want him to go.
16.	As we were walking out, actually attacked the officer by jumping on his back,
17.	and scratching and pulling at him.
18.	Um. So. again, we don't know what we're arriving on, or what we see
19.	until we're on scene.
20.	[Western] state laws can sometimes work against us,
21.	because it does state that we shall arrest,
22.	if there is evidence that a crime has probable cause to-
23.	that a crime has been committed.
24.	So, i— it's intended to protect the victim, and it can protect the victim, but
25.	sometimes it can ultimately be a hindrance,
26.	because if they don't want them to be booked into jail, or be charged,
27.	um, it can really reduce their cooperation with us.
28.	And in some regards it can create additional hardships for a- a-
29.	couple that is struggling,
30.	because now we have to arrest.

Detective Sidwell begins his narrative in Extract 4.5 with a common claim about victims, they "just want us to make him be nice" (line 1). According to Detective Sidwell, victims want an end to the violence, but not more; they do not necessarily desire incarceration for the abuser. Indeed, in lines 3 and 4, Detective Sidwell states that the only "tool" that he has, ostensibly to make the abusive party "be nice," is "incarceration." Incarceration is not the wish of the hypothetical victim he stories in this extract. However, as he narrates it, his hands are tied legally and ideologically. State law requires an arrest if there has been an assault, and Detective Sidwell clearly sees this as the best option, given the circumstances. Incarceration is thus the only readily available way for law enforcement to deal with a physically abusive partner. Yet, jail time is not the result that the hypothetical victim in Extract 4.5 desires.

When victims learn the law, according to Detective Sidwell and other officers, they can become recalcitrant. To make this point, Detective Sidwell turns to the use of quotations, putting words into a victim's mouth, but not just this specific victim (lines 6–9). He creates a sort of every-victim when he speaks through the victim, animating the victim using direct quotation. Using this technique, he indicates what he thinks the every-victim wants. The use of quotation puts the ideas and words in the mouth of the victim. Detective Sidwell does not present these ideas as his. Even though he is making assumptions about speaker goals, motivations, and ideas, using direct quotation, he presents them as though they are the victims. In response to learning about state mandatory arrest policies, this victim is characterized as saying, "well, I don't wanna cooperate" (line 6). The victim is characterized not just of behaving uncooperatively, whatever that looks like, but of saying directly that she does not want to cooperate with police. This ups the ante for the behavior that Detective Sidwell finds aberrant. The victim is also quoted as saying, "I just want him to leave for the night" (line 7). The use of quotation adds a feeling of realness and factuality to Detective Sidwell's claim, as though these are a real person's words rather than merely a paraphrase or gestures to what victims are likely to say in Detective Sidwell's opinion. Using this ventriloquism technique, it is as though the victim herself is saying that she is uncooperative.

Having also established his knowledge of the law at the beginning of the narrative, this construction of the victim as uncooperative, voiced by themselves, provides the backdrop against which a procedural, law-following identity emerges for the detective. What is interesting is that this identity emerges in concert with the production of an "uncooperative victim" persona that is attributed to the narrative other. His expertise becomes dependent not only on his experience but also on his characterization of a victim as recalcitrant.

Extract 4.5 amounts to a story about a victim of domestic violence who does not want her abusive partner taken away to jail. This a representation of the essential recalcitrant victim, the "every victim". Lines 15–18 are a narrative about a specific, individual woman who fought police when she found out that they were taking her partner to jail. Jail comes to equal recalcitrance and violence on the part of the victim in narratives like these. It is not, importantly, aligned with the abuser and their actions. Detective Sidwell's identity as law follower and law enforcer emerges in contrast to the victim's lack of cooperation and violence not the abuser's violence and actions. Detective Sidwell had found evidence that a crime had been committed (line 14), and in that case, the law required an arrest. He states this relationship between the law and arrest again in lines 22, 26, and 30, topicalizing the law further. Then on lines 27–30, he topicalizes law and the cooperation of victims together, moving again to a characterization of the every-victim, the general victim. "So, [the law] i-- it's intended to protect the victim, and it can protect the victim, but sometimes it can ultimately be a hindrance, because if they don't want them to be booked into jail, or be charged, [...] it can really reduce their cooperation with us." The law and the victim are topicalized together in the first two clauses about protecting the victim – law/protect/victim. Then the topic shifts to "it" (law)/hindrance, and then "they" (victims in general)/jail. We can see in the progression of the noun relationships a move from a relationship between law and victim to a relationship between victim and jail (law) to a relationship between cooperation and "us" (police). What Detective Sidwell really wants is cooperative victims that support him in his job – enforcing the law. The mandatory arrest law is positioned as a hindrance primarily to police who have to work with uncooperative victims. Victims make police work harder.

In the noun flow, relationships between subjects and objects, the primary relationship is between police and victim, not police and abuser. This is the process of policing the victim. "Victim" becomes the foil against which a semi-stable identity of law and procedure identity emerges for police. This identity is punctuated with a claim that Detective Sidwell does not want to make things harder for a "couple that is struggling" (line 29). This adds, again for Detective Sidwell, an identity of caring and a valuing of relationships that we have seen from him before, and it is one that sometimes forgets in fundamental ways that a person is being abused in the storied events.

In Extract 4.6, Detective Tyler tells a story quite similar to that told by Detective Sidwell. In this experience that he calls "typical," a couple with a child called police in the course of a fight.

Extract 4.6 Detective Tyler

1.	Det. Tyler:	Uh, I went on— and it's your typical—
2.		it was a boyfriend girlfriend.
3.		I don't know if they were married,
4.		but they were living together and they had a child.
5.		And, uh, we go in and—I believe they had been drinking,
6.		if I remember correct—Um,
7.		had gotten into an argument and he had thrown and broke some things and
8.		got a little bit—
9.		he didn't really hit her, but he threw some things and broke 'em.
10.		Based on the fact that he was—in his attitude towards us—
11.		he was very aggressive, uh, very—
12.		Uh, we decided that he needed to go to jail.
13.		That if we left the situation as is, that he was gonna—

14.		there could be further violence, so we decided to take him into custody.
15.		when we do, the fight's on. Um.
16.		The minute we start fighting with him, she gets involved
17.	*Jenny*:	Oh no.
18.	*Det. Tyler*:	because she doesn't want us to take him to jail.
19.		And, and we end up having to fight both of them.
20.		Luckily, nobody got hurt, you know, but
21.		that's just a kind of perfect example.
22.		There were several. I can say multiple that have been like that,
23.		or they'll phone in a complaint afterwards on excessive force or things like that.

[...]

24.	*Det. Tyler*:	At the time, I think they knew or just assumed that we wouldn't understand.
25.		They don't want us to do something. What they—
26.		Usually, they come to it, "Yeah, he broke this picture or broke something,
27.		but I don't wanna charge him with anything."
28.		They don't understand that we don't have a choice.
29.		That being said, we have to do our job.
30.	*Jenny*:	It's dangerous for them; for them to stay, that would be dangerous for them.
31.	*Det. Tyler:*	Yeah.
32.	*Jenny:*	Are they overlooking that because they don't want 'em to go to jail?
33.	*Det. Tyler:*	Well, I think that they probably perceive that it's gonna be more dangerous
34.		when he gets out and comes back.
35.		It's like, "I can probably handle what's coming at me right now but,
36.		later, if he blames me for this."

In Extract 4.6, Detective Tyler describes a fight, which he largely represents as between equals with the use of "they." On line 7, he says, "had gotten into an argument." The pronoun use/elision on line 8 is quite interesting. "Had gotten into an argument" apparently borrows the "they" from the line, "they had been drinking" (line 5). Using the "they" in the context of the "argument" distributes fault across both members of the couple. Later in line 7, he introduces the pronoun "he," the person who "broke some things." The abuser is referenced directly, as are Detective Tyler and his police officer partner. Together the two officers decided that because the abuser was behaving very aggressively, "he needed to go to jail" (line 12). In response to the police decision to make an arrest, the victim gets upset. "When we do [take him into custody], the fight is on" (line 15). This victim is storied as combative and uncooperative, working against the best practices of and legal constraints on police work. The recalcitrant victim is introduced alongside a discussion of law, good police practice, and procedure, as it was in Detective Sidwell's interview. This victim, though narrated as an individual, is essentially represented as a type, a common type. Detective Tyler makes it clear that this is not an isolated incident, but rather what he calls "a kind of perfect example" of "multiple that have been like that" (lines 21–23). This is a perfect example of the every-victim.

On lines 28 and 29, Detective Tyler makes a very direct identity statement that positions victims against police officers, and in it, he continues to discuss the every-victim, while placing the motivation for his decision to arrest on the "job." "[Victims] don't understand that we don't have a choice. That being said, we have to do our job" (lines 28 and 29). We see this equation emerge:

Victims do not get it + it is out of police hands (law) + just the job.

An identity emerges here in which police are doing the job they are sworn to do, and victims simply do not understand the "job" or the law. Victims disrupt police procedure and policy. Victims are treated as a interference for police, who are just following the law and doing their jobs.

Another identity emerges at the close of Extract 4.6, one of understanding and caring. When I asked Detective Tyler why he thought victims didn't want to see their abusive partners jailed, he said, "they probably perceive that it's gonna be more dangerous when he gets out and comes back" (lines 33, 34). He suggests that victims worry that abusers will blame them for the incarceration, even though it is state law and out of victim hands. This gentle, understanding discussion of victims shows a kind of caring for victims and a contextual understanding of the complexities of their plights.

Extract 4.7 gives an account of another situation in which the victim disagreed with police decisions against her abusive partner.

Extract 4.7 Detective Jacobs

1.	Det. Jacobs:	So: I had one—this was last year.
2.		Um, initially when the report came in to us,
3.		um, it was actually the suspect who called dispatch and said,
4.		"I need to be taken to jail. I just attacked my wife."
5.		When the officer arrived on scene, um he found the suspect outside, and
6.		he walked right up to him, and
7.		he said, "put handcuffs on me, and take me to jail. I— I hit her."
8.		And they made contact with her in the home.
9.		There wasn't really anything as far as evidentiary value there.
10.		Uh, but all she could say was that,
11.		"I can't remember what happened, why does my head hurt?"
12.		So the officer thought, he-- he must've hit her to the point she has concussion.
13.		Fire came out, evaluated her, and they took her to the hospital, and
14.		just based on that particular information, determined that—
15.		okay this guy's admitted he has assaulted her.
16.		She appears to have been assaulted.
17.		They book him in jail on a class B misdemeanor.
18.		About 6 to 8 hours later, she comes back and says she's starting to remember
19.		what happened, and
20.		actually, uh, says that he pointed a gun at her, and threatened to kill her.
21.		That kind of just got put as new— in— information in the report
22.		and it didn't really go much further until I got it.
23.		I saw that. Um, I followed up with her further information after I received it, and
24.		it sounds like a pretty solid case of, he did push her.
25.		Um, after he pushed her onto the ground, he retrieved a firearm, and
26.		he was going to attempt to—what he ended up later saying was a

27.	murder suicide, was his original plan.
28.	He just backed out of it.
29.	Um, so as soon as I got that information, I made contact with our district
30.	attorney, and it went from a class B misdemeanor to a secondary
31.	felony with a firearm.
32.	Um, she had been initially, been very happy about us doing something.
33.	Over that following weekend, I actually got a phone call from her,
34.	and it went to my voicemail, and
35.	she was leaving me a pretty upset message that I had just ruined her whole life.
36.	Um, so I called her back, I talked to her, and she said,
37.	"Why would you charge him with that?"
38.	"Now he's going to be even more mad, and he, he shouldn't be in jail."
39.	I asked her, "Why shouldn't he be in jail considering from what you've told me
40.	and what he's also told me he did."
41.	She just kept going on that he has mental illnesses, and
42.	that this was just something that happened, and
43.	she started making comments to me that if he's out of jail, he's going to kill me.
44.	"I know he'll kill me,"
45.	but kept begging me at the same time to not go through.
46.	I kept at it, why would you want us to let this person out of jail if you truly
47.	believe he's going to kill you, and
48.	he has almost acted on that?
49.	And, uh, it really just came back to her just saying
50.	he doesn't deserve to be there.

| 51. | *Det. Sidwell:* | She still loved him. |
| 52. | *Det. Jacobs:* | Still loved him, still wanted to be there for him |

In Extract 4.7, Detective Jacobs painstakingly walks us through law enforcement and legal procedure. In lines 28–32, he makes the following claims:

- He noticed details in a report that hadn't been followed up on.
- He called the victim to follow up.

- He determined that "it sound[ed] like a pretty solid case of, he [the assailant] did push her."
- "[The abuser] retrieved a firearm," and
- The abuser had planned to use it in a murder suicide, which he backed out of.

These details add up to jail and a felony charge because of the use of a gun. As was the case in the previous two extracts, the victim fought the police officer on the upgraded charges, because she was afraid of her abusive partner. "Why would you charge him with that?" she says on line 37. "Now he's going to be even more mad," she goes on to say on line 38. The victim is represented as fearing her husband's fury at the felony charges, and even though Detective Jacobs represents this fear, he does not seem to understand it. Fear of an abusive partner and fear of angering an abusive partner do not resonate with him. He understands and trusts the law and law enforcement's ability to keep her safe. He is confused by the victim's behavior, leading him to editorialize about her position. If she is afraid of him, why would she want him out of jail? Jail will keep the abuser away from a victim, if only for a few months. There is no recognition that abuse may escalate after incarceration. As Detective Jacobs talks through his bewilderment at the victim's response, Detective Sidwell gives an answer as to why she wants to keep her abuser out of jail: "She still loved him" (line 51). As we have seen multiple times, Detective Sidwell is deeply invested in a cultural narrative of romantic love, and thus, he attributes loving feelings to this victim. Detective Jacobs supports Detective Sidwell's statement when he responds with "Still loved him, still wanted to be there for him" (line 52). While that may be true, it may not be, or love may just be one of a number of reasons. She may be afraid of retaliation, which she is represented as expressing. She may feel like her abuser is misunderstood. She may feel a number of things. What the officers go to is love, drawing on and reinforcing social notions about relationships and romantic love.

Against a backdrop of stories about recalcitrant victims, police officers situate, perform, and construct identities of procedural knowledge and law enforcement. It is as though the group that needs to be schooled by the law are the victims rather than the abusers. In these stories, it is the victim who is policed. Alongside this identity founded in accusing victims of misbehavior, an identity of caring also emerges. One that is rich with concern. This is a complex, multifaceted identity, indeed, and it is one that is echoed in the complicated responses of victims to police in their own storying of police encounters.

4.5 Conclusions

Identity is produced from without and within. It emerges in relationship to constructions and characterizations of others and to identities that are assigned to others. It also draws on prior discourses and performances of identity that were successful and that link the speaker to a group identity. Identity qualities are assigned in narratives, ascribed to other active others narrated in the course of the story as a way of performing identity for the speaker. What we find in the police narratives about domestic violence victims is a recapitulation of general and specific events and descriptions of victims/survivors, both of which aid in the performance and emergence of their own identities individually and of a kind of group identity for police officers in general. This all takes place within a field of policing discourse that is saturated by topics such as policy, procedure, and law. Following and enforcing the law, and following proper policy and procedure are fundamental elements of a generalized police identity that circulates within the discourse of policing. In that field of indexicality, we also find complicated notions about frustration with and caring for victims/survivors of domestic violence. These views are circulating in the discourse of policing, acting as a resource for identity emergence (police) and identity attribution (victims/survivors) alike. This discourse creates an indexical link between victims/survivors as frustrating and in need of help and police officers as both frustrated and caring, and providing help. In the assignment of identity to the victims/survivors, there is a heavy emphasis on their lack of cooperation and recalcitrance. Police identity emerges against this backdrop of victim/survivor identity assignment. Police identity is oppositionally constructed and performed against the assumed identity of recalcitrance for victims/survivors.

Identity, then, can be formed in narrative in relationship to others who are framed, explained, described, and generally talked about. In the telling of a story, the selection of details, the ordering of events, and the editorializing of an "other" are all presented in such a way as to allow identity for the teller to emerge and be performed. Identity emerges in the interview interaction, where the performance of identity constructed and performed in the narrated interactions may or may not be taken up. That notwithstanding, it is clear that an identity can be performed in the careful construction of recapitulated events in a narrative about something that is not the self, but in which the self emerges, nonetheless.

Conclusions
Toward a Reconceptualization of Domestic Violence

This book has dealt with issues of identity and indexicality as those issues emerge in the stories of domestic violence victims/survivors and the police officers who answer domestic calls. Complex issues of emotional and physical violence, family, pregnancy, policing, and agency have emerged. The question of leaving has loomed heavy over these analyses, as victims/survivors and the police grapple with the huge social issue that is domestic violence. I want to begin this conclusion where I began the book – with the story of Killingsworth, specifically, her leaving story. Not only was I physically present when she made the decision to leave a decade ago, but I had the opportunity to interview her for this project. What follows is her leaving story. As we saw in other leaving stories, it is filled with the emotional and physical violence that she lived with on a daily basis for at least four years. As we saw in other such stories, Killingsworth's story is punctuated with resolve and insight into abuse and violence. She also explains why she did not ever call the police, and the role that emotional violence/coercive control played in that decision. In what follows, Killingworth begins by recalling a feeling that the abuse was escalating.

Extract C.1 Killingsworth

1.	*Killingsworth:*	"This is just—this is - this is clearly, like, I'm not allowed to do things,
2.		uh, and this is bad."
3.		And I remember, um, I think I must have been
4.		having back pain, or cramps, or something.
5.		And he used to—he was a huge pill popper and
6.		would feed me as many pills as I wanted
7.		that he got from his dad.
8.		So I think I remember I had— I had asked for a muscle relaxer or a pain pill and
9.		I was lying on my back in the entry way and

10.		he sat on top of me so that his crotch was on my chest.
11.		And his— his knees were on my biceps, so he had pinned me down that way.
12.		And he had the pill and he was shoving it in my mouth.
13.		And mocking—and laughing and
14.		I was resisting and saying, "Stop it. Stop it. Stop it."
15.		And he started slapping my face.
16.		And I was so immobile—
17.		and that's, like, when I—that was kinda, like, that moment where I was like,
18.		"Oh my god. This has - this has never been to this degree before."
19.		"And, um, I can't move, and this is serious."
20.		And when he got up off of me I said to him, "You're breaking my heart."
21.		And he said, "Shut the fuck up." And he kicked me in the vagina.
22.		And I think that was, among everything else, that was just the signal that,
23.		like, there's—this - this could get so bad I - I don't even know.
24.		And then, of course, um, all of the loaded guns in the house.
25.		And he had threatened to kill me many, many, many times in a joking way.
26.		But - so it was just like the perfect storm of all of these things coming together.
27.		And me saying that I think it really it was, "I don't want to have a baby with this man."
28.		And my only way—my only—I can't talk my way out of this.
29.		My only way to do this is to completely disappear.

[...]

30.	*Jenny:*	Why didn't you call the police?
31.	*Killingsworth:*	Because it didn't seem like, um, it wasn't loud violence.
32.		Everything was so quiet, and everything was so—
33.		because I was waiting— I knew it would quiet down afterwards.
34.		So I knew that all I had to do was get through it.

35.	I understood the logic and the rules of the violence.
36.	Um, and I just— I— it was mostly because it never crossed my mind that what I
37.	was going through merited a phone call to the police.

In Extract C.1, Killingsworth clearly articulates a moment of physical and emotional abuse. Her abuser had trapped her in a violent relationship in which she had internalized the rules and logics of violence. He joked about killing her; he mocked and laughed at her; he pinned her down and stopped her from moving. He also physically assaulted her, holding her down and slapping her. She was rendered immobile and physically and emotionally assaulted. It was in this moment that Killingsworth knew she couldn't survive, literally and emotionally, in this marriage. In this moment, she felt the violence and intuited the patterns of escalation, and she was afraid. In lines 16–22, she says, "And I was so immobile – and that's, like, when I – that was kinda, like, that moment where I was like, 'Oh my god. This has - this has never been to this degree before.'" She connects the emotional/ physical violence of immobility with escalation and her need to leave the relationship. This was the moment when she realized that it was getting and could continue to get worse, more violent.

Following this story of violence and resolve, Killingsworth explains why she never called the police. Even though the violence she describes is heinous and serious, her everyday regime of "coercive control" (Stark) had been internalized and normalized for her in some ways. It did not seem like a big enough deal to call the police. As Killingsworth puts it, "Because it didn't seem like, um— it wasn't loud violence" (line 31). That is, it did not seem like the kind of violence that warranted a call to the police. It didn't match the volume and type of physical violence that Killingsworth, and so many, have come to associate with domestic violence. Images of extreme physical violence run through our culture as domestic violence, the black eye, the broken ribs. We also have ideas about fighting and verbal abuse, such as the childhood adage, "sticks and stones may break my bones, but names will never hurt me," which is, in effect, a commentary on verbal violence that negates its effects. These two discursive formations come together in domestic violence, making verbal and emotional abuses hard to recognize as violence, let alone as reportable to law enforcement. To further complicate social messaging, the regime of emotional violence under which Killingsworth lived, her subjugation, stopped her from recognizing that it was possible to report events that had until this moment seemed everyday and normal. Before this, events of violence were just waited out; she would wait for it to "quiet down afterwards" (line 33). So, she was stuck between expectations of what is required to call the police, social narratives of domestic violence, and her own experiences of emotional violence. Yet, she escaped that relationship. Domestic violence victims do leave. They leave every day.

Killingsworth has told these stories before. She has told them in many different venues, for different audiences, and with different purposes. Like most victims of domestic violence, she has told these stories to judges, to paralegals, to attorneys, to friends, to therapists, to strangers, and to family. She is adept at managing the content differently as the situation demands. In each telling, an identity emerges in interaction with her interlocutor and in context. When I've listened to her tell her story as a friend, she is more vulnerable and emotional, for example, than she was telling the story in a research setting. She sometimes focuses more on being a victim, sometimes a survivor, sometimes as strong, sometimes as pained. None of these identities emerge in solo, but more typically in concert with each other, partial and multiple. Each identity that emerges becomes a resource to be used strategically or accidentally in future performances of the narrative, which comes with attendant identities. That is, once an identity is ratified by an audience and for a teller, it becomes a resource for future identities. While none of these identities are fully durable and stable, neither are they fully ethereal and diffuse. An identity can be/come a feature of an indexical field, where the identity has the potential to be activated, turned on, so to speak, as the speaker does identity work in future tellings and contexts. Again, there is not macro- super-identity, but there are smaller, fragmented, partial, and fluid identities, which emerge in the telling, sometimes by animating a potential identity resourced from the indexical field. As I have argued here, identity work occurs in a field of indexicality that constrains, limits, and enables identity work, a process we see Killingsworth work through in Extract C.1.

One theme that has run through the preceding chapters is the idea of the recalcitrant victim, the victim who returns to her/his abuser time and time again. The idea of recalcitrance is established in the discourses of the police, who are consistently "frustrated" that people living in abusive relationships do not leave post haste. The recalcitrant victim is also often emotionally and verbally abused, calling the police for matters that are noncriminal. The police seem to see such behaviors as time-wasters – answering calls that are civil rather than criminal for people who aren't going to leave the relationship anyway. I want to make two points in this conclusion: First, lacking the immediate decision to leave immediately does not make a person recalcitrant. Indeed, there are other ways of understanding what is going on, factors that the police refer to as "bad excuses" (Officer Angel). Second, emotional violence is real violence, demanding and deserving the attention of the police officers.

In this conclusion, I will continue to work with aspects of Killingsworth's story as I pull together the major strands of theory, analysis, and thought in this book. In particular, I will focus my discussion on indexicality and ideology, identity and narrative, policing discourses and the expectation of recalcitrance from victims, emotional violence and coercive control. I will conclude with a discussion of the limitations of this study, in particular, the exclusion of the macro-social categories of race, gender, and class. These issues certainly impact domestic violence, and domestic violence certainly manifests itself differently with regard to issues of race, class, and gender. They have been avoided because they did not emerge in the data and because I had to keep my participants' identities completely secret. There is, nevertheless, important and relevant research on these topics that I will discuss at the end of this conclusion.

C.1 Indexicality, Ideology, and Agency

As a way of beginning and of reminding the reader, Eckert (2008) defines an indexical field, as "a constellation of ideologically related meanings." An indexical field, then, is a discursive formation peppered with variables that are related via a value or belief system to which those speakers have access. Each variable has multiple potential meanings that can be animated by a speaker in order to produce social meaning in some fashion. I have argued in the preceding chapters that in the process of animating variables within the ideological framework of the indexical field, identities are performed and emerge, identities that are themselves often part of the indexical field. That is, identities are sometimes semistable, accessible formations that circulate in the indexical field, and as a speaker tells stories that animate identity variables, as well as other variables that take the form of words, phrases, and pronoun uses, identity emerges.

Blommaert (2007) argues for a type of indexicality that is both emergent and structured. "Indexicality, even though largely operating at the implicit level of linguistic/semiotic structuring, is not understood but *ordered*, [...] account[ing] for 'normativity in semiosis" (Blommaert, 2007, p. 116). That is, through indexicality, we find normativity – typified ways of interacting discursively in order to produce meanings that are both social and ideological. These are fields of indices that are available for meaning-making. For example, there are normalized, regularized ways of talking about domestic violence that make presumptions about what the best course of action for the victim is, discourses that normalize home life, discourses that presuppose the harmlessness of emotional and verbal violence, all of which show up in police discourses – all of which are animated in the indexical field in police officer speech and narrative. Thus, the indexical field is patterned. Blommaert (2007,pp. 116–117) explains Silverstein's "indexical order" this way: "Indexical meanings occur in patterns offering perceptions of similarity and stability that can be perceived as 'types' of semiotic practice with predictable (presupposable/ entailing) directions." Meaning- making is expected because of the patterns and potentialities of the indexical field, patterns that are recognizable and animatable because of and within ideological frameworks.

Victims/survivors of domestic violence and police officers animate different variables differently, because they are operating with different worldviews, experiences, and ideological frames. "Clustered and patterned language forms that index specific social personae and roles, can be invoked to organize interactional practices" (Blommaert, 2007, p. 117). Blommaert thus also sees something like identity as circulating in the indexical field. These identities are neither static nor fully dynamic. We might say, instead, that they are rhetorical. They can be operationalized to perform particular functions and do identity work, but they are not stagnant. They are deployed in ways that match the expectations and interests of the situation and interlocutors, who of course participate in the emergence of identity. Emergent, of course, but also available for performance in important ways – as clusters of practices that have been performed more than once. Performances that work, that have been ratified, and that are thus available within the indexical field.

Not only is identity a feature of the indexical order, the indexical field for individuals, but also for groups. Indeed, individual identity is related to and indexes group identity in important ways. That is, the indexical field is productive – it creates that which it names, both ideologically and materially. In laying out potentialities, meaning-making is constrained in productive ways, in ways that produce subject positions. This productive process takes place at the group and individual levels, creating hierarchies.

> Indexical order of this sort is a positive force, it processes [?] social categories, recognizable semiotic emblems for groups and individuals, a more or less coherent semiotic habitat. It does so, however, within the confines of a stratified general repertoire, in which particular indexical orders relate to others in relations of mutual valuation – higher/lower, better/worse. (Blommaert, 2007, p. 117)

Thus, within the patterned, ordered indexical field, ideology comes to play in making some variables, some ways of talking, some ways of making meaning, some stories more desirable than others. We see this in the relationship between police discourse and victim/survivor discourse. Having institutional power as they do, having the power to arrest, which they do, the ways in which the police describe emotional violence, for example, are more effective than victim discourses on the same topic. The meaning of the policing variable is granted more weight. Further, it is more hearable in the society at large, given its weight, and given its affinities with popular discourses on domestic violence. Thus, as Blommaert (2007, 117) puts it, "Systematic patterns of indexicality are also systemic patterns of authority, of control and evaluation, and hence of inclusion and exclusion *by real or perceived others.*" The patterning and structuration, however much they exist, are ideological. Not only is the pattern a product of ideology, of value systems and hierarchies in which female victims of domestic violence fall to the bottom, it is also an ideological framework that performs the function of ideology.

So far, I have been primarily considering the ways that individuals animate elements of the indexical field to perform acts of identity. Indeed, that is only one use of the indexical field. It is also animated in order to think about, constrain, enable, and story the other, other people and groups of people in the story being told. In their storytelling, the participants in this study often animate particular identities for themselves in the process of labeling other groups, often by animating variables within the indexical field. Thus, interactional structures are deeply indexical, with meaning being partially assigned by those who story the interaction. Likewise, events are indexical. Domestic violence is an indexical formation that is produced and reproduced when elements of the indexical field are animated, especially in different sometimes competing ways. The indexical formation that is domestic violence has elements that are animated differently by victims/survivors and police officers, and it is enriched, the clusters and patterns more detailed *because* of the competing modes and sources of information and indexical field element animation.

C.2 Identity and Narrative

In the preceding pages, we have heard many stories. Stories about pain; stories of strength; stories of authority; stories of work and procedure; stories that sometimes wonder about and consider the future. Stories that, frankly, are sometimes hard to hear, read, and reexperience. In the telling of these stories there is an account, but there is also an action, a social achievement in which the teller connects with, instructs, and believes with their interlocutor in a specific moment in time. Thus, accounting for narrative is a way of accounting for experience, the situated actions, behaviors, and identities of life, but it is also a doing. That is, narrative is more than a recapitulation of past actions, but it is an action in and of itself. "Tellers perform numerous social actions while telling a story and do rhetorical work through stories" (De Fina & Georgakopoulou, 2008,p. 181). Telling a story is contextual, told to an audience in a particular location and context. It performs a number of actions and does social work such as connection, performance of authority, and analysis of self and other as part of the interaction of narrative. "Narratives are [...] aspects of situated language use, employed by speakers/narrators to position a display of contextualized identities" (Bamberg & Georgakopoulou, 2008, p. 379). Narrative is an achievement that often includes an achievement of identity. Identities are performed and displayed in situationally rich ways that erupt and emerge in narrative, in storytelling. According to Bamberg and Georgakopoulou (2008, p. 378), narratives, contextual as they are, perform "social actions/functions" – they happen between people, socially. People also use "stories in everyday, mundane situations in order to create (and perpetuate) a sense of who they are" (Bamberg & Georgakopoulou, 2008, p. 378). That is, people tell stories to other people in order to perform identities, which in some ways emerge in the telling and in other ways are borrowed and imported in contextually relevant ways from previous moments of identity work.

Narratives do not simply reiterate past, isolated events. They also do identity work. The stories we have heard in this book often fall into what Georgakopoulou (2006, p. 130) calls "a gamut of under-represented narrative activities, such as tellings of ongoing events, future hypothetical events, shared (known) events, but also allusions to tellings, deferrals of tellings, and refusals to tell." We see each of these unfold as people do identity work in their narratives. For example, police officers told story fragments about victims of domestic violence staying with their abusers, bailing them out of jail, and calling the police over and over. These are presentations of ongoing behaviors, and thus the stories do not always isolate a single example of some behavior, or they use both story forms one after the other. In the group interviews with the police, there are allusions to the fact that the stories have already been told amongst themselves without me present. This generalizing work is also the work of narrative. It builds community with the telling and the group retelling. And perhaps most importantly, the use of general stories creates a mythological system for the police. A set of truisms about victims of domestic violence. These stories teach the police what to expect from domestic calls, helping them safely navigate a volatile and dangerous situation. They also help police understand a behavior – returning to and staying with an abusive partner – in policing terms that make sense to them.

Generalized stories about domestic violence and the victims thereof circulate in police discourse that is saturated with ideological expectations as well as sociocultural information. Police values and ideologies must impact their responses and storying of domestic violence and domestic violence victims, and the storying of the same feeds back into policing discourse, creating and circulating epic stories about how victims behave and how they should behave. Critical ideas about victims come from and circulate in such generalized/ing stories, infiltrating the indexical field, populating the indexical field of domestic violence. Ideas from stories, big and small, that are told over and over, alluded to over and over, become resources in the indexical field for both meaning-making and identity work. Narrative pieces that come up over and over become elements in the indexical field that can be animated and reanimated in order to make sense of an event, story, situation, utterance, etc. that one encounters within the expansive framework of domestic violence.

Victims/survivors of domestic violence also add and animate elements of the indexical field through their storying; they also attach new and different meanings to elements of the indexical field through narrative. As one would expect, not all victims attach the same meaning to an indexical form. It is the multiple storying of the same events that create indexical fields and give them nuance. Take, for example, stories about "pregnancy" and "black eye." For some, pregnancy was a reason to stay in order to maintain a "whole" family. For others, it was a reason to leave, to escape the abuse. The black eye sometimes appears in stories about physical violence and a beating, or being hit, but sometimes it appears in stories about emotional violence, where it is described as less injurious than emotional violence.

Police and victims/survivors story staying in dramatically different ways. For the police, staying is a sign of weakness, defunct agency, and in at least one case, people who stay are described as "stupid." Victims/survivors story staying and leaving as thought-out decisions about home life, economic status, family structure, love, and being a helpmate. The women and men interviewed for this research were not the dupes of violence, forced for psychological reasons to stay in bad relationships. Nor are they "stupid." Through the work that their narratives do, we can see that they are strong and thoughtful, interested in creating and maintaining a good life. Put another way, when we pay attention to what victims/survivors story and how they story it, we see that there is more going on to staying and leaving decisions than the pared down version of such events we get in either popular culture discourses or police discourses. Through the work of the stories told by victims/survivors, we see that there is thinking and considerations going into decisions about staying and leaving that we do not always see in the storying of the same events by police officers. A dispatcher, Vera, gets it when she says as in Extract C.2.

Extract C.2 Vera

1.	*Vera:*	I think they're scared of what's gonna happen afterwards,
2.		especially if it's your husband or your boyfriend who you're living with and
3.		you guys have kids together.
4.		"Do I stand up for myself and put an end to this or
5.		do I suck it up because the kids or because we're married or because we live together, and
6.		I have nowhere else to go?"
7.		It's a big deal when they call because that's how much help they need in that moment.

As a police dispatcher and call taker, Vera knows that it is hard to call 9-1-1; it's hard to pick up the phone because "they're scared of what's gonna happen afterwards" – because the abusive party might go to jail (line 1). If they do go to jail, according to Vera, that might disrupt the whole family structure. As we have seen across the pages of this book, she turns to quotation to put the words of complication into the mouth of victims – victims/survivors, to speak for and through the person who is being abused, to speak both generally and specifically at the same time. Divided from a specific story, this move creates a general sense of victim reasoning, typified, typical reasoning. Such storying feeds back into the indexical field and the mythology of victim behavior in policing discourse, in this case adding some nuance and caring.

C.3 Identity, Policing Discourse, and Recalcitrant Victims

A number of identities emerge in the stories recounted in this book. Some identities are semistable, circulating in the indexical field, and they are both attributable by another and performable by the storyteller. Other identities are fleeting and ethereal, emerging in the telling moment. Discourse and context provide resources for both identities, and indeed, they are not a binary pair. They occur and emerge together, each performance of an identity category emerging anew within the contextual constraints, depending on the discourses in circulation, and depending on the contributions of the interlocutor.

Identity emerges when one stories themselves and their own action. What this analysis shows is that identity can also be constructed in relationship with other characters in the story, who are also a real group of people in the world. That is, identity is formed, performed, constrained, and enabled by a real/imagined group of people, who are also accounted for in stories about domestic violence and police work. Identity is also constrained, created, performed, and enabled by discourses circulating in the context; in this case, there are those that instruct in and enable police behavior, and those that instruct in and create the resources for interpreting, making meaning out of, victim/survivor behavior. In the narratives told by police officers, the focus was on recalcitrant victims, or victims who do not do what officers want and expect them to do. These victims are storied multiple times as attacking police as they attempted to remove the abuser from the home. It is not uncommon in these stories for victims to seem or be presented as either hysterical or unreasonable or as habitually making poor decisions.

Police represent themselves as neutral in relationship with victims. They perform identities rooted in procedure, law enforcement, fact-finding, and authority. While their stories about victim/survivor behavior may critique victims/survivors, the stories about events and interactions often begin with descriptions of neutral procedure that is followed to the letter as well as fact-finding. When the story becomes preoccupied with victim behavior, authority comes up – authority to arrest and to follow the law, which they know and control better than the victims do.

Victims/survivors challenge the attributions of identity when they story domestic violence themselves. In those stories, they tend to focus on the severity of abuse and the difficulties associated with leaving an abusive relationship. They focus on their own strength, their children, family support or the lack thereof, and hope for the future. This identity is significantly different than the pared down, iconicized identities attributed to victims by the police officers. When victims/survivors story police, they attribute a similar identity to police as emerged in police discourse itself – authority, policy, law. That is, victims/survivors attributed and assigned a police identity that in many ways matched that performed by the police themselves. Such attributions are made whether the storyteller had a positive or a negative experience with police officers.

C.4 Emotional Violence

One important point that has been thematized in the forgoing pages is the fact that the elements and performance of emotional and verbal violence are not illegal. "The lack of accountability for the emotional violence is a great injustice to me that seems like it's not gonna get rectified" (Killingsworth). When saying this, Killingsworth is hurt and angry that emotional violence does not get taken more seriously. She uses the term injustice to describe the limited ways that abusers are held liable for emotional violence. She is a survivor of extreme physical violence *and* emotional violence, and she is concerned that only physical violence, big explosive violence, is understood as violent. Indeed, emotional and verbal violence has filled the pages of this book, working in concert in stories in which abusers have asserted control over victims cum survivors of domestic violence. While victims of domestic violence do experience extreme and dangerous physical attacks, they also often experience and live under regimes of control. In his clinical work with domestic violence victims, Stark (2007) learned that long-running, low-level physical and verbal attacks were more concerning to victims themselves. He writes, "[Domestic violence victims'] typical experience involved frequent, but largely low-level, assaults combined with non-violent tactics that ranged from being deprived of basic necessities and being cut off from the outside world to rules about how they should dress, cook, or clean" (Stark, 2013, p. 18). Deprivation, isolation, regimented assaults that are ongoing and regular make up the everyday horror that is domestic violence. "Moreover, my clients insisted that being isolated and controlled could be even more devastating than being beaten" (Stark, 2013, p. 18). My own data support Stark's finding. In this section, I will sum up my arguments regarding emotional violence and "coercive control."

C.4.1 Coercion and Control, Agency and Choice

Many of the victims/survivors in this study complained of emotional violence and verbal attacks, the kind of ongoing, low-intensity but constant threats to body and mind. This regime of emotional violence and control is not illegal, but such regimes make it hard to leave an abusive relationship; having been isolated, deprived, and controlled, make leaving difficult. Police cannot arrest for emotional and verbal attacks, and indeed, as I have argued and explained, they downplay them as "just arguments," or they attribute equal blame to the victim asserting that it is just a "bad relationship." Police also insist that victims should leave such bad relationships, walk away from the arguments; police assign full sovereign agency, while in the very same breath complaining that they will never leave. In some cases, it is the emotional violence, the noncriminal domestics, that keep the victims in the relationship, operating under a cruel regime of control. According to Stark (2007, p. 5), the "key dynamic" of coercive control "involves an objective state of subordination" in which men and women are made to feel inferior to their abusers, beholden to them, and stuck with them. This happens through emotional violence. As Stark importantly notes, and as my data attest, survivors of domestic violence do fight coercive control. They mount "resistance [and] free themselves from domination" (Stark, 2007, p. 5). Strength, persistence, support, and sheer force of will allow victims of domestic violence to leave and survive. Police officers need to work toward understanding emotional violence in order to better support and facilitate the leaving process for which they yearn.

A situation of coercive control is described by Killingsworth, who describes constant, violent attacks that kept her in the relationship by controlling her, but also because they were low-level with what seemed like middling violence to her, she did not think it worthy of calling the police (Extract C.3).

Extract C.3 Killingsworth

1.	*Killingsworth:*	Um, he would—also there was a very, very detailed kind of, um,
2.		record-keeping situation
3.		where if he - he would not tolerate me getting any kind of, um,
4.		one step ahead of him, or to be in a position over him.
5.		So if he felt that I did something to put him at a disadvantage
6.		I would kind of have to pay for it in some way.

[...]

7.	*Killingsworth:*	Um, he would—yeah, so he would leave garbage, he would refuse to do things
8.		Uh, so that my labor around the household, which was already disproportionate
9.		anyway, was pretty much constant.

10.		And I was constantly cleaning, um, just to—a- as a form of penance.
11.		As a form of punishment.
12.	*Jenny:*	Yeah. Yeah, it sounds—
13.	*Killingsworth:*	So it was this com- this complex system of punishments.
14.		Um, that was the thing that really, really over the years
15.		greatly conditioned me—

On line 15, Killingsworth uses the term "conditioned" – a system of punishments habituated her behavior and response, regularizing the abuse and leading her to accept it as an unavoidable part of everyday life. Elsewhere she calls this violence that was neither loud nor explosive – a kind of constant, intense, small, and quiet set of attacks meant to keep her under thumb. Nevertheless, she left, after careful safety planning. She denounced the system of control and made her way out of the abusive relationship.

C.4.2 Policing Discourse and Power

While the police help victims of domestic violence in many important ways, it is important to note that policing discourse is controlling in many of the same ways that domestic violence is. In many ways, victims/survivors leaving an abusive relationship go from a system of control at home to a system of control within law enforcement and adjudication. In no context are their ideas, convictions, and choices taken seriously, or in some cases, even taken account of. A police encounter comes stocked with discourses about authority and control – who is in charge; who has a gun; who can arrest; who can cite; who will press charges; ultimately, who has the power to decide what will happen with the couple, the relationship. These decisions are not up to the victim/survivor, who may have and often do have their own ideas. Police officers in this study often complained that victims just wanted help cooling down the situation; they did not want their partners arrested, in some cases acting out against police when their partners were being arrested. All of the legal decisions that will impact both the abuser *and* the victim/survivor are entirely up to the officer who responds to the call and the district attorney and judge who will work with the case as it moves through the system. In some ways, this mirrors the violent relationship of control, discussed above, in which the abuser absolutely controls the home, their partner, and all of the decisions made in the home and about the relationship. For these reasons and more, an encounter with the police can feel scary for a victim/survivor of domestic violence who is trying to manage a chaotic relationship and live a life.

We can think about the relationship between victims and survivors in terms of the indexical field. Within the field, different elements can be animated to mean in a number of ways. Not all of the meanings will be taken as seriously as others, some will have more weight and authority than others. As Blommaert (2007, p. 17) puts it, "Some forms of semiosis are systemically perceived as valuable, others as less valuable, and some are not taken into account at all, while all are subject to rules of access and regulations as to circulation." Within the indexical field there are regularized patterns of meaning-making that affect the ways that speakers animate key features of the discourse. In terms of domestic violence, the police have more power and authority, and once in the legal system, their ways of knowing and modes of representation are authorized in ways that victims/survivors are not. "Orders of indexicality are stratified and impose differences in value onto the different modes of semiosis, systematically give preference to some over others and exclude or disqualify particular modes" (Blommaert, 2007, p. 120). Ideology infiltrates indexical fields, ordering them according to the rules of the society in which they operate. The stratification that Blommaert discusses positions policing discourses, and the expectations and values embedded therein, above those of the victims/survivors. Police and other officers of the law get to make decisions that at the least lay blame on victims and their choices and agency, and at the worst impact victims/survivors, the way they live their lives (cf. Stanko, 1989). As I discussed in Chapter 2, police make assumptions and assertions about agency from the privileged perspective of policing that surreptitiously ignore the very real, strategic, yet constrained agency that victims/survivors operationalize. These effects of agency are authorized within the ideologically saturated indexical field for domestic violence within which such discussions, presuppositions, and representations take place. That is, meaning-making happens in the indexical field, and neither meaning nor indexicality is neutral, value-free.

C.5 Other and Future Topics

Early work on domestic violence came out of feminist studies, which worked ardently to make the private assault of people, typically women, behind closed doors available for public scrutiny, critique, and change. Not surprisingly, the topic of discussion was the battery of *women*. In the last two decades, a growing body of literature has revamped this discussion, moving beyond a purely feminist account of domestic violence.

> Scholars adopting these approaches have challenged the primacy of gender as an explanatory model of domestic violence and have emphasized the need to examine how other forms of inequality and oppression, such as racism, ethnocentrism, class privilege, and heterosexism, intersect with gender oppression. (Sokoloff & Dupont, 2005, p. 39)

In other words, this research is looking for ways that other factors, beyond gender or intersecting with gender, play a role in domestic violence, importantly paying attention to issues of socioeconomics and race, and equally importantly, creating space to recognize and grapple with abuses against men. As Anderson (1997, p. 655) puts it, "feminist [scholars] contend that issues of gender and power are the ultimate root of intimate violence" while others "argue that patriarchy is just one variable in a complex constellation of causes." For issues of privacy of my research participants and because my focus has been on the micro experience, I have not delved into issues of race and ethnicity, class, and gender, which are nevertheless an increasingly important body of scholarship. I want to briefly discuss these issues, here, however, as they will apply in future studies and because they impact the reading of my findings in important ways.

In the development of this new literature, two strains or directions of research have emerged, that Sokoloff and Dupont (2005, p. 39) among others (cf. Andersen & Collins, 2001; Mann & Grimes, 2001) call "the race, class, gender perspective" and the "structural perspective." The race, class, gender approach focuses on intersectionality, often with the goal of giving voice to marginalized peoples. An additional goal of this approach is to understand the different ways that domestic violence is experienced depending on different embodied experiences. The structural perspective focuses on structural systems of privilege, power, and exclusion. "This means recognizing an analyzing the hierarchies and systems of domination that permeate society and that systematically exploit and control people" (Andersen & Collins, 2001, p. 6). That is, understanding ideological systems of oppression and domination is necessary for understanding the sociocultural why and how of domestic violence. The research presented here takes a structural approach, albeit by largely leaving out macro sociocultural categories of race, gender, and class, but by paying attention to the systems of power and hierarchy of policing discourses in which interactions between victims/survivors of domestic violence and police officers are embedded. I have argued that there is a field of indexicality that has potential social meanings that are hierarchically organized, with the meanings attributed by police officers falling at the top. Scholars have thus recently made moves to understand domestic violence using a variety of factors and structures. This research shows, "strong relationships between domestic violence and age, cohabiting status, unemployment, and socioeconomic status that suggest that other characteristics of the social structure may engender violence" (Anderson, 1997, pp. 655–656). That is, there are a variety of confounding factors that group to create the space for domestic violence.

An interesting and important conversation in recent literature has to do with the inclusion of literature that takes the analysis of male victims/ survivors as its center. Some of this research makes the argument that domestic violence is not only a gender issue but actually a human issue (McNeely, Cook, & Torres, 2001), therefore including men within the purview of domestic violence. Others think of it in terms of "gender symmetry," arguing that men are the victims of domestic violence as often or more than women are, and thus the response to and resources for both genders need to be equal (Kimmel, 2002). Kimmel (2002, p. 1333) argues that "more than 100 empirical studies or reports [...] suggest that rates of domestic violence [between men and women] are equivalent." While domestic violence is violent and abusive regardless of the gender of either the abuser or the victim, feminist scholars have critiqued the cited research arguing "that these methods [national surveys] ignore the context in which violence occurs and thus the issues of gender and power" (Anderson, 1997, p. 656). That is, quantitative studies do not look at the nuance, severity, and other factors of the abusive context to understand the relationship between gender, violence, and other factors such as age, education, cohabitation status, and the like. I have remained purposefully neutral on macro-categories such as gender, because they did not come up for my participants during the interviews, and because of my need to fully protect my participants' identities. Nevertheless, I readily recognize that domestic violence cuts across gender, and that men are often an invisible group of victims/survivors. This study only includes one male victim, because though I spoke with three others, they would not opt into the study.

Finally, issues of race loom heavy over domestic violence. "Sociodemographic correlates of domestic assault reveal higher rates of violence among younger, poorer, less educated, unmarried, African American, Hispanic [*sic*], and urban couples" (Anderson, 1997, p. 656). Some studies have found that factors such as education, age (18–30), cohabitation status (living together but unmarried), and especially race lead to higher rates of domestic violence. Until fairly recently, domestic violence studies have focused on white households. Now, a number of studies have taken up the issue of race, paying attention to the complex constellation of factors, including race that impact rates of domestic violence (Grossman & Lundy, 2007). Citing two decades of reports, including the National Violence Against Women Survey and the National Survey of Families and Households, Benson et al. (2004) find that African-American women are substantially more likely to be victims of domestic violence than their white counterparts (see also Bent-Goodley, 2004). They correlate the factor of race back with the other factors that lead to domestic violence, such as isolation in urban neighborhoods and joblessness (Benson et al., 2004, pp. 327–328).

Explaining why domestic, intimate-partner violence is higher in African-American, Latinx, and other disenfranchised populations is a fraught conversation (Ellison et al., 2007). I will attempt to account for the debate with caution and carefulness. Benson et al. (2004) suggest that widespread racism and its effects have "destroyed the social fabric of African American urban communities" (Benson et al., 2004, p. 327). Structural racism has, according to these scholars, broken down community sensibilities and rules. "Structural characteristics of neighborhoods affect neighborhood collective efficacy" (Benson et al., 2004, p. 328). Structural racism has certainly reshaped and damaged African-American communities. Grossman and Lundy (2007) argue that another issue involving race and domestic violence is the fact that there are so many studies on African-American and Latinx communities, ignoring the issues impacting other demographic groups. Grossman and Lundy's stated goal is to bring light to the set of factors that impact Asian-American women and Native American women (for them, women specifically). Certainly, issues of structural domination and racism impact other minority groups in ways that have damaged structures of self and community. Tjaden and Thoennes (2000) offer an important caution. They argue against the practice of combining all non-white populations and comparing them with white populations, because "such practices may exaggerate differences between Whites and non-Whites" (Grossman & Lundy, 2007, p. 1031), leading to arguments of white exceptionalism or racist overstatements. Therefore, it is important to consider the different ways domestic violence impacts different groups, but only in ways that treat race carefully and without judgement or discrimination.

I want to return briefly to the issue of domestic violence in African-American communities, in order to delve more deeply into some factors specific to African-American communities that can make it difficult for women to get help, but there are also structural things in these communities that can reduce domestic violence. In terms of getting help and services, there are barriers grounded in problematic stereotypes of African-American women. According to Bent-Goodley (2004, p. 309), "Shelters have denied housing to African American women for not sounding fearful enough or sounding too strong." That is, they do not seem weak enough to need services. Bent-Goodley (2004, p. 309) goes on to quote from Kupenda (1998): "In many minds a picture has been painted of Black women as hardened, tough, back-talking, strong, permissive, and undeserving of protection, women for whom blows might not be considered cruelty." This stereotype of African-American women works against her need for care and support; it is incredibly damaging. Another confounding factor that Bent-Goodley (2004, p. 309) identifies is something she calls "racial loyalty." Racial loyalty can be defined as an African-American woman's decision "to withstand abuse and make conscious self-sacrifice for what she perceives as the greater good of the community but to her own physical, psychological, and spiritual detriment" (Bent-Goodley, 2001 quoted in Bent-Goodley, 2004, p. 309). That is, because of long-standing mechanisms of racism and in order to protect the reputation of the community, an African-American woman may sacrifice her own well-being.

Community is known to play a strong role in keeping domestic violence rates down. Isolation is a key way that abusers keep control over their victims. Isolation and control are harder to instigate when there is a strong, well-developed, dense, multiplex community. According to a few studies, both African-American and Latinx communities may get this through religious community, or that church life sits at the center of community, providing well-regarded and important resources.

> African Americans tend to rely on and receive more assistance from religious congregations to a greater degree than Whites. In particular, a considerable body of research has documented the role of relation in reducing feelings of depression, distress, and other negative emotions, as well as mitigating the effect of economic and other social stressors on well-being among African Americans (and to a lesser extent, among Latin[x]s. (Ellison et al., 2007, p. 1099)

Ellison et al. (2007) have analyzed the relationship between domestic violence and regular church attendance in African-American and Latinx communities, and their findings are remarkable:

> The frequency of religious attendance is inversely associated with the likelihood of victimization. [...] [C]ompared with a woman who never

attends religious services, a woman who shares similar demographic
characteristics but attends several times a week is roughly 40% less likely
to be the victim of domestic violence. (Ellison et al., 2007, p. 1104)

Dense multiplex community structure provides resources, in the form of
classes, role models, and community standards that are internalized by
victims and abusers and enforced by the community. Although this is a
limited case – two religions – the findings are hopeful. Though not talking
about religion specifically, Bent-Goodley also calls for community changes
rather than only law enforcement strategies. She writes, "the community
approach is more culturally competent and produces a more positive
outcome by not playing blame but promoting the idea that the men accept
responsibility for their behavior" (Bent-Goodley, 2004, p. 313). The goal is
to stop domestic violence, to heal communities, to take responsibility and
change, not, or not only, to discipline the abusers by legal means. We need
to stop domestic assault before it happens, as much as we need to punish
abusers after it happens.

C.6 Sexual Assault

I would be remiss if I did not comment on sexual assault and sexual violence
in the context of domestic violence. Indeed, my comments here will be too
brief. Though rape in intimate relationships is a centuries old problem,
it has only been criminalized in the last few decades (Woolley, 2007, p.
269). "Social attitudes and legislation regarding domestic violence are often
caught in a tension between family privacy and victim/survivor protection,
whereas non-marital rape is often lodged between problems of consent
and evidentiary proof" (Woolley, 2007, pp. 269–270). That is, intimate
partner rape puts victims/survivors in a double-bind of rape *and* domestic
violence. Both rape and domestic violence come with damages, issues, and
complaints that are unique, and thus when they occur together, double
damage is done. Thus, as Woolley (2007, p. 270) puts it, there are "unique
circumstances and consequences of rape that is perpetrated by one's own
[intimate partner]." Being sexually abused by your intimate partner is a
psychological minefield. Intimate partner rape combines the intricacies and
issues associated with rape in general – where is the proof and how do we
measure consent – with the problems of intimate violence and family life
that are endemic in domestic violence. That is, sexual assault in an intimate
relationship is two problems in one. It is hard to report and even harder to
prove, and all of the actions the victim/survivor takes against her partner

may fall on deaf ears. Many of the women I spoke with had been raped by their partners, and all felt the tension Woolley (2007) describes.

Many of the women I interviewed had been the victims of rape within their intimate relationships, with none mentioning that they were able to successfully prosecute though a few had tried. Sexual assault and spousal rape are significant problems within the context of intimate partner violence because they are hard to report to the police, as Crystal found out (Extract C.4).

Extract C.4 Crystal

1.	Crystal:	Yeah. Even with sexual, rape.
2.		I took some things to the police office, and
3.		nothing was ever done with that as well.
4.		They said because I was married there was nothing that they could do.
5.		I was like, "I physically brought you evidence of things that were going on in our home
6.		in front of the kids, and
7.		that's what you do with it?"

[...]

| 8. | Jenny: | That's frustrating. |

9.	Crystal:	I was like, "as a whole that was really hard for me to do,
10.		to put all that out there, and then
11.		be told there's nothing they can do."

In Extract C.4, Crystal talks about trying to report a rape perpetrated by her husband and being turned away, even though there is a spousal rape law on the books in the state where she lives. She articulates that it was hard, embarrassing to put together evidence of a violent sexual nature, bring it in to be perused by strangers, and then have the police turn her away. Little Bird also talked about sexual violence – being forced to have sex and being forced to do things she did not want to do (Extract C.5).

Extract C.5 Little Bird

| 1. | Little Bird: | Then he starts sexually assaulting me right—pretty much right after the baby was born. |
| 2. | | Horrible stuff, made me do horrible stuff to him. |

[...]

3.	I wouldn't go to the next apartment that he wanted me to go to.
4.	'Cause he started raping me again in July.
5.	There was a couple of rapes in July that were really brutal *[crying]*.

[...]

6.	I don't even know about a DV shelter.
7.	I don't even know that exists, because I grew up in a privileged home, Mormon.
8.	We didn't talk about this crap.
9.	I didn't even really understand I was getting raped.
10	I didn't understand any of what had happened to me, okay?
11.	Nobody was helping.

For Little Bird, there was an added dimension. Not only was she being raped, violently, terribly, she didn't understand what was happening; she did not understand that she was being sexually assaulted in her marriage, and further, that that was illegal. Spousal rape is not talked about in many social circles, for one, and beyond that, she had been habituated to a life of violence and denigration such that the sexual violence perpetrated against her did not register. Little Bird had to be told that what her husband was doing to her was rape, which added pain and anguish while also adding much needed explanation.

One feature that persists across both sexual assault narratives is a lack of detail language. Both Crystal and Little Bird talk in broad strokes about their sexual assault and rape without getting into details about what happened, even though both had given detailed accounts of physical and emotional violence. It is possible that the details were too sexual, and an account would have come off as titillating or lascivious. In other words, both women had been socialized not to talk about sex in public forums, like an interview with a stranger. Another explanation is that it was simply too difficult to recall and describe humiliating and painful sex acts – demanded, forced, and coerced. In the end, neither Crystal's nor Little Bird's pleas to be taken legally seriously regarding sexual assault were heard. Police and district attorneys ignored their allegations, due to the fact that evidence is hard to come by and questions of consent are difficult to prove in matters of spousal rape. Thus, "The history of domestic violence and marital rape reveals that these offenses are sanctioned and perpetuated by the criminal justice system" (Schelong, 1994, p. 81). In yet one more instance, the patriarchal structure of institutions hides and runs cover for domestic violence.

C.7 Conclusions

I'm not going to exactly conclude with a call to action, beyond the one I opened with. Domestic violence must cease, and police and victims/ survivors need to communicate more clearly when they interact about domestic violence. We need to increase police officer and victim/survivor fluency. In order to finally think through this issue and to give final voice to my participants, I turn again to the victims/survivors: their speech, their stories, their ideas. These men and women have clear ideas about the social problem of domestic violence and what they need when they interact with the police. This issue came up in a few interviews, leading me to ask directly, "if you could say anything to police officers, what would you say." I have selected three answers to talk through as a way of calling attention again to the insights of victims/survivors and of drawing this work to a conclusion. The answers describe the context of domestic violence, the fear, the constraints, the control, and the yearning the victims have to be understood, trusted, and believed.

When I asked Beth what she would say to the police, given the opportunity, she focuses on the victim, and asks that the police pay attention to the victim, trying to understand what they are going through (Extract C.6).

Extract C.6 Beth

1.	*Beth:*	Honestly, I just think that just being aware of the characteristics of an abusive partner
2.		going into a DV call, or going into a DV whatever, and
3.		knowing what to watch for, what to see in the victim.
4.		Of course, a victim is going to defend themselves. What do you expect?
5.		If you were getting beat up, and then they're terrified, and
6.		they're overwhelmed and they're panicking.
7.		They can't speak.
8.		They don't even know what to say.
9.		[Police] are like, "Did you start this?"
10.		"Oh, no!"

11.   It's like just know that when a DV call is made,
12.   that it's not made for no reason.
13.   [Police] need to understand more about the characteristics of an
             abusive partner,
14.   whether it be drugs, alcohol, mental illness, whatever it is.
15.   Be aware of those signs going into them.

In this small story, Beth reminds the police that even when the call seems ridiculous, the call for help was *not* made for "no reason" (line 12). The call for help was serious and made in earnest. The victim/survivor who calls the police feels that they were at risk for violence and in need of help. Beth also suggests that the police need to learn more about a typical "abusive partner" (line 13) carefully weighing involvement and recognizing that the victim may well be "terrified," "overwhelmed," and "panicking" (lines 5 and 6). Beth's story is a plea to be seen by police – seen, understood, and cared for.

Similarly, Nikki is concerned with being taken seriously and understood as truthful by the police (Extract C.7).

Extract C.7 Nikki

1.   Nikki: Take our word for it.

[…]

2.   I'm telling you that he hurt me, and
3.   I'm telling you there are visible red marks on my thigh, and
4.   he's telling you, "Oh, no, she's just clumsy."
5.   Please just believe me because I may not have the power or the
                 guts
6.   to just walk out of that house, but
7.   I called you because I figured, with your help, I could.

Nikki is articulate when she urges the police to believe that her injuries are real – to "just believe me." She claims that victims need to be believed and supported by police officers. She clearly explains that victims/survivors want to leave, and sometimes they need to rely on the strength of the police to do so. "I may not have the power or the guts to just walk out of that house, but I called you because I figured, with your help, I could" (lines 5–7). She clearly explains that being in a violent relationship is scary; she may not dare to leave. However, if she gets support and strength from the authority of the police, support that is shored up by their belief in her, she just may have the "guts" to leave.

Finally, in her answer to the question, what would you say to the police if you could, Katherine comes back to the issue of being scared. She asks the police to investigate, because victims may not be in a position to explain what happened to them, due to the shock of the event and the presence of their abuser (Extract C.8).

Extract C.8 Katherine

1.	*Katherine:*	Um, I would just say that you need to just be more detailed and
2.		when you come across the scene because sometimes, you know,
3.		the woman's gonna be scared, and so all the details—
4.		She's not gonna blurt out everything.
5.		She's wanting you to do your investigation, you know—
6.		and protect her and so—
7.		I think it's important to just make sure that they're safe.
8.		If they need to get, you know, the woman away
9.		to, you know, interview them, do that.

The focus for Katherine is safety, which she gets to at the end. The victim needs to feel safe in the presence of the police, safe from her abuser. Because the victim is afraid of the abuser, "scared" (line 3), they need the police to investigate and to have the presence of mind to interview her out of the presence of the abuser. Like others, Katherine makes an argument for context. She wants the police to keep the contextual factors of the victim/survivor in mind. That is, Katherine is commenting on context and situational constraints, asking the police to notice those constraints and act with them in mind. "She," Katherine articulates a female victim, will be too scared in the presence of the abuser to give a statement that includes details.

Katherine, Nikki, and Beth lay out some information for the police to consider. They urge the police to take into account context and the situated actions of victims. They want the police to see domestic violence as a kind of intimate violence deeply entrenched in structures of control and intimidation. They want the police to believe them. The issue that comes up across the three statements is that victims are going to be afraid – too afraid to give details, too afraid to speak in front of the abuser, and too afraid to leave. Police officers need to *see* victims/survivors and consider the fact that she is being abused when they interact with her. The fact that they are being abused is going to affect everything, from how she narrates what happened, to the words selected to describe the abuse. Thus, the police need to believe victims, understanding the abuser behaviors, and recognizing the abuser lies (Beth). Police need to trust that victims are being honest and that victims are struggling against the great weight of abuse.

In this struggle, in these stories, in these social processes, identities emerge. Identities include that of victim, all identify to some degree with the category of victimization that they lived within. However, the identities that emerge also include beauty, hope, reality, struggle, hard work, family and parenthood, and leaving – and this list is not comprehensive. Identities emerge and multiply. Nobody in this data is a single, monolithic identity. Most of the individuals interviewed expressed that leaving was the hardest thing they had to do in their lives. And they did it.

Interactions with the police are difficult and fraught, but policing identities are not. They appear to have a myriad of regularized, approved identities to select from within the indexical fields of policing and domestic violence. The work, then, will be bringing these two groups of identities together and increasing the facility of victim/survivor–police officer interaction. One way to begin quelling domestic violence is increasing the fluency of victim/survivor and police communication, for the police to begin believing victims, and for victims to begin trusting police officers.

References

Ahearn, L. M. (2001). Language and agency. *Annual Review of Anthropology*, 30(1), 109–137.

Anderson, K. L. (1997). Gender, status, and domestic violence: An integration of feminist and family violence approaches. *Journal of Marriage and the Family*, 59(3), 655–669.

Andersen, M., & Collins, P. H. (2001). Introduction. In M. Andersen & P. H. Collins (Eds.), *Race, class and gender: An anthology* (4th ed., pp. 1–9). Belmont, CA: Wadsworth.

Andrus, J. (2015). *Entextualizing domestic violence: Language ideology and violence against women in the Anglo-American hearsay principle*. New York, NY: Oxford University Press.

Bamberg, M. (2006). Stories: Big or small: Why do we care? *Narrative Inquiry*, 16(1), 139–147.

Bamberg, M., & Georgakopoulou, A. (2008). Small stories as a new perspective in narrative and identity analysis. *Text & Talk*, 28(3), 377–396.

Bathurst, E. H. B., & Buller, F. (1768). *An introduction to the law relative to trials at Nisi Prius*. Retrieved from heinonline.org.

Benson, M., Woolridge, A., Thistlethwaite, B., & Fox, G. (2004). The correlation between race and domestic violence is confounded with community context. *Social Problems*, 51(3), 326–342.

Bent-Goodley, T. B. (2001). Eradicating domestic violence in the African American community: A literature review and action agenda. *Trauma, Violence, & Abuse*, 2(4), 316–330.

Bent-Goodley, T. B. (2004). Perceptions of domestic violence: A dialogue with African American women. *Health & Social Work*, 29(4), 307–316.

Benwell, B., & Stokoe, E. (2006). *Discourse and identity*. Edinburgh: Edinburgh University Press.

Berk, S. F., & Loseke, D. R. (1980). "Handling" family violence: Situational determinants of police arrest in domestic disturbances. *Law & Society Review*, 15(2), 317–346.

Berry, D. B. (2000). *The domestic violence sourcebook*. Los Angeles, CA: Lowell House.

Black, M. C., Basile, K. C., Breiding, M. J., Smith, S. G., Walters, M. L., Merrick, M. T., ... Stevens, M. R. (2011). *The National Intimate Partner and*

Sexual Violence Survey. Washington, DC: US Department of Health and Human Services. Retrieved from www.cdc.gov/violenceprevention/pdf/nisvs_report2010-a.pdf.

Blommaert, J. (2005). *Discourse: A critical introduction.* New York, NY: Cambridge University Press.

Blommaert, J. (2007). Sociolinguistics and discourse analysis: Orders of indexicality and polycentricity. *Journal of Multicultural Discourses,* 2(2), 115–130.

Bradley v.State, 1 Miss. 156, 1 Miss.(1 Walker) 156, 1 Mississippi 156 (1824).

Brooks, P. (1996). The law as narrative and rhetoric. In P. Brooks & P. Gerwirtz (Eds.), *Law's stories: Narrative and rhetoric in the law* (pp. 14–22). New Haven, CT: Yale University Press.

Brooks, P., & Gewirtz, P. (Eds.). (1996). *Law's stories: Narrative and rhetoric in the law.* New Haven, CT: Yale University Press.

Bucholtz, M., & Hall, K. (2005). Identity and interaction: A sociocultural linguistic approach. *Discourse Studies,* 7(4–5), 585–614.

Bucholtz, M., & Hall, K. (2008). Finding identity: Theory and data. *Journal of Cross-Cultural & Interlanguage Communication,* 27(1–2), 151–163.

Butler, J. (1997). *Excitable speech: A politics of the performative.* New York, NY: Routledge.

Buzawa, E. S., & Austin, T. (1993). Determining police response to domestic violence victims: The role of victim preference. *American Behavioral Scientist,* 36(5), 610–623.

Cameron, D. (1998). Gender, language, and discourse: A review essay. *Signs: Journal of Women in Culture and Society,* 23(4), 945–973.

Coker, D. (2001). Crime control and feminist law reform in domestic violence law: A critical review. *Buffalo Criminal Law Review,* 4(2), 801–860.

Coker, D. (2004). Race, poverty, and the crime-centered response to domestic violence: A comment on Linda Mills's insult to injury: Rethinking our responses to intimate abuse. *Violence against Women,* 10(11), 1331–1353.

Coulter, M. L., Kuehnle, K., Byers, R., & Alfonso, M. (1999). Police-reporting behavior and victim-police interactions as described by women in a domestic violence shelter. *Journal of Interpersonal Violence,* 14(12), 1290–1298.

Dando, C., Geiselman, E., MacLeod, N., & Griffiths, A. (2015). Interviewing adult witnesses, including vulnerable witnesses. In G. Oxburgh, T. Myklebust, T. Grant, & B. Milne (Eds.), *Communication in forensic contexts: Integrated approaches from psychology, linguistics and law enforcement* (pp. 79–106). Chichester: Wiley.

De Fina, A., & Georgakopoulou, A. (2008). Analysing narratives as practices. *Qualitative Research,* 8(3), 379–387.

De Fina, A., & King, K. A. (2011). Language problem or language conflict? Narratives of immigrant women's experiences in the US. *Discourse Studies,* 13(2), 163–188.

De Fina, A., & Perrino, S. (2011). Introduction: Interviews vs. 'natural' contexts: A false dilemma. *Language in Society,* 40(1), 1–11.

Dettmer, C. (2004). Increased sentencing for repeat offenders of domestic violence in Ohio: Will this end the suffering. *University of Cincinnati Law Review*, 73, 705.

Dobash, R. E., & Dobash, R. P. (1992). *Women, violence and social change*. London: Routledge.

Eckert, P. (2008). Variation and the indexical field. *Journal of Sociolinguistics*, 12(4), 453–476.

Ehrlich, S. (2003). *Representing rape: Language and sexual consent*. New York, NY: Routledge.

Ehrlich, S. (2015). "Inferring" consent in the context of rape and sexual assault. In L. M. Sloan, J. Ainsworth, & R. W. Shuy (Eds.), *Speaking of language and law: Conversations on the work of Peter Tiersma* (pp. 141–144). Oxford: Oxford University Press.

Ellison, C. G., Trinitapoli, J. A., Anderson, K. L., & Johnson, B. R. (2007). Race/ethnicity, religious involvement, and domestic violence. *Violence against Women*, 13(11), 1094–1112.

English reports: Ecclesiastical, admiralty, and probate and divorce, Volume 161: 616. Retrieved from heinonline.org

Fairclough, N. (1995). *Critical discourse analysis: The critical study of language. Language in social life* (1st ed.). New York, NY: Pearson Education Limited.

Fairclough, N. (2001). *Language and power* (2nd ed.). New York, NY: Routledge.

Felson, R. B., Messner, S. F., Hoskin, A. W., & Deane, G. (2002). Reasons for reporting and not reporting domestic violence to the police. *Criminology*, 40(3), 617–648.

Ferraro, K. J. (1995). Cops, courts, and woman battering. In B. R. Price & N. J. Sokoloff (Eds.), *The criminal justice system and women: Offenders, victims, and workers* (pp. 262–271). New York, NY: McGraw-Hill.

Foucault, M. (1972). *The archaeology of knowledge, with discourse on language* (A. M. Sheridan Smith, Trans.). New York, NY: Pantheon.

Foucault, M. (1975). *Discipline and punish: The birth of the prison* (A. Sheridan, Trans.). Paris, France: Gallimard.

Gagné, I. (2008). Urban princesses: Performance and "women's language" in Japan's Gothic/Lolita subculture. *Journal of Linguistic Anthropology*, 18(1), 130–150.

Georgakopoulou, A. (2006). Thinking big with small stories in narrative and identity analysis. *Narrative Inquiry*, 16(1), 122–130.

Goodwin, M. H. (1997). Toward families of stories in context. *Journal of Narrative & Life History*, 7(1–4), 107–112.

Grossman, S. F., & Lundy, M. (2007). Domestic violence across race and ethnicity: Implications for social work practice and policy. *Violence against Women*, 13(10), 1029–1052.

Gubrium, J. F., & Holstein, J. A. (Eds.). (2003). *Postmodern interviewing*. Thousand Oaks, CA: Sage.

Haworth, K. (2009). *An analysis of police interview discourse and its role(s) in the judicial process*. Nottingham: University of Nottingham. Retrieved from http://eprints.nottingham.ac.uk/12253/.

Heydon, G. (2005). *The language of police interviewing*. Hampshire: Palgrave Macmillan.

Heydon, G. (2013). From legislation to the courts: Providing safe passage for legal texts through the challenges of a police interview. In C. Heffer, F. Rock, & J. Conley (Eds.), *Legal-lay communication: Textual travels in the law* (pp. 55–77). Oxford: Oxford University Press.

Holden v. Holden, 1 Hag. Con. 453 (1810).

Hoyle, C., & Sanders, A. (2000). Police response to domestic violence. *British Journal of Criminology*, 40(1), 14–36.

Hymes, D. (1967). Models of the interaction of language and social setting. *Journal of Social Issues*, 23(2), 8–28.

Irvine, J. T., & Gal, S. (2000). Language ideology and linguistic differentiation. In A. Duranti (Ed.), *Linguistic anthropology: A reader* (pp. 402–434). Malden, MA: Wiley-Blackwell.

Irvine, J. T., & Gal, S. (2009). Language ideology and linguistic differentiation. In A. Duranti (Ed.), *Linguistic anthropology: A reader* (pp. 402–434). Malden, MA: Wiley-Blackwell.

Johnson, A. J. (2008a). Changing stories – achieving a change of state in suspect and witness knowledge through evaluation in police interviews with suspects and witnesses. *Functions of Language*, 15(1), 84–114.

Johnson, A. J. (2008b). 'From where we're sat...' negotiating narrative transformation through interaction in the police interview. *Text and Talk*, 28(3), pp. 327–349.

Johnson, M. P. (1995). Patriarchal terrorism and common couple violence: Two forms of violence against women. *Journal of Marriage and the Family, 57*, 283–294.

Johnson, M. P., & Ferraro, K. J. (2000). Research on domestic violence in the 1990s: Making distinctions. *Journal of Marriage and Family*, 62(4), 948–963.

Johnstone, B. (1995). Sociolinguistic resources, individual identities, and public speech styles of Texas women. *Journal of Linguistic Anthropology*, 5(2), 183–202.

Johnstone, B. (2008). *Discourse analysis* (2nd ed.). Hoboken, NJ: Wiley-Blackwell.

Johnstone, B. (2010). Locating language in identity. In C. Llamas & D. Watts (Eds.), *Language & identities* (pp. 29–36). Edinburgh: Edinburgh University Press.

Johnstone, B. (2013). *Speaking Pittsburghese: The sory of a dialect*. Oxford: Oxford University Press.

Johnstone, B., Andrus, J., & Danielson, A. E. (2006). Mobility, indexicality, and the enregisterment of "Pittsburghese". *Journal of English Linguistics*, 34(2), 77–104.

Johnstone, B., & Kiesling, S. F. (2008). Indexicality and experience: Exploring the meanings of/aw/-monophthongization in Pittsburgh. *Journal of Sociolinguistics*, 12(1), 5–33.

Kimmel, M. S. (2002). "Gender symmetry" in domestic violence: A substantive and methodological research review. *Violence against Women*, 8(11), 1332–1363.

Kitzinger, C., & Frith, H. (1999). Just say no? The use of conversation analysis in developing a feminist perspective on sexual refusal. *Discourse & Society*, 10(3), 293–316.

Kupenda, A. M. (1998). Law, life, and literature: A critical reflection of life and literature to illuminate how laws of domestic violence, race and class bind black women based on Alice Walker's book *The Third Life of Grange Copeland*. *Howard Law Journal*, 42, 1–26.

Labov, W., & Waletzky, J. (1967). Narrative analysis. Essays on the verbal and visual arts. In R. F. Spencer (Ed.), *Proceedings of the 1966 Spring Meeting of the American Ethnological Society*. Seattle: University of Washington Press.

Lamb, S. (1999). Constructing the victim: Popular images and lasting labels. In S. Lamb (Ed.), *New versions of victims: Feminists struggle with the concept* (pp. 108–138). New York: New York University Press.

Latour, B. (2000). When things strike back: A possible contribution of 'science studies' to the social sciences. *The British Journal of Sociology*, 51(1), 107–123.

Linell, P. (1998). *Approaching dialogue: Talk, interaction and contexts in dialogical perspectives* (Vol. III). Amsterdam: John Benjamins.

MacLeod, N. (2016). "I thought I'd be safe there": Pre-empting blame in the talk of women reporting rape. *Journal of Pragmatics*, 96, 96–109.

Mann, S. A., & Grimes, M. D. (2001). Common and contested gound: Marxism and race, gender & class analysis. *Race, Gender & Class*, 8(2), 3–22.

Matoesian, G. M. (1993). *Reproducing rape: Domination through talk in the courtroom*. Chicago, IL: University of Chicago Press.

Matoesian, G. M. (2001). *Law and the language of identity: Discourse in the William Kennedy Smith rape trial*. Oxford: Oxford University Press.

McElhinny, B. S. (1995). Challenging hegemonic masculinities: Female and male police officers handling domestic violence. In K. Hall & M. Bucholtz (Eds.), *Gender articulated: Language and the socially constructed self* (pp. 217–244). New York, NY: Routledge.

McNeely, R. L., Cook, P. W., & Torres, J. B. (2001). Is domestic violence a gender issue, or a human issue? *Journal of Human Behavior in the Social Environment*, 4(4), 227–251.

Milani, T. M. (2010). What's in a name? Language ideology and social differentiation in a Swedish print-mediated debate. *Journal of Sociolinguistics*, 14(1), 116–142.

Milroy, J. (2012). Sociolinguistics and ideologies in language history. In J. M. Hernández-Campoy & J. C. Conde-Silvestre (Eds.), *The handbook of historical sociolinguistics* (pp. 569–584). Malden, MA: Wiley-Blackwell.

Mulla, S. (2011). Facing victims: Forensics, visual technologies, and sexual assault examination. *Medical Anthropology: Cross-Cultural Studies in Health & Illness*, 30(3), 271–294.

Murphy, J. (1993). Lawyering for social change: The power of the narrative in domestic violence law reform. *Hofstra Law Review*, 21(4), 1243–1293.

Murray, C. E., & Mobley, A. K. (2009). Empirical research about same-sex intimate partner violence: A methodological review. *Journal of Homosexuality*, 56, 361–386.

Murray, C. E., Mobley, A. K., Buford, A. P., & Seaman-DeJohn, M. M. (2007). Same-sex intimate partner violence: Dynamics, social context, and counseling implications. *The Journal of LGBT Issues in Counseling*, 1, 7–30.

National Coalition against Domestic Violence. (2018). *Who is doing what to whom?* Retrieved from https://ncadv.org/statistics.

Newbury, P., & Johnson, A. (2007). Suspects' resistance to constraining and coercive questioning strategies in the police interview. *International Journal of Speech Language & the Law*, 13(2), 213–240.

State v. Black, 60 N.C. 262 (1864).

Ochs, E. (1979). Transcription as theory. *Developmental Pragmatics*, 10(1), 43–72.

Ochs, E. (1993). Constructing social identity: A language socialization perspective. *Research on Language and Social Interaction*, 26(3), 287–306.

Ochs, E., & Capps, L. (1996). Narrating the self. *Annual Review of Anthropology*, 25(1), 19–43.

Ochs, E., & Capps, L. (2001). *Living narrative: Creating lives in everyday storytelling*. Cambridge, MA: Harvard University Press.

Peirce, C.S., 1940. Logic as Semiotic: The Theory of Signs. In Justus Buchler (Ed.), *Philosophical Writings of Peirce*, (pp. 98–119).

Pence, E., & Paymar, M. (1993). *Education groups for men who batter: The Duluth model*. New York, NY: Springer.

Raphael, J., & Tolman, R. M. (1997). *Trapped by poverty, trapped by abuse: New evidence documenting the relationship between domestic violence and welfare*. Chicago, IL: Taylor Institute.

Renzetti, C. M. (1992). *Violent betrayal: Partner abuse in Lesbian relationships*. Newbury Park, CA: Sage.

Rock, F. (2013). Every link in the chain. In C. Heffer, F. Rock, & J. Conley (Eds.), *Legal-lay communication: Textual travels in the law* (pp. 78–104). Oxford: Oxford University Press.

Roulston, K., & Shelton, S. A. (2015). Reconceptualizing bias in teaching qualitative research methods. *Qualitative Inquiry*, 21(4), 332–342.

Schelong, K. M. (1994). Domestic violence and the state: Response to and rationales for spousal battering, marital rape and stalking. *Marquette Law Review*, 78, 79.

Schiffrin, D. (1996). Narrative as self-portrait: Sociolinguistic constructions of identity. *Language in Society*, 25(2), 167–203.

Schiffrin, D., De Fina, A., & Nylund, A. (Eds.). (2010). *Telling stories: Language, narrative, and social life*. Washington, DC: Georgetown University Press.

Schneider, E. M. (2000). *Battered women and feminist lawmaking*. New Haven, CT: Yale University Press.

Sherman, L. (1992). *Policing domestic violence: Experiments and dilemmas*. New York, NY: Free Press.

Shuy, R. W. (1998). *The language of confession, interrogation, and deception* (1st ed., Vol. II). Thousand Oaks, CA: Sage.

Silverstein, M. (1995). Shifters, linguistic categories, and cultural description. In B. G. Blount (Ed.), *Language, culture, and society: A book of readings* (pp. 187–221). Prospect Heights, IL: Waveland.

Silverstein, M. (2003). Indexical order and the dialectics of sociolinguistic life. *Language & Communication*, 23(3–4), 193–229.

Smart, C. (1989). *Feminism and the power of law*. New York, NY: Routledge.

Sokoloff, N. J., & Dupont, I. (2005). Domestic violence at the intersections of race, class, and gender: Challenges and contributions to understanding violence against marginalized women in diverse communities. *Violence against Women*, 11(1), 38–64.

Stanko, E. A. (1989). Missing the mark? Policing battering. In J. Hanmer, J. Radford, & E. A. Stanko (Eds.), *Women, policing, and male violence: International perspectives* (pp. 46–69). New York, NY: Routledge.

Stark, E. (2007). *Coercive control: How men entrap women in personal life*. New York, NY: Oxford University Press.

Stark, E. (2013). Coercive control. In N. Lombard & L. McMillian (Eds.), *Violence against women: Current theory and practice in domestic abuse, sexual violence and exploitation* (pp. 17–33). London: Jessica Kingsley Publishers.

Stiles-Shields, C., & Carroll, R. A. (2015). Same-sex domestic violence: Prevalence, unique aspects, and clinical implications. *Journal of Sex & Marital Therapy*, 41(6), 636–648.

Stokoe, E., & Edwards, D. (2007). Story formulations in talk-in-interaction. In M. Bamberg (Ed.), *Narrative – State of the art* (pp. 69–79). Amsterdam: John Benjamins.

Thornborrow, J. (2002). *Power talk: Language and interaction in institutional discourse*. New York, NY: Pearson Education Limited.

Tjaden, P. G., & Thoennes, N. (2000). *Full report of the prevalence, incidence, and consequences of violence against women: Findings from the National Violence against Women Survey* (pp. 1–71). Washington, DC: US Department of Justice, Office of Justice Programs, National Institute of Justice.

Tolman, R. M., & Raphael, J. (2000). A review of research on welfare and domestic violence. *Journal of Social Issues*, 56(4), 655–682.

Trinch, S. (2003). *Latinas' narratives of domestic abuse: Discrepant versions of violence* (Vol. XVII). Amsterdam: John Benjamins.

Trinch, S. (2010). Disappearing discourse: Performative texts and identity in legal contexts. *Critical Inquiry in Language Studies*, 7(2–3), 207–229.

Violence Against Women Act. Title IV, Sec. 40001-40703 of the Violent Crime Control and Law Enforcement Act, H.R. 3355.

Williams, S. L., & Mickelson, K. D. (2004). The nexus of domestic violence and poverty: Resilience in women's anxiety. *Violence against Women*, 10(3), 283–293.

Woolley, M. L. (2007). Marital rape: A unique blend of domestic violence and non-marital rape issues. *Hastings Women's Law Journal*, 18, 269.

Worden, R. E., & Pollitz, A. A. (1984). Police arrests in domestic disturbances: A further look. *Law & Society Review*, 18, 105.

Young, K. G. (1987). *Taleworlds and storyrealms*. Dordrecht: Martinus Nijhoff.

Index

abuse, 9–10, 48, 67, 70, 93, 99, 107, 135,
    see also violence
  emotional, 9, 49, 69, 100, 112,
    see also violence, emotional
  emotional and physical, 147, 189
  material conditions, 147
  physical, 9
  verbal, 142
abuser, 132, 153, 165, 179
age, 51
agencies, 155
agency, 3, 119, 135, 138–139, 145, 148, 154
  constrained, 120, 123, 127, 131, 139, 142
  discursive, 120
  in narrative, 122
  practical, 139, 147–148, 154
  situated, 120
  sovereign, 120, 127–129, 138
agented nonagency, 122–123, 127, 131, 138, 143,
    145, 151, 154–156
Ahearn, 119
Andrus, 40
arrest, 12, 27–29, 60, 65, 182
authority, 165

Bamberg, 16, 20, 82–83, 194
Benwell & Stokoe, 16, 18, 20, 24, 159, 162
Blommaert, 201
Bradley v. *State of Mississippi*, 56
Bucholtz and Hall, 3, 15, 20, 26, 160
Butler, 122, 124, 127, 155

caring, 170, 180, 182
challenge identity, 197
characters, 158, 161
children, 101–102, 104
class, 202
coercive control, 8–9, 48, 60–62, 64, 66,
    69–70,
  73–74, 147, 198–199
community, 205

context, 14, 24, 31, 119, 138, 160, 162
control, 36, 47–48, 50, 59, 61, 65, 70–71, 74–75,
    85, 198
"crazy", 138
criminal, 88, 112, 151, 153

direct quotation, 178
discipline, 121
discourse, 18, 37, 61, 81, 102, 159
  agency, 155
  coupling, 170
  domestic violence, 160
  patriarchal, 48, 79
  police, 31, 38, 57–58, 120, 122, 125, 128, 131,
    138, 143, 145, 148, 158, 160, 195
  policing, 200
  social, 20
Discourse analysis, 37
discrimination, 63
discursive formation, 117
discursive practices, 14
domestic call, 13, 32, 176
  criminal, 10, 49, 112
  non-criminal, 86, 112–113
domestic violence, 2, 5, 28, 37, 50, 54, 62, 71,
    79, 80, 102, 113, 115
  narrate differently, 3
  narrative, 32
  same-sex, 73
  social meaning, 110
domination, 47, 70–71, 75, 202
"double closet", 73

Eckert, 3, 26, 44, 80–81, 101, 191
Ehrlich, 39
empirical, 37
erasure, 15, 28, 101, 122–126, 128, 133, 143, 148, 151
escalation, 185
"every-victim", 178–179, 182
evidence, 165, 175
  nonlinguistic, 17

fact-finders, 100
fact-finding, 165
factors, 203
facts, 100
family, 82, 84, 99–100, 102
family narratives, 2
family values, 101
father, 94, 101, 104
fear, 108, 146, 149, 185
forensic discourse analysis, 37
Foucault, 44, 120–121, 127, 138
frustration, 12, 30, 34–35, 115, 163, 171

gender, 202
Georgakopoulou, 20, 24, 82–83, 194

hedging, 109
heterosexual, 75, 110
heterosexual privilege, 73
history of domestic violence, 54
husband's property, 55

icon, 25
iconic victim, 127, 131, 135, 138, 171
iconicized identity, 197
iconization, 15, 28, 122–126, 128, 131, 145
ideal victim, 122
identity, 3, 5, 15, 17–18, 20, 26–27, 110, 119, 129,
        142, 154, 159, 161–162, 165, 169–170, 177, 197
    attribution, 186
    emerge, 3
    emergence, 15–16, 39, 145, 157, 162, 164, 186
    fragmented, 23
    interactional, 161
    partial, 23
    performance, 39, 145
    police, 39, 158, 163
    policing, 36, 173
    procedural, 176
    procedure, 197
    procedure and law, 180
    ratified, 20
    semi-stable, 21, 158–159, 174, 191
    social, 20
    victim, 124
ideological, 27, 158
ideological structures, 26
ideologies, 14
ideology, 18, 24, 26–27, 80, 94, 119, 159, 162,
        191, 193, 201
    agency, 120
    victim, 126
incarceration, 178, 182, 185
index, 25, 112
indexical, 15, 104, 131, 133, 159

indexical field, 3–4, 16, 21, 26, 37, 80–82, 84–91,
        94, 96, 98, 100–102, 104–105, 113–114, 117,
        159–161, 190–193, 195–196, 201
    domestic violence, 91, 117
indexical order, 192
indexicality, 3, 25–27, 80–82, 144, 159–160, 191
indexicals, 84
intact family, 101, 105
interaction, 2–3, 15, 17, 157–158
    past, 16
    victim-police, 29, 41
interactional, 81, 84, 119, 161
intersectionality, 202
intertextuality, 38
interview, 18–19, 41–42
interview context, 157
intimate terrorism, 61, 73,
    see also patriarchal terrorism
intimidation, 48, 50, 65
isolation, 8, 63, 65, 70, 85
jail. *See* incarceration
Johnson, 38, 43, 49, 60–62, 75, 167
Johnstone, 3, 5, 14–16, 24–25, 37, 80–82
just an argument, 112

kinda, 109

Labov, 82
language, 37
law, 37
law enforcement, 13, 49, 65, 70, *see also* police
leave, 125, 133
leave safely, 142
leaving, 12, 21, 23, 72, 76, 89–91, 100, 104,
        116, 123, 127, 129, 130–131, 140, 142, 146,
        152–153, 165, 171, 187
legal facticity, 39
linguistic form, 81
love, 99, 105, 113, 145, 171, 185

male privilege, 63, 70
mandatory arrest, 12, 28, 58–59, 178–180
McElhinny, 13, 38
moral order, 16
motherhood, 142

name-calling, 52, 71, 77, 85, 112
narrate, 129
narrative, 3–5, 14–18, 20, 23–24, 34, 80, 83, 91,
        98, 157, 160, 193, 194
    family, 92, 94, 99
    identity, 16
    leaving, 140
    legal, 40
    police, 99, 110, 112, 168, 177, 186

staying, 107, 144
staying/leaving, 91
victim, 171
violence, 99, 144
narrative potentialities, 81
narrators, *See* storytellers
NCADV, 51, 79
NIPSVS, 51, 79
nonagency, 135
norms, 94, 104

objectivity, 19
Ochs, 15–16, 18, 20, 23–24, 158
Ochs & Capps, 18–19, 23–24, 158
officer safety, 174
other, 15, 27, 37, 158, 160–161, 179,
    193–194

parenthood. *See* motherhood, fatherhood
participants, 19
partner rape, 207
patriarchal, 47, 65, 67, 78
patriarchal terrorism, 50, 60–61, 66, 68, 70
patriarchy, 65, 79
patterns, 192, 193
Peirce, 25
Pence and Paymar, 49
performance, 18, 20, 37, 158, 192
    social identity, 3
police, 10, 28–30, 96, 100, 107–108, 116, 120,
    122, 124, *see also* law enforcement
    identity, 158
police policies and procedures, 58
police procedure and protocol, 38
police safety, 176
police situations, 38
policing, 31, 82, 84, 94, 158, 165
policing narratives, 2
policy and procedure, 173
positionality, 160
potential meanings, 26
poverty, 52, 60
power, 36, 50
pregnancy, 195
pregnant, 93, 102, 105, 108, 138
presupposition, 119, 128
primary aggressor, 2, 12, 59, 100
prior, 24
private, 17, 30–31, 55, 108
procedure, 161
pronoun usage, 112–113
protective order interviews, 40
public, 30, 31, 56, 108
public/private, 30
punishment, 200

race, 202, 203
rape, 39
recalcitrance, 179
relationality, 160
Renzetti, 73, 75
return to abuser, 30
rhetorical, 4

same-sex, 72, 75
scared. *See* fear
Schiffrin, 16, 162
Schneider, 55, 56, 57, 58, 79
self, 5, 7, 8, 15, 16, 23, 25, 27, 54, 127, 129, 148,
    158, 160, 166, 186, 194
shelter, 57, 58
Silverstein, 25
small stories, 82–83
social identity, 15, 81
    performance, 3
social meaning, 25, 26, 37, 80, 82, 159, 160
    love, 113
    of domestic violence, 28
    relationship, 113
spousal rape, 207, 208
Stark, 8, 9, 43, 48–50, 60, 62–63, 76, 140, 189,
    198–199
staying, 89–91, 105, 123, 129, 135, 139
staying and leaving narratives, 2
staying/leaving, 31–32, 34, 82, 84, 89, 91,
    99–100, 124, 129, 139, 143–144
stereotypes, 63, 69, 76
Stokoe & Edwards, 5, 158
stories. *See* narrative
story. *See* narrative
    narrative, 157
    police, 34, 116, 163, *see also* narrative, police;
        narrate
    victim/survivors, 196
story world, 157–158, 160, 162–163
storyteller, 157, 160–162, 196
storytelling, 82
subjugation, 9
subordination, 47, 56
survivor, 6–7, 19
symbol, 25

talk,
    about domestic violence, 2
    makes meaningful, 3
telling stories, 4
testimony, 17
topicalization, 179
Trinch, 13, 17, 24, 39, 40, 66, 83
trouble, 143
troubling, 139

two parents, 94

uncooperative victim. *See* recalcitrant
unhealthy relationship, 130, 170
unhealthy relationships, 133

victim, 6–7, 12–13, 34, 95, 116, 125, 127, 165, 176
   policing, 185
   recalcitrance, 80
   recalcitrant, 34, 114, 116, 171, 177, 185, 197
   uncooperative, 102
victimhood, 125
violence, 8, 47, 49, 52, 66, 71, 84, 88, 100, 148, 151
   emotional, 8–9, 31, 35–36, 50, 67, 70, 85, 102, 124, 139, 149, 151, 153, 198

emotional and physical, 60, 71, 82, 85, 108, 116, 123–124
   physical, 31, 35, 62, 68, 86
   sexual, 8, 39, 206
   verbal, 50, 151, 198
Violence Against Women Act, 58, 59
vows, 94

women, 53, 63, 201
   African-American, 205
women of color, 51
worldview, 24

Milton Keynes UK
Ingram Content Group UK Ltd.
UKHW031444290224
438440UK00022B/167